Descartes' *Meditati*
Philosoph,

Edinburgh Philosophical Guides Series

Titles in the series include:

Kant's *Critique of Pure Reason*
Douglas Burnham with Harvey Young

Derrida's *Of Grammatology*
Arthur Bradley

Heidegger's *Being and Time*
William Large

Plato's *Republic*
D. J. Sheppard

Spinoza's *Ethics*
Beth Lord

Descartes' *Meditations on First Philosophy*
Kurt Brandhorst

Husserl's *The Crisis of European Sciences and Transcendental Phenomenology*
Katrin Joost

Nietzsche's *Thus Spoke Zarathustra*
Douglas Burnham and Martin Jesinghausen

Descartes'
Meditations on First Philosophy

An Edinburgh Philosophical Guide

Kurt Brandhorst

Edinburgh University Press

© Kurt Brandhorst, 2010

Edinburgh University Press Ltd
22 George Square, Edinburgh

www.euppublishing.com

Typeset in 11/13pt Monotype Baskerville
by Servis Filmsetting Ltd, Stockport, Cheshire, and
printed and bound in Great Britain by
CPI Antony Rowe, Chippenham and Eastbourne

A CIP record for this book is available from the British Library

ISBN 978 0 7486 3479 8 (hardback)
ISBN 978 0 7486 3480 4 (paperback)

The right of Kurt Brandhorst
to be identified as author of this work
has been asserted in accordance with
the Copyright, Designs and Patents Act 1988.

Contents

Series Editor's Preface   vii
Note on Texts Cited   viii

1. Introduction and Historical Context   1

2. A Guide to the Text   17
    The First Meditation   17
    The Second Meditation   47
    The Third Meditation   84
    The Fourth Meditation   134
    The Fifth Meditation   156
    The Sixth Meditation   176

3. Study Aids   197
    Glossary   197
    Types of Question You Will Encounter   199
    Tips for Writing about *Meditations*   200

Further Reading   203
Index   207

Series Editor's Preface

To us, the principle of this series of books is clear and simple: what readers new to philosophical classics need first and foremost is help with *reading* these key texts. That is to say, help with the often antique or artificial style, the twists and turns of arguments on the page, as well as the vocabulary found in many philosophical works. New readers also need help with those first few daunting and disorienting sections of these books, the point of which are not at all obvious. The books in this series take you through each text step-by-step, explaining complex key terms and difficult passages which help to illustrate the way a philosopher thinks in prose.

We have designed each volume in the series to correspond to the way the texts are actually taught at universities around the world, and have included helpful guidance on writing university-level essays or examination answers. Designed to be read alongside the text, our aim is to enable you to *read* philosophical texts with confidence and perception. This will enable you to make your own judgements on the texts, and on the variety of opinions to be found concerning them. We want you to feel able to join the great dialogue of philosophy, rather than remain a well-informed eavesdropper.

Douglas Burnham

Note on Texts Cited

Citations to Descartes' *Meditations on First Philosophy* use the pagination of the modern standard edition of the original Latin and French: *Oeuvres de Descartes*, ed. Charles Adam and Paul Tannery, revised edition (Paris: Vrin/CRNS, 1964–76). This edition is designated by 'AT' followed by the volume (7) and page number. I have used the translation by Donald Cress which can be found in *René Descartes: Meditations, Objections, and Replies*, ed. and trans. Roger Ariew and Donald Cress (Indianapolis: Hackett, 2006. Reprinted by permission of Hackett Publishing Company, Inc. All rights reserved). Citations can be located using the AT numbers which are printed in the margins of the Cress translation (and most other translations of *Meditations*).

The citation from Georg Christoph Lichtenberg on page 69 is from §18, Notebook K (1793–1796) in *The Waste Books*, trans. R. J. Hollingdale (New York: New York Review Books Classics, 2000).

1. Introduction and Historical Context

This is a book on *Meditations on First Philosophy* (1641). While this might seem to go without saying, I think it is important to emphasise this point because this is a book only about *Meditations on First Philosophy*; this is not a book about Descartes, Descartes' philosophy in general or the place of this philosophy in the tradition of western thought. There are other books that address these issues but this book is nothing more than an attempt to address the text of *Meditations* in order to better understand what it has to say.

This is also therefore an attempt to take seriously what the text says rather than what has been said about the text. Perhaps the greatest challenge a reader faces when approaching an iconic text such as *Meditations* is finding the text under the layers of tradition. Everyone seems to have an opinion about what Descartes is up to in *Meditations* and some very illustrious and influential thinkers have contributed to the understanding of what we might call Cartesian Philosophy. The role that this form of Cartesianism plays in the tradition of western philosophy is indisputable and if we want to understand Gilbert Ryle's or Martin Heidegger's, Richard Rorty's or Luce Irigaray's quarrel with the tradition of Cartesian Philosophy we ought to take it seriously. Unfortunately, the text of *Meditations* is rarely the target when criticisms are raised against the tradition of Cartesianism. Indeed, the text of *Meditations* has little to do with much of the tradition that claims it as ancestor.

The text of *Meditations* seems to have been mislaid and the industry of commenting upon it has come to be dominated by attempts to say what the text ought to have said and attempts to coax the text into making sense in terms of current philosophical debates. *Meditations* has perhaps been too influential for its own good. When the likes of Locke, Spinoza, Leibniz, Hume and Kant offer glosses of Descartes' philosophy as a backdrop for their own philosophical projects it is only natural that the traditions that take these thinkers as touchstones would be likely to defer to their judgement about what is going on in the original text. Thus a tale of what *Meditations* is meant to be doing often supplants what the text says. In this regard, Hume and Kant stand out for particular merit because of the degree to which they managed to transform the philosophical tradition into an epistemological tradition.

Roughly put, the Anglo-American view of the history of sixteenth- and seventeenth-century philosophy is largely shaped by the Enlightenment projects of Hume and Kant. This is no accident. Both thinkers saw themselves as revolutionary and, in keeping with the practice of modern revolution, actively (if perhaps not consciously) added a historiographical dimension to their work. In other words, Hume and Kant not only presented their own work as new and important but also explicitly stated how their work was progress on (and yet the culmination of) previous philosophical projects. As progress becomes an integral part of the philosophical project it becomes necessary to show that the philosophers you claim to have progressed beyond were involved in the same project you are now involved in. Thus Hume explicitly characterises Locke's project as his own, badly executed, and Kant bemoans the failure of Plato to investigate the possibility of synthetic *a priori* propositions! This historiographic tendency in Kant most notably results in the positing of two competing traditions in modern philosophy (what will come to be known as rationalism and empiricism) neither of which tells the whole story but which Kant's revolution happily reconciles.

These historiographic flourishes could be dismissed as so much bluff and bluster were it not the case that they have been so successful in characterising the early modern period as primarily if not exclusively about the questions Hume and Kant want answered: questions of knowledge, mind and experience – the epistemological bias. This is not the place to go into the way that this bias sells the likes of Locke and Leibniz short; nor is it my task to deny that Descartes' philosophy is not also concerned in various important ways with the 'problem of knowledge'. Rather it is crucial to note at the outset that this bias does serious harm to *Meditations on First Philosophy*. Thus, part of the task of this book will be to explore what can be meant by 'first philosophy' as well as to emphasise the ways in which *Meditations* is concerned with ontology and subjectivity rather than epistemology and philosophy of mind – after all, its most famous proclamation is primarily about being and existence and only secondarily about knowledge and certainty.

A contributing factor in the reinterpretation of *Meditations* as an epistemological text is, of course, that Descartes wrote more than one book. Taken as a whole, therefore, there might be good reason to believe that Descartes is interested in questions of knowledge. But here again *Meditations* suffers from a well-meaning misapprehension. *Meditations on First Philosophy* is a book that is almost immediately accessible to beginners in philosophy. Often it is taught as if it were a primer, a substitute for the more technical books of Descartes' corpus. If, however, *Meditations* is not undertaking the same project as *Rules for the Direction of the Mind* (abandoned in 1628), *Discourse on Method* (1637) or *Principles of Philosophy* (1644) then the text suffers serious distortion through this approach.

It is worth remembering that *Meditations on First Philosophy* is neither a discourse nor on method, and this is a good place to begin when trying to understand what sets *Meditations* apart from Descartes' earlier text. By the same token, *Meditations* is not immediately about rules or principles no matter how many rules and principles can be derived from it. Therefore, taking the text of *Meditations* seriously requires that we take meditation seriously. In order to understand what the text has to say we have to understand how approaching a meditation necessarily differs from approaching a discourse, essay or treatise.

Thus far I have emphasised the need to treat *Meditations* in itself and as a unitary entity. There remains, therefore, only the difficulty of determining just where the boundaries of *Meditations* lie. For such a compact text *Meditations* has a surprisingly large penumbra. The grey area of supporting documents is indeed imposing. To the core six meditations, Descartes has appended a title, a dedicatory letter, a preface, a synopsis, and – most dauntingly – seven sets of objections and replies. Add to this the de facto eighth set of objections and replies to be found in his correspondence with Princess Elisabeth of Bohemia and the waters are well and truly muddied. So what counts as *Meditations*?

Rather than answer this difficult question, I have adopted a strategy meant to enable readers to navigate the grey area around the text for themselves. Thus, I take the core of *Meditations* to include the features that would have been addressed to a 'first reader'. That is, the dedicatory letter, while available to us as readers, is addressed to specific readers that we cannot be; in other words, in reading it we are eavesdropping on someone else's conversation. Similarly, the objections and replies are by their very nature an exchange after the fact. That is, the objections are evidence of someone else having been a 'first reader', while the replies are necessarily responses to someone else's first reading. The exclusion of the objections and replies complicates the way in which I must treat the preface for it is in the conclusion of this preface that the reader is asked to withhold judgement until they have read the objections and replies. At the very least this indicates that the preface itself, as with most prefaces, is a reply of sorts: a reply by a first reader named Descartes. As a result, the text as available to a first reader would only include the title, the synopsis and the six meditations. I will occasionally make use of the remaining documents but always with a caveat: commentaries on *Meditations*, even Descartes' own, are evidence of a first reading. It is the purpose of this book to make it possible for each reader to take up the position of first reader – and then it will be possible to compare notes with other first readers such as Kurt Brandhorst or indeed René Descartes.

Meditations

Perhaps the most distinctive feature of *Meditations on First Philosophy* is that this text is composed of meditations. But what does this mean? To the modern ear 'meditation' calls to mind certain religious practices or the mental exercises that are derived from these – and we would not be far wrong in thinking of Descartes' *Meditations* in this way. Certainly, this is better than pretending that the text is a treatise, discourse, or essay.

By treating the text as we would a philosophical treatise or discourse, we would be forced to assume that the literary form of *Meditations* is irrelevant to the reading and interpretation of the text. This is perhaps the most common approach to Descartes' text. Practitioners of this sort of approach range from those who express dismay at Descartes' foray into such an esoteric literary form and bemoan his failure to present us with a proper treatise, to those who acknowledge that the form of *Meditations* displays Descartes' literary merits and rhetorical skills and yet deny these any significant role in the interpretation of the text so presented.

In each case, so the argument goes, the 'philosophical' reading should attempt to disentangle the content of *Meditations* from its form. In this sort of approach the task of the interpretation is to extract arguments and conclusions, derive premises and principles; in short, this approach to the text takes up the task of trying to set out clearly what the text 'fails' to set out clearly – to say clearly what Descartes does not say but 'meant to say' or 'ought to have said'. While I think that this approach is intrinsically damaging to the text, and will attempt to avoid talking over the text in this way, this is not the only problem faced by this sort of reading.

Deciding what counts as an argument is a crucial first step in deciding what can – and what cannot – be extracted from a text. Not all arguments are attempts at logical persuasion and, given that this text is a meditation, consideration must be given to rhetorical, psychological and even spiritual argument. But more importantly, one must first ask whether the text is proposing an argument of any kind at all. What harm might one do to a text that does not argue if one finds and extracts arguments from it? It is worth noting that relatively few philosophical forms take argument to be their primary task. Limiting the field to examples which precede Descartes, we should keep in mind the therapy of the Stoics, the strategy of Sextus Empiricus and Epicurus, the rhetorical and poetic persuasion of Plato, the autobiography of Augustine, and the reassurances of Anselm. In these cases, argument is employed but is never the whole or even the main story.

While each of the above forms might be of use in understanding *Meditations*, perhaps the best example we can look to for an understanding of the meditational literary form is that of Ignatius of Loyola's *Spiritual Exercises* (c. 1524). As a devotional meditation, *Spiritual Exercises* does not propound an argument or put forth a set of principles to defend. Instead the text is meant to serve as a guide for a journey of spiritual enlightenment. Various attempts have been made to draw parallels between the two texts, and biographically there is good reason to believe that Descartes had come into contact with Ignatius' text in some form or other in his early education. Unfortunately, most of this attention has focused on possible similarities of either the form or the content of these texts. This, I believe, is the wrong way forward. Rather than looking for ways in which *Meditations* and *Spiritual Exercises* are saying the same thing or saying things in the same way, we ought to be looking to *Spiritual Exercises* for guidance on how to use a meditational text.

Devotional Meditation and Ignatius Loyola

Ignatius (1491–1556) founded the Society of Jesus, or Jesuits, and developed the *Spiritual Exercises* as a course of meditative practices and prayers for those seeking a deepening of spirituality and a closer contact with God. Over time these *Spiritual Exercises* became the basis for the

Jesuit order and a pedagogical tool in Jesuit schools. Despite the fact that Descartes' early education was at the Jesuit college at La Flèche in Anjou and there is therefore little reason to believe that he would not have been exposed, at least in passing, to the *Spiritual Exercises* of the founder of that order, Descartes is not writing a guidebook to spiritual enlightenment in the precise theological sense of Ignatius.

Moreover, Descartes' text is both a challenge to authority in philosophy and an enquiry into the nature of knowledge rather than faith. Still, we should be cautious to avoid enforcing too strict a division between the spiritual and the philosophical here. As we shall see, one of the things that *Meditations* accomplishes is a transformation of the notion of spirit into that of mind. A transformation, however, is not the same as a rejection. Indeed, while it is clear that Descartes and Ignatius have a different understanding of the spiritual and the religious, it is far from clear that Descartes' *Meditations* is not intending to induce a religious experience in his own 'spiritual' work.

There is little doubt that Descartes is *not* intending to induce the same sort of religious experience that Ignatius seeks to induce. But, we should be careful not to assume that there is a meaningful distinction to be had between metaphysical knowledge and religious experience. The medieval tradition in philosophy, of which Descartes is among the final flowers, takes it largely for granted that metaphysical knowledge is both a way to and a form of religious experience. This assumption is particularly strong in the Neoplatonic/Augustinian strand of Christian philosophy which most truly informs Descartes' view of philosophy.

That Descartes' text does not espouse a particular dogmatism is hardly sufficient to support the claim that his *Meditations* are not meant to induce a religious experience. It is only in a decidedly post-Cartesian climate that one could assume that philosophy, or the quest for metaphysical knowledge, could be wholly detached from religious commitment. Indeed, Descartes is advocating no less a religious conversion than any 'religious' writer of his day; the commitment to a method and orientation to the world is not something that requires the trappings of a particular God, set of dogmatic beliefs or rituals to make it religious. It is only prejudice that leads us to assume otherwise. To sequester religious experience from philosophical or scientific experience on the grounds that the former cannot avoid being dogmatic only serves to rob the latter of precisely the sort of life-changing and revolutionary orientation that the tradition is so keen to affirm in Descartes.

Moreover, we should be careful not to confuse the cognitive revolution of the second meditation with a rejection of the spiritual. As we will see in Chapter Two, it is true that Descartes re-brands the mind in terms of cognition but it is no less true that this rebranding is in the service of the soul. Indeed, for Descartes, as for the tradition since the time of Plato, the distinction between mind, soul and spirit is not firmly fixed. Saying that the mind is essentially cognitive is not clearly distinguishable in Descartes' usage from saying that soul or spirit is essentially cognitive. Given that the explicit point of the second meditation in which the cognitive revolution occurs is to establish that the mind is distinguishable from the body, and given that the explicit point of establishing *this* is to secure the possibility that the soul will survive the death of the body, it seems remarkably difficult to make sense of the claim that while *Meditations* are cognitive they are not spiritual.

What Ignatius' *Spiritual Exercises* brings to the reading of Descartes' *Meditations* has little to do with the content or indeed the particular form of the texts. Instead Ignatius provides a model for the sort of commitment involved in the reading of a meditational text. The reading of a meditational text is distinct from the reading of most texts but perhaps most of all from the reading of a traditional philosophical discourse. The reader does not approach the text for information as one might an encyclopaedia or textbook; a meditational text is not a resource. The reader does not approach the text as one might a set of instructions or a manual; the meditational text is not description. The reader does not approach the text as one might an essay or treatise; the meditational text has nothing to prove. Ignatius' text is not called *Spiritual Exercises* by accident. Like a book on physical exercise, this text is useless unless the reader does the exercise. It would be odd to read a book on how to do yoga as a treatise, a textbook, or even a set of instructions without ever actually doing any yoga.

In the case of a meditational text like *Spiritual Exercises* the doing involves thinking (meditating, praying) rather than any particular physical activity. And for this reason it might be easier to conclude that the non-physical activity of reading would be sufficient. But just as teachers do not usually equate the turning of the pages of a book all the way to the end with having actually read it, Ignatius is unlikely to be sympathetic with a meditant who claims merely to have read *Spiritual Exercises*. There is a presumption in a meditational text that time must be spent in the reading, in thinking over what has been read; there is a presumption that there will be layers of understanding corresponding to the level of commitment one makes in the meditational practice. One's bodily understanding of yoga changes over time and through practice. Likewise, a meditational text is meant to take time and the reader is meant to take time with the text. And it is not incidental that Descartes invites only those readers who have the desire to meditate *seriously*.

It is at this point in the comparison that the reading of *Meditations* as a meditational text runs up against the reason most people read the text in the first place. The text is very easy to read and is thus perfectly suited to classes for beginners and introductory philosophy courses. Unfortunately, what I am arguing is that this is precisely the wrong reason to read the text and that any reading that begins with this assumption is bound to be unsatisfactory. *Meditations* will be as easy or as difficult as the reader allows it to be, but a reading that takes it seriously as a meditational text will find that the whole piece hangs together much more convincingly and fruitfully than one which approaches the text as a discourse or textbook.

Descartes' *Meditations* is not as structured as *Spiritual Exercises* but we should not conclude from this that it is not meditational. By inviting us to meditate with him, Descartes invokes a literary form that has expectations of the reader. We will eavesdrop on Descartes' own meditational practice; we will allow the text to appeal to our imagination as well as our reason; we will take the time with the text to make Descartes' practice our own; we will think hard about the things Descartes thinks through before us; and in the end we just might discover that we really are better persuaded by the reasons which we have discovered for ourselves in the process than we could ever be by those dictated to us by an other.

First Philosophy

Descartes presents his meditations as *Meditations on First Philosophy*. What, then, is 'first philosophy'? To explain this, as is often done, by saying that 'first philosophy' is another name for 'metaphysics' is not entirely helpful if one does not already know what 'metaphysics' means. More to the point one would have to know in advance what metaphysics means to Descartes for this to be a helpful explanation. And here is yet another opportunity for prejudice to enter our reading of *Meditations on First Philosophy*, for it is not likely that what Descartes means by metaphysics will be what is meant by metaphysics today. Fortunately, all this can be avoided if we explore what might be meant by 'first philosophy' instead.

The notion of 'first philosophy' is first invoked by Aristotle in a series of writings that came to be known as *Metaphysics* (*meta ta physica*) because it came after the writings called *Physics* in the standard ancient collection of Aristotle's writings. In invoking 'first philosophy' Descartes casts us back into the Aristotelian roots of metaphysical philosophy. Descartes' relation to the Aristotelian/Scholastic philosophy of his day was largely hostile and this evocation of Aristotle's usage is both a challenge to this Scholastic tradition and a reminder that perhaps his philosophy is closer to the spirit of Aristotle than to the tradition of Aristotelianism.

According to Aristotle, first philosophy is the study of being qua being (or being in itself). That is, it is not the study of any particular being (a dog, a cloud) or even of any particular kind of being (animals, meteorological phenomena) but of what it means to be. In Aristotle's philosophy this question of what it means to be would involve that which all beings have in common. Just as the study of dogs would set out to determine that which all dogs have in common (dog-ness) which makes each one of them a dog (and not a cat or a cloud), first philosophy sets out to determine what all beings (things that are) have in common as beings. First philosophy asks after the being of being.

Given this, the notion of 'first' in play in first philosophy might initially seem counterintuitive. Aristotle is clear that all speculation *begins* with the experience of particular beings and we progress to the study of more general categories of being by the method of abstraction, by asking what each member of a set has in common. As the largest set is the set of all beings and it is the study of this set that concerns first philosophy it might seem that Aristotle ought to talk of 'last philosophy' as the philosophy of being qua being. But it is not *temporal priority* that is in question when we speak of first philosophy. We find first philosophy last but when we find it we understand what must in fact have been first for the particulars to be the way they are.

The key to understanding this reversal is to be found in Aristotle's analysis by causes which is the centrepiece of his philosophy. 'Cause' (*aita*) for Aristotle has a very technical meaning that is much broader than the common meaning we might associate with the word. Without going into too much detail, there are four causes (material, efficient, formal and final) by which all things that are (beings) can be analysed. And this analysis is possible because everything that is, every particular thing that we experience, owes its being as it is (its particular being) to these causes (understood as grounds of being). To use a simple example, to give a complete analysis of the being of a particular soup bowl, we must ask after: the matter (clay) of the soup bowl (material cause – that which makes up the particular being); the maker (the potter) of the soup bowl (efficient cause – that which brings the particular thing into being); the 'form' of the soup bowl (formal cause – that which identifies the soup bowl as a soup bowl and not a wine chalice); and the purpose or *telos* (to hold soup) of the soup bowl (final cause – that toward which the being of the particular is directed).

A complete understanding of a particular being will give an account in terms of these four causes. Without putting too much weight on the term, everything that is, every particular that we experience, is the 'effect' of these causes and thus these four causes are the ground for anything that is. It is in this sense that, while the experience of the particular being must always be temporally first, the proper understanding of this particular being involves the understanding of what must have preceded it for it to be. And as not all the four causes function temporally, this precedence is not entirely temporal but logical (concerning thought) or ontological (concerning being). In this sense, first philosophy concerns that which is most abstracted from any particular being but must have priority for any less abstract being to be. Ultimately, the proper understanding of particular beings (or sets of particular beings), what Aristotle calls physics, rests on a proper understanding of the study of first philosophy; and yet the method of abstraction from particular beings grounds this first philosophy.

Here is where Descartes differs from Aristotle. Like Aristotle, Descartes embraces the idea that a proper understanding of first philosophy is essential to the understanding of physics (science). But Descartes rejects the method of abstraction that the Scholastic philosophy of his day, derived from Aristotle, advocates for this. Descartes doubts that a science of ultimate generality (metaphysics) can be achieved by greater and greater abstraction from particulars. He also doubts that any metaphysics developed in this way has the right to be called first philosophy. At root this worry is twofold. First there is the suspicion that by starting with the experience of particulars and applying the method of abstraction science will forever be limited to taxonomy (albeit a remarkably complicated one). But more importantly for the reading of *Meditations*, Descartes is worried that there is no clear method for reliably picking out the particulars to start with – there is little doubt that if your initial sample of particular beings is unreliable then any general science derived from it will be faulty.

So Descartes clings to Aristotle's insistence that the question of first philosophy is paramount but abandons Aristotle's methodology. In doing so he reverses the Aristotelian approach. For Descartes, first philosophy is the study of that which is necessary for the experience of particulars rather than the study of that which is necessary for the being of particulars. In effect, Descartes is attempting to ground the Aristotelian starting point by suggesting that the experience of particular beings is not as easy as it appears. Descartes thereby realigns the 'first' of first philosophy with the 'first' knowledge. For this reason Descartes is sometimes called a foundational philosopher. Rather than admit that any of his naïve opinions be given the status of knowledge and the basis for future investigations, he insists that first philosophy deal with those things that we are able to know first. And this means first jettisoning everything that we *think* we know.

While this shift is revolutionary, however, we should not immediately assume that Descartes is abandoning ontology for epistemology. The revolution is much more subtle. Descartes does problematise the naïve experience at the heart of Aristotle's philosophy but he has not abandoned Aristotle's ontological definition of first philosophy: ultimately, what Descartes discovers as the first principles for experience are the being of the ego and the being of God. And for this reason Descartes' metaphysics can be seen as the legitimate heir to Aristotle's concern with the nature of original, or first, being.

The Title

Having already discussed the words of the main title of Descartes' text, we now turn to the *full* title, of which there are famously two versions:

First Edition: *Meditations on First Philosophy in which the existence of God and the immortality of the soul are demonstrated*

Second Edition: *Meditations on First Philosophy in which the existence of God and the distinction between the soul and the body are demonstrated*

Apart from the historical contingency that Descartes was not entirely happy with the publisher of his first edition and that, apparently, this first publisher was responsible for the wording of the title, this change is instructive.

On the one hand, the change is perfectly sound because one thing that *Meditations* most definitely does not do is demonstrate the immortality of the soul. Rather, as the second subtitle indicates, *Meditations* demonstrates the distinction of the soul from the body and thereby satisfies a necessary, but not sufficient, condition – that the soul need not die with the body – for the further proof of the immortality of the soul. On the other hand, the change is entirely fitting to the project because the proof of the immortality of the soul would not be a question for first philosophy as Descartes understands it.

First philosophy traditionally deals with the ontologically first questions and therefore with the being of being. In the vocabulary of *Meditations* this question is resolved in terms of the question of substance. We will deal with the question of substance in more detail later but for here it is enough to say that 'substance' is that which bears properties. Thus in everyday terms a hat is something that might have the property (or attribute) black. As we are dealing with *first* philosophy, however, 'hat' will not be sufficiently general to qualify as substance. Instead, first philosophy will attempt to isolate the most general types of substance and those ultimate substances which cannot be resolved into more fundamental terms. Thus, in our example we can see that 'hat' quickly resolves into something more fundamental, for example tweed; were we to continue on this line of thought we would discover that it will ultimately resolve itself into matter – which, appropriately enough, is one of the substances Descartes deals with.

In this model the question of the nature, or being, of the soul is appropriate for first philosophy, while the question of the immortality of the soul is a more contingent question – something like the shape matter takes on in being a hat. Put another way, the distinction of the soul from the body is a question appropriate to metaphysics while the question of the immortality of the soul is better left to physics. For Descartes, of course, no reliable physics (or second philosophy) is possible unless we get the underlying metaphysics sorted out. And so, it is crucial to any meaningful answer to the question of the soul's possible immortality that we know just what it is to be a soul – what the substance in question is.

The Meditator

Much has been made of the first person pronoun, the 'I', that runs through *Meditations*. On the one hand everyone is determined to show that this 'I' cannot refer to Descartes and that we ought not to take the reports of what this 'I' thinks and does as actual reports about Descartes. On the other hand, with this initial and standard referent for the 'I' out of play, there is a general consensus that *some* philosophical significance ought to be given to the use of 'I' and there are various competing, and sometimes baroque, solutions to this supposed problem.

There is an almost knee-jerk rejection of the possibility that the 'I' refers to Descartes. The possibility that Descartes might be made to say, in his own name, something obviously false strikes these commentators as unthinkable. The idea that these six meditations may correspond to a literal six day period in the life of Descartes seems to them ludicrous. The notion that Descartes could espouse opinions and positions that we claim to know he had already rejected prior to his thirty-second year must not, they claim, be taken seriously. But what of lies, fiction and literary method? No one doubts, to take but one striking example, that the hero in many of Hemingway's stories is Hemingway either in part or in essence; some go further to claim that Hemingway's non-fictional life is in some way an enactment of the fictional characters he created. Why should we assume anything other in the case of Descartes?

At the other extreme of the debate about the 'I' is the claim that it functions allegorically. Since the latter half of the twentieth century there has been a movement to fill the position of the 'I' not with a simple character referent (the most obvious of which would be Descartes) but with a type, attitude, or set of beliefs. In other words, the assumption of a philosophical significance for the 'I' seems to have moved the debate into more and more complicated allegorical referents. Thus for example, John Carriero suggests that the 'I' represents someone who has been educated in the scholastic tradition (if not a scholastic philosopher); Harry Frankfurt argues that the 'I' refers to the perspective of common sense; Bernard Williams presents the position of the 'I' as that of our everyday standards for judgement pushed to their natural extreme.

The supposed problem of the 'I' in *Meditations* thus tends to be forced upon us by too strong an opposition between the two extremes: either the 'I' is strictly identified with Descartes or the 'I' encapsulates a philo-sophically articulate structure of beliefs and attitudes. While the former case is rejected out of hand, the assumption latent in the latter is that Descartes is involved in a more or less standard philosophical project of persuasion. In taking up a more literary reading of *Meditations* I am both less worried about the implication that there is indeed a pseudo-autobiographical reference and less inclined to assume the prerequisites for philosophical persuasion.

The prejudice that the 'I' must serve some argumentative purpose in *Meditations* drives the philosophically loaded allegorical readings of the 'I'. The belief that the autobiographical 'I' must bear a strict referential relation to an empirical individual (as a pronoun bears in a rigorous philosophical vocabulary) drives the presumption that *Meditations* cannot be in the least autobiographical. However, as I have suggested by my discussion of meditational literature, the literary device of meditation neither implicates the author in strict autobiography nor sets out to persuade in a purely logical or rational way. By asking the reader to meditate along with him, Descartes is most definitely employing an 'I' that bears *some* relation to him as first or lead meditator. But by deploying the literary device of meditation he also takes on the guise of literary character who leads as first meditator. As a literary character, who I shall call Descartes, this 'I' is free to indulge in fictional assertions. It would be odd to insist that these assertions be entirely fictional, however, for part of the point of the meditational exercise is for the reader to enter into the practice along with the lead meditator; and for this process to be successful the practice must be real and not purely fictional. By following the lead of the first meditator, Descartes, the reader is put into a position to persuade themself.

Neither the purely autobiographical 'I' nor the pure allegorical 'I' can persuade the reader; only the reader can do this and for this purpose the literary 'I' is more than sufficient. For these reasons, I will refer to the 'I' of *Meditations* as Descartes while at the same time noting that this use of 'Descartes' is not a reference to the author of *Meditations*.

The *Cogito*

Descartes' most famous pronouncement, *cogito ergo sum* (I think therefore I am) does not appear in the main text of *Meditations*. Strictly speaking this exact Latin phrase does not occur in Descartes' published works at all. There are variants of this phrase and the French of the *Discourse on Method* has '*je pense, donc je suis*' (I think therefore I am) but in *Meditations*

Descartes only talks around this point which is famously not stated therein. Instead, Descartes in the second meditation builds up to the claim '*ego sum, ego existo*' (I am, I exist) as true whenever he thinks it.

Nonetheless, in philosophical language the *cogito* has come to represent the philosophical moment of certain self-consciousness. Therefore, I will use 'the *cogito*' freely in this book to indicate this philosophical moment despite the awkward fact that the phrase to which it most directly applies in *Meditations* (I am, I exist) does not make use of '*cogito*'.

How To Use This Book

This text is not a substitute for reading *Meditations*; rather it is a guide to Descartes' text and should be read alongside it. More importantly, however, neither this text nor the reading of *Meditations* is a substitute for meditation. *Meditations on First Philosophy* is a difficult text. It makes demands of a reader that go beyond those that most texts make, for it asks that you do the work yourself rather than letting Descartes do the work for you. For *Meditations* to be genuinely transformative each reader must guard against letting *any* text (even *Meditations*) stand in the way of undertaking such a project 'once in their life'.

2. A Guide to the Text

The First Meditation

The first meditation is entitled 'Concerning Those Things That Can Be Called into Doubt' and it is with the so-called 'method of doubt' that Descartes enters into *Meditations*. The justification for the application of this method is biographical but as this is a meditational exercise we are asked to meditate on this justification as well. The impetus for the meditational cycle is the realisation that much if not all of what Descartes currently believes to be true is dubious. This is because he currently holds many opinions which he has never thought to examine and, at the same time, has had the experience of discovering that many such unscrutinised opinions he formerly held had turned out to be false.

At first glance this crisis might seem less than devastating. On the one hand, this is an experience common to everyone and it seems to be a fairly good description of the process of learning that we all go through. At some point in our intellectual growth the belief that thunder is the sound of angels bowling on the clouds fails to satisfy and we then revise our belief in line with our current intellectual capacity and the available data. Moreover, some beliefs that may in fact be false may never interfere in enough of a way to demand revising. The false belief that the line 'Play it again, Sam' occurs in the film *Casablanca* will almost certainly never be in need of revision – although it probably has just been revised for some readers. Indeed, Descartes admits to being able to cope with having a good many false beliefs and to being able to manage the business of life by means of the *ad hoc* revisionism that he now seems to find inadequate.

On the other hand, because Descartes is speaking to an experience common to all readers, this is an ideal point of departure on the meditational journey. In order to justify his *Meditations*, and first and foremost his method of doubt, Descartes does not need to make a case for this experience being commonly shared; he only needs to make a case for the unacceptability of the *ad hoc* revision of belief necessitated by this experience.

The most commonly cited justification is the one that Descartes spells out explicitly in the first meditation: that *ad hoc* revisionism is inadequate 'if I wanted to establish anything firm and lasting in the sciences.' (AT7:17) There is little doubt that this, as it stands, is a compelling reason for Descartes. However, were this the only reason to abandon *ad hoc* revisionism then he would lose the interest of the majority of his readers who (correctly) think that the theoretical foundations of science are beyond both their needs and their interests if not also their capacities. Without elaboration this justification will not support a meditational reading for most readers.

Upon meditation, however, there are obvious reasons beyond this narrow scientific remit for the worry about the strategy of *ad hoc* revisionism. It should be pointed out that Descartes' use of '*scientia*' has a broader meaning than does 'science' to the contemporary reader; we will return to this. But for our purposes as meditational readers, the most powerful reason becomes clear when we reflect on the image Descartes draws for us of the state of his current opinions:

> Several years have now passed since I first realized how numerous were the false opinions that in my youth I had taken to be true, and thus how doubtful were all those that I had subsequently built upon them. And thus I realized that once in my life I had to raze everything to the ground and begin again from the original foundations, if I wanted to establish anything firm and lasting in the sciences. (AT7:17)

The image he calls up is both powerful and devastating. Through the analogy of building and foundations Descartes presents our collected beliefs in the image of a house. An imaginative extension of this description makes the house of our opinions the dwelling in which we live – our position in the world.

As any homeowner will testify the process of day-to-day maintenance is not one of major renovation but of *ad hoc* revision – replacing and fixing each bit of the house as it becomes damaged or falls into disrepair. And so, like any house, this imaginative house can be successfully managed through the same process of *ad hoc* revision. But what is troubling to Descartes is not the maintenance aspect of the analogy but the question of origin involved. Upon reflection it becomes clear that, unlike most homes, this imaginative house of our opinions was constructed not only partly but entirely *ad hoc*. Descartes' initial reflection upon those opinions he had held to be true in his youth forces us to realise that there is no original 'new' house that we moved into at some point in the past. Rather through the course of our lives we built this house piecemeal and from scratch.

When we map this imaginative house onto the course of a human life we suddenly realise that there never was a blueprint or architectural drawing; there never was a long-term plan when construction began. What three year old makes such plans? What three year old is even aware of the fact that they have begun construction of the house they will live in for the rest of their lives? And this is an important thought because it is as two or three year olds that each of us began the construction of this house. More worryingly, however, is that no matter how handy we are in repairing the fixtures of the house and making it liveable, the parts of the house that were laid down first, the foundations and weight bearing structural support, are the work of our three-year-old selves.

If this image holds any power it ought to cause us to ask whether we really want our position in the world to be determined by a three year old; we ought to ask whether we should trust the stability of a dwelling that was constructed entirely from a method better suited to repairs and minor fix-it jobs. And our meditation on this ought to lead us to accept, if it were offered, the opportunity to start over. What Descartes is offering in the first meditation is a chance to do just this. As extreme as it may seem, to start the construction of our dwelling in the world on our own (more) mature terms and with the knowledge of the importance of the undertaking – knowledge unavailable to our three-year-old selves – will require the demolition of our old dwelling. No amount of *ad hoc* revision will serve this end.

Through this imaginative meditation, however, something more is revealed about Descartes' more narrowly construed concern with science. The Aristotelian/Scholastic science of his day was built on the notion, encapsulated in the dictum 'nothing in the intellect that is not first in the senses', that prior to all theorising was naïve observation of the world. But, given our imaginative construct, this is cast into relief as a glorified version of the same *ad hoc* approach that would not serve in house building and is hardly enticing in opinion formation. By approaching the question of science through these autobiographical images, Descartes illustrates just what is weakest in the science he hopes to revise by his new approach: the lack of a guiding principle, blueprint or prior plan. Descartes' take on first philosophy will, if nothing else, provide the basis for the new science by offering an account of guiding principles.

As indicated by the Latin word '*scientia*', the science that is being critiqued has a particular scope in Descartes' usage that binds together the concern with science as a field of enquiry and the broader worry of the world of opinions in which we dwell. While it can be used to indicate specific fields of knowledge (what we would call 'sciences'), '*scientia*' itself simply means 'knowledge'. Descartes' concern, then, extends to the question of knowledge generally. However, the full import of this extension cannot be understood without a proper understanding of what is at stake in the fields of knowledge '*scientia*' comprises. We should be careful not to assume that '*scientia*' is limited to those fields that bear the title of science today. More than the hard sciences (such as physics or biology), or even the human sciences (such as sociology and economics), Descartes' use of '*scientia*' extends to metaphysics and morals as these are just as clearly fields of knowledge as physics or sociology. In fact, elsewhere Descartes ranks moral science as the highest degree of wisdom as it comprises and presupposes all the other sciences.

Given that the full title of *Meditations* directs us to the proof of the existence of God and the question of the soul, this status for moral science should give us pause. That is, Descartes' interest in establishing the principles of first philosophy extends not only to the sciences narrowly construed but ultimately to morality and action. More to the point, the 'hard sciences' are subordinate to the proper fulfilment of moral wisdom – the knowledge of how to live. For Descartes, the epistemological, physical and moral form a unified project which is in the end grounded in the metaphysical (ontological) questions of God and the soul. It is this that makes Descartes' case for *Meditations* so compelling because getting the starting point, first philosophy, wrong jeopardises our moral well-being.

The method of doubt

The method Descartes advocates for beginning the process of meditation has come to be known as the method of doubt. This process is also sometimes, and somewhat misleadingly, referred to as methodological scepticism. While this latter label captures the essential features of the method in the first meditation, it also imports unnecessary debates into the text by tacitly referring Descartes to scepticism, ancient or modern. While Descartes is most certainly concerned with the problem posed by both epistemological and moral scepticism, and while he deploys some of the techniques and language of the sceptic, he never uses the term 'scepticism' in the text of *Meditations*. By inserting the term into the discussion of the first meditation in this way several pseudo-questions arise: what is Descartes' relation to ancient scepticism? To what extent is *Meditations* a response to the scepticism of Montaigne? Is the first meditation sceptical enough? In the end, while there is nothing essential brought to the discussion by 'methodological scepticism' that is not covered by 'method of doubt', a great many distractions are imported. Rather than showing how Descartes' supposed scepticism is different from other scepticisms, therefore, it will save time if we focus on Descartes' use of doubt.

The crucial feature of Descartes' doubt is that it is part of a method. He does not doubt because he wants to; he does not doubt because he is predisposed to being suspicious; he doubts because it is the method he has chosen to arrive at a solid starting point for his philosophy. The method of doubt, therefore, is purely propaedeutic and the doubting, while radical, is never an end in itself. This has two important implications that we must keep in mind: first, that Descartes is not obliged to keep doubting once the aim of the doubt has been achieved; and second, that he is not obliged to doubt everything.

The method only requires that he doubt as long (and as much) as is necessary to serve his purpose. This purpose is to find, if at all possible, a starting point that is entirely impossible to doubt. The method of doubt, therefore, is a search and the doubt is the method of testing things in order to see if they measure up.

It is important to stress this feature of the method of doubt because once one enters into the doubt Descartes proposes it is tempting to take it too far and to forget what the point of the whole exercise was. It is tempting to do this because Descartes is proposing a very radical form of doubt that, like a powerful drug, can be addictive. So the meditator should take a moment to remind themself that the doubt ought not turn into an end in itself.

Imagine, for example, that you cannot find your house keys amidst the clutter of your house but that you need to find them before you can leave home. Rather than hunting randomly for your keys you adopt the following unusual but effective method: you decide to tidy your house methodically until you find them. To an outside observer it might appear that you are tidying up for the sake of tidiness; if the process takes a significant amount of time someone might even assume that you had neatness issues. You, however, are not in the least bothered by the untidiness; you know that the reason you are going through the tidying process is to find your keys. And it would be odd, once you found them, for an outside observer to say that you ought to continue to tidy up. In fact, were you to adopt this strategy for finding your keys and, by chance, find your keys under the first bit of clutter you move you *ought to* stop tidying then and there so you can go out. In such a case no outside observer would be able to judge what method you had been employing and would therefore be unable to comment on the fact that you have stopped it. It should make no difference if the process takes longer than this.

Descartes' method does take longer and is more intense but for all this it is still essentially a method for finding something. In this case what Descartes seeks is something that is incapable of being doubted that will be able to serve as the strongest possible starting point for his new philosophy. The method of doubt, then, is a method of searching for and testing possible candidates for this first principle or undoubtable foundation. By exposing each potentially certain opinion to doubt, Descartes will be able to weed out the field of candidates. But this is, as it were, the bare bones of the method of doubt. Descartes' method is modified in two ways before he even begins: first, he notes an important feature of the standard he has set himself; secondly, he notes an important feature of the opinions he is testing.

The standard of certainty

The first observation that Descartes makes about his proposed method is that saying that something is dubious is not the same as saying that something is false. This is an important observation because it not only quickens the testing procedure but it also leaves open the possibility that some opinions he is temporarily putting aside could turn out to be true. This is based in the nature of the relation of doubt to certainty. The standard of certainty that Descartes has adopted in his search is 'that which is not capable of being doubted'. It is reasonable to ask whether this standard is too stringent, but given that doubt is his chosen testing agent there is little other choice for Descartes because this is what doubt tests.

Doubt is a negative test: it cannot reveal the truth of an opinion but only the possible falsity of the opinion. At the same time, however, it cannot guarantee the falsity of an opinion. The method of doubt relies on the fact that whatever is open to the possibility of doubt may in fact be false and is therefore not guaranteed to be true. Given the parameters of his test, Descartes must adopt the standard of absolute certainty. Of course we would have good reason to reject or revise this standard if *nothing* were to survive the test of doubt; but until this test fails it would be difficult to argue that we ought to settle for anything less stringent. This would be like settling for inferior medical treatment because you have decided, in advance of any investigation of availability or cost, that you cannot get or cannot afford the superior treatment; this attitude might be common in the modern economic reality but it is probably not the best approach to something as important as health, or indeed to the foundations of your scientific and moral world.

By adopting such a strict standard, however, Descartes also provides a workable way forward for his method. As there is no need to determine once and for all the falsity of an opinion in order to rule it out as a candidate for undoubtable first principle, the process will be much more manageable. An opinion can be put aside upon the discovery of the mere possibility of doubt. Many if not most of these rejected opinions will turn out to be useful and perhaps even contingently true. But a contingent truth, one which depends upon what happens to be the case, will not satisfy the demands Descartes has set: to build a house on a plot of land that happens to be hard and solid in January may prove to be a difficulty when the spring thaw comes in March. An absolute truth is not contingent upon what happens to be the case and so, in our metaphor, will be a hard and solid foundation in all conceivable circumstances.

It is important to remember, however, that the method of doubt is designed to test for solid and undoubtable foundations. That a particular building material, say plaster, is not suitable as a foundation stone is no reason to throw it away altogether; it might serve some other purpose in the construction process. Similarly, that an opinion does not pass the test of absolute certainty is no reason to reject it completely. It is, however, justification to reject it from the current context – the search for certain foundations. Thus, an important side-effect of the method of doubt is that it does not indict opinions with falsity and they can therefore be recovered later in the process once we know how to use them properly. Within the context of the method of doubt, however, Descartes will treat all opinions that are in the least bit uncertain *as if* they were patently false. It will be very important to recall this 'as if' later in *Meditations*.

First foundations

The second observation Descartes makes about his method concerns the nature of the opinions he is seeking to test. Descartes could adopt a method that tests each and every opinion he has, and some years later, if he lives long enough, he might succeed in testing all the opinions he has. Fortunately Descartes is able to sharpen his method by observing that his opinions form themselves into groups, categories and types. Indeed, the nature of his structure of belief is such that opinions are supported by other, more basic, opinions. Like the house he has invited us to imagine, the quickest way to sort all this out is to test the foundations directly. If he can identify the type or source of opinions that are the most basic and most foundational in his structure of beliefs then he can take the test of doubt directly to this level. If these foundations pass the test then the worries that started the whole process are unfounded and he can set about repairing the upper levels piecemeal; but if these foundations fail then the whole of his belief structure will come down with them.

Thus, with this initial strategy, Descartes is not faced with the insurmountable task of itemising all his opinions and sifting through them one by one. Instead, he claims to have found the starting point for testing these foundations: 'whatever I had admitted until now as most true I received either from the senses or through the senses.' (AT7:18) There are two things going on here that need to be meditated on: first he has moved very quickly to this supposition and secondly he has moved away from the examination of opinions to examining the source of his opinions.

As this is a meditation we need to be sure that we are in a position to follow Descartes and affirm what he affirms. In this case, the initial and apparently unexamined declaration that 'those opinions I consider most true I have received through the senses' needs to be thought through. There are two obvious sorts of opinions that would seem to conflict with this initial claim: on the one hand, there are the opinions of religious belief; on the other, those of mathematics. It might reasonably be assumed that someone (or even Descartes) would hold the truths of religion or the truths of mathematics to be more true than those that are admitted through the senses. So then why does Descartes start with the senses?

The answer is twofold. First, identifying the opinions that I hold to be most true constitutes only half of the criterion for identifying the starting point. The second half involves identifying those beliefs that are most foundational. Thus, it is no objection to say that there are opinions that I deem to be more true than those I receive through the senses if these 'more true' opinions do not fulfil the function of providing a foundation for the rest of my opinions. So it may be that I hold the truth of transubstantiation to be true beyond reproach, so it may be that I hold the truth of the Pythagorean Theorem to be true beyond reproach, but unless I can claim that these opinions also function as the ultimate foundations of my opinions then they are not where I should start the method of doubt. Indeed, when I ask about these opinions I discover that neither is foundational even within their specified fields: transubstantiation relies on the prior notion of substance and the Pythagorean Theorem relies on prior axioms and postulates about triangles.

This leads on to the second part of the answer to our question. For both the sciences that Descartes is critiquing and the ordinary formation of beliefs of our imaginary three year old, the senses *do* provide the basis for our most true opinions. Aristotelian science is explicit about this: 'nothing in the intellect that is not first in the senses'. Thus even the truths of religion and mathematics, while no doubt logically prior to truths of sensation, do not precede the first experience; put another way, we come to these truths (as meaningful for us) by means of our experience of the world. In the same way, the three year old's experience of the world must precede (temporally) the discovery of the truths of religion and mathematics. Indeed, if we take an inventory of the opinions we deem to be most true, we are unlikely to discover that the truths of religion and mathematics are older than our commitment to the opinion (belief) that the world of sense exists, that there are hard things and soft things in this world, that bright light hurts the eyes, or more to the point that I have eyes and that they register visible objects. These sorts of opinions have as compelling a degree of truth as any belief about the Trinity or triangles. But more importantly, they also satisfy the second condition: they serve as first foundations for all the opinions that we may later accrue.

Given that both Aristotelian science and our imaginary three-year-old self give priority to the opinions derived from the senses, Descartes seems to be on firm footing in beginning his method of doubt with this set of opinions. But this set of opinions has nothing in common other than something outside the set: their origin. As a result, if Descartes intends to make use of the discovery of these foundational opinions, he will have to modify his method of doubt in a significant way. As it is originally presented to us, the method of doubt is designed to be a test applicable to opinions (beliefs). But now Descartes is asking us to apply this method to a faculty (or set of faculties): the senses. Is this legitimate?

The short answer is, 'yes, of course'. It is, after all his method and if he wants to modify it in this way then we ought to do our best to accommodate this modification. The better question to ask is, 'will it work?' This is a better question because it brings into focus just what is at stake in accommodating this modification. Our understanding of the method of doubt must be modified so that it will allow for the testing of the senses in a way that still allows for the discovery of certain foundations; and this means that we might *not* find a foundational opinion but something else entirely.

An outline of the method of doubt

Because of the hierarchical structure of opinion and Descartes' decision to test sets (or types) of opinion rather than individual opinions, the method of doubt supports an analogy with the process of cleaning. As with any analogical explanation, this example is only useful up to a point so we must be careful not to push it too far. More importantly, we must remember that this is a way of explaining how Descartes *expects* the method of doubt to work rather than an account of how it does in fact work. As we shall see when we turn to the second meditation, the method of doubt catches Descartes out in various ways.

Nonetheless, thinking of the method of doubt as a process of cleansing brings out the notion that this is a process that seeks to reveal what is hidden. In our analogy, the absolutely true opinion that we seek is hidden under years of accumulated opinions which must be removed by the process of cleansing. But cleaning can take many forms and it is important to have the right cleansing agent for each step of the job. Take for example a silver spoon recovered from a sunken ship. In order to reveal the silver of the spoon we must overcome several layers of build-up. For the first layer of sand and dirt a good scrub with water might be sufficient. But this only reveals the outline of a spoon encrusted with barnacles and other such stubborn sea-creatures. To remove this layer we need another sort of agent or another process of cleansing. At the end of this process we might still discover that the spoon is tarnished and yet another agent must be employed. At each stage of the process something new and more spoon-like is revealed but no single process or cleansing agent is sufficient for every stage.

In the method of doubt, of course, the only 'cleansing agent' we have to apply is doubt. But we have already seen in the shift from opinions to faculties that *how* this is applied is open to modification. At each stage we should be aware that Descartes is modifying the process, modifying the way he applies doubt in order to continue toward the goal. The treasure at the end, the *cogito*, is very much like a burnished silver spoon insofar as once you see it you immediately know that you do not need to carry the process any further. Just as the polished silver in our example is as clean as it can get, the *cogito* is precisely that which cannot be doubted and so the process of doubt must come to an end.

But this is where the analogy begins to break down. Comparing Descartes to such a treasure hunter is only useful up to a point. Unlike our treasure hunter who knows he has a spoon of some description or other, Descartes does not know that what he is looking for is the *cogito*. The process Descartes has devised will reveal *whatever* is buried under all these doubtable opinions, but apart from that he has no idea what it will be. In fact, his expectations for what it will look like are importantly thwarted at the opening of the second meditation. Thus, while it is clear that Descartes has a plan when he deploys the method of doubt, it is also important to remember that even the best laid plans can lead to some startling surprises.

The analogy with a process of cleansing, however, does bring to light one further question about the method of doubt: why does the doubt work in stages? That is, why not apply the strongest possible cleansing agent at the outset and thereby save time? To understand why the staging of doubt is necessary in the first meditation we must recall both the meditational nature of the text and the greater project of *Meditations*. On the one hand, within the context of the first meditation, it is crucial that the reader not become alienated from the project. That is, they must be led step by step into the doubt and be allowed to meditate on each stage in turn. There is little point in providing a meditational text – say, on the goodness of God – that consists only of the assertion 'God is good'. The point of the meditational process is that the reader takes each stage in turn, meditates upon it, takes seriously what is at stake in this stage, and takes this to heart; the process does not move on unless or until it is made real for the meditator. This is not an academic exercise in which the reader moves from step one to step two with the caveat 'for the sake of argument'; read in this way, the meditational text cannot be properly transformative of the reader. Put another way, the reader confronted at the outset with the most powerful doubt available might not really take on board the full import of this power. But the reader who takes seriously each stage of the doubt in its power and import only to see this supposedly great doubt surpassed by an even greater doubt has a genuine sense of what is at stake.

The second reason for the staging has to do with the structure of the project as a whole. In the heat of the first meditation it is sometimes forgotten that Descartes would really like to recover as much of the world as possible. Ultimately, the project of *Meditations* has to bring us back round to our original opinions but reordered or seen differently. In this light, the staging of the doubt in the first meditation is like a trail of breadcrumbs. As we progress through the six meditations we will be able to mark our progress (in reverse) against the stages of the first meditation. Once we set about to recover the world from this self-imposed doubt, such a roadmap is crucial to the undertaking.

And so, as we turn to the method of doubt we will take care to meditate on the successive stages in turn: sensory illusion, the dream argument and the various stages within dreams, and the deceiving God.

Stage one: sensory deception

It is easy to miss the first stage of the doubt both because of its brevity and because of its familiarity. Indeed, the whole of the first stage of doubt is presented in less than one sentence in the Latin original. Having announced that those opinions that he has taken to be the most true (and most fundamental) are those received from the senses, Descartes immediately declares: 'However, I have noticed that the senses are sometimes deceptive; and it is a mark of prudence never to place our complete trust in those who have deceived us even once.' (AT7:18) This is the first stage of the method of doubt in its entirety.

Given its brevity it is tempting to move on quickly to the later more exciting stages – as, it would appear, Descartes is in a hurry to do. Indeed, the case of sensory illusions and error is so commonplace in psychological and philosophical literature that we are likely to assume that nothing special is going on. Even Descartes fails to provide specific examples for this stage of the method of doubt. Nonetheless, we would do well to meditate on this a moment.

Descartes only offers the special cases of distant objects and very small things after the fact, but specific examples of the sort of error he has in mind are not hard to find: the stick that appears to be bent when it is in a glass of water but appears to be straight when it is removed from the glass; the tower that appears square from afar but from closer up turns out to be round; and so on. Before moving on to the next stage it is important that we make an effort to categorise the sort of error Descartes is invoking. The first thing to note is that, precisely by not invoking any particular examples, Descartes amalgamates the different senses into one faculty thus facilitating his procedure but leaving open the question of the relative reliability of the individual senses. For our purposes, however, it is clear that we are meant to treat the senses as a unitary faculty.

In each case the error consists in the necessary incompatibility of two conflicting reports from the senses. Thus the senses tell us that the tower is square but later say of the same tower that it is round; the error here is not dependent on either one of these reports being true of the tower but on the impossibility of both reports being true. As it stands the senses were either wrong about the tower when they said it was square or they wrong when they later claimed that it was round. Similarly, in the case of the stick in water the eyes report that the stick is bent while the sense of touch reports that it is straight. Thus for the purposes of this stage of the method of doubt, Descartes does not need to establish the truth or falsity of any particular claim because the unreliability of the senses is founded in their inability to keep their story straight. It is safer, therefore, to treat the senses as if they were wholly unreliable until we are in a better position to judge.

It is not the purpose of the first meditation to attempt any sort of solution to these errors because there is enough doubt here to guarantee that the testimony of the senses is not to be naïvely trusted. Still it is telling that the basic outlines of solutions present themselves fairly quickly because of the way that Descartes has simplified the problems. Berkeley, for example, solves optical illusions by refusing the amalgamation of the senses; thus conflict only arises when the sense of sight, which ought to be dealing with light and colour, attempts to make reports about spatiality, which is the proper province of touch. The illusions as they are set up also seem to dissolve with the addition of time: the tower does genuinely appear to be square at one time but appears to be round at another. These 'solutions' and others like them import new problems and worries (for example about the status of objects and continuity of experience) but the ease with which Descartes' supposed worries can be dealt with ought to signal that he is worried about something other than solutions.

We must always remember that the method of doubt is a search and, as contrived and simplified as the first stage of doubt might be, it cannot be a criticism of Descartes that he fails to solve these problems at this point. Instead we should focus on what it is that the initial doubt of the senses reveals to us about the process thus far. In this case, the important feature to keep in mind is that the unreliability of the senses has nothing whatsoever to do with the nature of the world or the true state of affairs. Rather the senses are unreliable because they give us reports that, on occasion, directly contradict each other. And this is not a good sign for absolute certainty.

Before we move on, however, we must comment on an often over-looked but nonetheless remarkable feature of the first stage of doubt. In presenting this first stage Descartes adopts the strategy of personifying the senses. Philosophers do this more or less unwittingly every time they refer to the 'testimony of the senses' for it is a person first and foremost who gives testimony, who can be a witness. However, while talk of 'what the senses tell us' or 'the reports of the senses' might be explained away as nothing more than a convenient way of talking about an abstruse and complicated process, Descartes' argument rests on taking the elements of the personification seriously. Thus, the personification in the brief passage in which the senses are introduced is both more explicit than is usually the case and has profound implications for how we should read *Meditations*.

'However, I have noticed that the senses are sometimes deceptive; and it is a mark of prudence never to place our complete trust in those who have deceived us even once.' (AT7:18) Here Descartes invokes a double comparison between sensory activity and personal activity. Not only is it the case that the senses provide testimony, but that testimony can be deceptive. This is crucial because for the comparison to hold we must forego weaker claims about sensory illusion or mistaken testimony. Descartes' account of the parallel with human interaction is explicitly couched in the moral terms of prudence and trust. It is not the case that we would withhold our trust from someone whose testimony was simply in error; it would not be prudent to suspect a friend who has made an honest mistake. Indeed the phrase 'honest mistake' is only meaningful in a world where there is dishonest testimony and it is the latter that is most readily identified as deceptive. Moreover, it is only in the face of dishonest testimony, of deception, that it makes sense to withhold our trust. This is remarkable because, for all its intuitive force, Descartes' brief argument for the first stage of doubt rests entirely on the application of these moral categories.

In making this comparison between the testimony of the senses and that of a personal witness Descartes reveals a great deal about his understanding of the faculties. So what is involved in the notion of the senses deceiving us? First, and at the very least, this way of thinking of the senses reveals a distance between them and me. There is a gap between my senses and me in a way that implies that the senses enjoy a certain degree of autonomous existence. Otherwise there would be no question of testimony at all; I would not be in need of a witness, trustworthy or otherwise, if this gap did not exist. The senses are, in fact, treated as agents. More interestingly, they are treated as moral agents. In the case of deception there is the twin assumption of will and knowledge, which are imported into the faculties in the process of personification. That is, for a person to deceive us with their testimony there is the assumption that they both know the true state of affairs and choose to tell us otherwise. By asking us to think of the senses as involved in deception, Descartes is asking us to believe, at least implicitly, that the senses are personal witnesses who on occasion wilfully pass on information that they know to be false.

At this point it is important simply to note this feature of Descartes' relation to the senses as we must await further implications and finally a transformed perspective in the fourth and sixth meditations.

Stage two: madness and dreaming

In the second stage of the method of doubt Descartes takes a quick inventory of the opinions that survived the first stage. Thus, while the first stage advocates a hard line against the reliability of the sense faculties in general, it soon becomes clear that the implicit arguments deployed there in fact have a more limited efficacy. So, while he admits that the senses ought not to be trusted in extraordinary circumstances there are plenty of quite ordinary circumstances where it would be foolish to doubt their testimony. Descartes, therefore, urges a more cautious approach that recognises that there are many occasions in which the senses simply do not offer conflicting testimony. Thus, that he is sitting by his fire, wearing his dressing gown and holding his pen and paper is testified to unequivocally by his senses and, more importantly, this picture of the situation is confirmed in a coherent way by each of his senses. One would have to be mad to suspect the testimony of the senses in such circumstances – which is, of course, the problem.

Descartes deploys the hypothesis that he is in fact mad. Now it is important to note that even within the already hypothetical method of doubt, Descartes is careful not to commit to being mad. Nonetheless, it must be admitted that were one mad the reliability of such opinions as 'I am sitting in my study now' would be called into question and it is through the introduction of this possibility that Descartes first seeks to dislodge the 'opinions of ordinary circumstances' that had survived the first stage of doubt. Before turning to Descartes' sudden disavowal of the madness hypothesis, we should take a moment to understand just how Descartes' understanding of madness might serve as a useful way to disrupt the opinions of the senses.

First, it must be noted that if we follow through with the madness hypothesis we are no longer dealing with opinions received through the senses. Instead, as in the case of hallucinations, we are dealing with opinions that we believe to be received through the senses. This is significant because this means we are no longer calling the reliability of the senses in ordinary circumstances into doubt. Rather we are calling into doubt our capacity to recognise the very source of our opinions. In a visual hallucination I would believe I was receiving the testimony of my eyes when in fact my eyes are not involved in the process. This means that there are no certain markers that an opinion originated in the senses; or more worrying still, the markers that we rely on to call something a visual sensation are also the markers we use to call something a visual hallucination. Thus, by introducing madness, Descartes shifts the focus slightly but significantly. The reliability of our faculties is still under examination but now before we can make claims about the reliability of the senses we must examine the reliability of a meta-faculty: the 'sense' of what counts as an opinion of sense in the first place.

When applied to the testimony of the senses in 'ordinary circumstances' this observation has a devastating effect. In our attempt to save some of the opinions of sense we appeal to the internal coherence of a set of opinions that we take to correspond to 'ordinary circumstances'. That is, as in a court of law, if the testimony of any single witness hangs together and coheres with the testimony of other witnesses we would be likely to assume that all of these witnesses are reliable. Descartes is relying on this being the case where the testimony of the senses under ordinary circumstances is concerned. Unfortunately, Descartes has no criterion other than this coherence to determine that these are in fact ordinary circumstances. By introducing madness, Descartes exposes the limits of the criterion of internal coherence. Unless we are able to identify the 'ordinary circumstances' in advance or independently of the coherent reports of the senses, then we will never be able to say that this coherence guarantees reliability.

Among the ordinary circumstances involved in the example of court testimony is the belief that the witnesses will not all be unreliable rigorously and in the same way. Thus, a competent attorney would be able to uncover inconsistencies in deceptive testimony given by the various witnesses. The court would be less likely to accept coherent testimony as an indicator of reliable witnesses if it were the case that all the witnesses were of the same family. But what would happen in the extraordinary event that all the witnesses turned out to be the very same person? In such a case no amount of examination would be able to turn up disqualifying inconsistency if the witness chose to deceive the court.

Unfortunately, in the case of the sense faculties all the witnesses are very closely related to each other as part of the same organism. And it is therefore likely that if one were to be corrupted by illness or deranged by madness the others would be as well. Thus, the appeal to the coherent and non-conflicting reports of the senses in a particular circumstance is not sufficient to mark that circumstance as one of ordinary sensation; it could just as well be a coherent hallucination. All that we can guarantee by an appeal to internal coherence is that the opinions will cohere within this particular frame. Madness calls the frame into question.

But Descartes' account of madness is not explicitly limited to simple hallucinations. His examples include those who constantly insist they are kings when they are paupers, or that they are dressed in purple robes when they are naked. And he offers more extreme cases such as those who believe they are made of glass. In these cases the testimony of the senses is less like that of a family and more like that of a single absolutely convinced witness. The degree of coherence in these examples is total and their testimony is compelling. To believe that one is a king is not simply to succumb to sensory hallucination but to adopt a bearing and character that coheres with that belief. To believe that one is made of glass might involve sensory hallucination but the belief is so compelling that it necessarily dictates one's actions. It might be difficult to identify the specific opinion that led one to believe that one is made of glass but once that belief is in place one's behaviour is necessarily and coherently modified; it is far too risky to do otherwise with a body so fragile. It is precisely because the life of the mad can be so totally coherent that the madness hypothesis is devastating.

Thus, the madness hypothesis not only calls into question the framed coherence but it also demonstrates the degree to which foundational opinions do generate a web of further necessary (and in this case necessarily false) opinions that govern behaviour, action and character. In other words the madness hypothesis serves to strengthen Descartes' original contention that the foundations of one's belief structure are crucial to both a meaningful and a moral life.

Given the power and usefulness of this hypothesis why does Descartes abandon madness as a way forward? A first answer can be made by drawing on our previous analogy of cleansing; madness is simply too strong. In the cleansing example, we have to remember that we *want* the silver spoon. Thus one would be correct to say that we could remove the barnacles by vaporising them, say with a nuclear device; but one would be mad to take such steps because this process of barnacle removal would destroy the spoon as well. Indeed, if the spoon represents the *cogito* the madness example does just that. Whatever else the *cogito* turns out to be it is only useful if it is not the *cogito* of a madman. This is captured in the manner by which Descartes dismisses the possibility of his own madness: 'But such people are mad, and I would appear no less mad, were I to take their behaviour as an example for myself.' (AT7:19) If I am really trying to put my house in order then it would be a singular sign of madness to model my new house on one that I have already deemed mad.

This is not to say that Descartes can rule out the possibility that he is mad for this is never possible from within that framework. But to consciously deploy the model of madness is an utterly self-defeating exercise. At the very least, even if he really is mad, it is necessary to act *as if* he is not mad. But more than that, Descartes is involved in a meditational exercise and so it is necessary that he only employ steps that can be carried out by a meditator. An appeal to his own madness is unlikely to be compelling to a reader who has a great deal invested in not being mad. In short the madness hypothesis is too strong both for the methodical doubt and for the meditational form he has adopted.

Instead, Descartes moves on to what is now famously referred to as the dream argument. Having noted that he is not mad, or at the very least ought not to admit this possibility into his method, he immediately notes that he is in the habit of sleeping and having dreams. This is important, for as exotic and unacceptable as the madness hypothesis is for a meditational text, the experience of dreaming is both common and acceptable to the meditator. In shifting to the dream argument, then, he is able to keep the features of the madness hypothesis that are most useful in challenging the frame of experience while not offending or alienating the reader. Moreover, the experience of dreams extends to entirely common occurrences such as 'I am sitting here by the fire now' and is not limited to the extravagances of madness. That is, in fact, by being a more moderate form of doubt than the madness hypothesis the dream argument is more effective. Not only does it leave in place the possibility of a sane foundational starting point, but it is also more attuned to destabilising ordinary experience because the content of dreams is often quite ordinary.

So why, if he has no intention of using the madness hypothesis, does he introduce it at all? There are two basic explanations for the detour through madness. First, by implicitly comparing dreams to 'little madnesses' or 'self-contained episodes of madness' Descartes has positioned the reader to realise just how strange dreams are and hence how powerful the dream argument is. That is, Descartes imports the power of madness into the safe environment of dreams so that the meditator has the opportunity to meditate seriously on something that they would normally be likely to dismiss out of hand. Descartes' strategy in this regard is very straightforward: you might not be ready to declare that you are mad but you might be willing to consider the possibility that you are dreaming right now.

The second reason is more involved. By introducing and then rejecting madness as a hypothesis Descartes is establishing the centrality of reason in his project. One reason that madness is too strong for his purposes is because it undermines the very ground of the exercise. The method of doubt and the process of meditation presume rational capacity. An irrational agent would not be able to undertake the meditations because at every turn you are asked to consider thoughtfully the object of meditation. In effect the reader is cautioned that the method of doubt is not free licence to abandon reason in favour of fancy. In this way, Descartes reveals his commitment to reason as the necessary ground for his philosophy. Just what this commitment to reason entails is open for debate. At the very least, however, the rejection of madness indicates to the reader that there needs to be some capacity for rational thought in order to proceed: otherwise we have gone through the looking glass and should just enjoy the ride.

Within the safety of the dream, however, Descartes is able to deploy all the doubts involved in madness. In addition, because the dream is a circumscribed episode, Descartes is able to appeal to the meditator's memory of dreams. In other words, the meditator is in a position to think back on the experience of being in a dream in a way that a madman would not be able look back on the madness he is in. And, as Descartes argues, the experience of being in a dream can have all the marks of reality that we have in waking experience. This is crucial because Descartes does not insist that the meditator claim that they are now in a dream; Descartes only insists that the reader meditate on the fact that they have had experiences that at the time, while they were dreaming, they took to be entirely real and coherent. That the reader later woke up and declared that those experiences had been a mere dream is not sufficient to dispel the doubt. As Descartes puts it, 'I see so plainly that there are no definite signs by which to distinguish being awake from being asleep.' (AT7:19)

At the end of the sixth meditation, Descartes will identify the 'definite signs' that elude us within the circumscribed purpose of the dream argument. By then, not only will Descartes have more resources available to him, but he will no longer need to apply the strict requirements of the method of doubt. For now, it is worth pointing out that within the method of doubt, definite signs that appeal beyond the dream state are doomed to fail. In the meditational exercise the meditator is asked to judge the experience they are having now and so an appeal beyond that frame is impossible. In the case of dreams, there are of course definite signs that are available after the fact: for instance you wake up in your bed; but experience happens in the present and it is incumbent upon us to judge that experience whilst we are in the midst of it. Descartes' claim is simply that *in the midst of experience* there are no definite signs regarding the frame (dream or waking life) available. But identifying this frame is essential to any appeal to ordinary sense experience.

Interlude: within dreams

The dream argument has called into doubt the reliability of determining which opinions are derived from the senses and which are not. The internal coherence of the set of opinions, while perhaps sufficient to establish the reliability of the senses as long as the set is already framed as opinions derived from the senses, is not sufficient to identify the frame of this set itself. Unfortunately neither the opinions themselves nor their set as a whole bears a mark that distinguishes these opinions as genuinely derived from the senses. Nonetheless, Descartes hopes to determine to what extent the sense faculties might still be reliable. And to do this he turns to the set of opinions that lay claim to being opinions of sense. Even in dreams, Descartes argues, the opinions I am likely to suppose (wrongly) to be derived from the senses, must bear some mark of reality or I would never be likely to make this supposition. About these marks perhaps the senses do make reliable reports.

Put another way, there may be features of sensory reality that will survive the dream argument because these features are precisely the ones that make sense-like (dream) opinions compelling. While in dreams I do not in fact rely on my senses to report about these features, these are the sorts of features that I expect the senses to report on. And as a result, I can be sure that these features would be reliably reported by the senses if I were awake. The fact that these same features occur in dreams merely indicates that I can be certain about these being genuine features of reality. As long as I limit my opinions to only these features I will be on solid ground.

Thus Descartes introduces another modification of the method of doubt. Having shifted from examining opinions to examining the reliability of the faculties (the senses), Descartes now finds it necessary to narrow the focus of his enquiry. Like a psychoanalyst who assumes that much of what is being reported is unreliable, Descartes now tries to find what features must be reliable even in a generally unreliable report. It is in this extended interlude between the second and third stages of doubt that we discover what features of the opinions derived from experience generally will remain true to reality whether or not we are able to determine the nature of the experience (sense-experience or dream experience).

To pursue this line, Descartes introduces what has come to be known as the painter's analogy. Descartes makes a comparison between the imaginative production of appearances in dreams and the real production of images in painting. His claim is that in order for dreams to be compellingly real to us they must follow rules similar to the rules a painter must follow in creating a compelling scene. Like the method of doubt itself, however, the painter's analogy follows careful steps that lead the reader from the familiar to the more extreme. Descartes passes from the sorts of painted images a reader would be most likely to call realistic, through a series of more fanciful images, to abstract images that the seventeenth-century reader would hardly have considered under the rubric of painting at all. This parallels the passage from the sorts of dreams one would naturally find most compelling, through those which upon reflection we can hardly believe we believed to be real at the time, to those with *features* that we must admit we would find compelling no matter how absurd the dream.

Thus Descartes' first claim is that painted images are produced in the likeness of things: for example, those in a landscape or still-life. Corresponding to these paintings are the ordinary dreams one has of having a picnic with friends or riding a bus. Descartes then passes to those paintings that are produced by the creative transposition of parts of ordinary things: for example the depiction of a centaur or satyr in a mythological painting. Corresponding to these paintings would be extraordinary dreams such as picnicking with a talking rabbit or riding a flying bus. But then Descartes suggests that even if a painter were to create an image 'so utterly novel that nothing like it has ever been seen before' (AT7:20) they would still be bound by the restriction that the most basic features of painted images (size and shape) would have to remain familiar to our sense experience. From this analogy, Descartes claims that even in the most extravagant dream there would have to be basic features that would remain consonant with our waking sense experience. These general components of images

include corporeal nature in general, together with its extension; the shape of extended things; their quantity, that is, their size and number; as well as the place where they exist; the time through which they endure, and the like. (AT7:20)

These constitute the features of opinions that survive the dream argument; those that are trustworthy even in dreams.

What would it mean, then, to say of a mere feature of an opinion that it is trustworthy? When we say of an opinion derived from the senses that it is trustworthy, we seem to be making a claim about things in the world that correspond to these opinions. For Descartes to take his belief that he is sitting by the fire as an example of a trustworthy opinion would be for Descartes to believe that the situation so described actually obtains: that there really is a fire (and presumably a room in which there is a fire) and that Descartes really is sitting (in that room) by that fire. But when we shift away from the reliability of even simple opinions of experience to the reliability of mere features of those opinions we can no longer make such claims about any particular situation given in experience. Instead we are making claims about what such situations must be like. That is, we have abstracted away from claims about particular situations, which may in fact have been framed by dream experience, to the general features of experience. Thus, our claim about the 'real things' corresponding to both sense-derived and sense-like opinions is reduced to a claim about the general features of any correspondent reality. And so just as visual experience must involve some colour or other, those features of sensory reality that we can reliably claim to be true are extension, shape, size, number, position, and persistence.

While the process thus far might seem to have reduced the meaningful content of reality to nought, Descartes finds reason to celebrate. For with these basic features in place he is actually in a position to declare the certainty of a number of sciences. Any discipline that relies on the knowledge of composite things, situations or the observation of particular experience will be doubtful. Thus, medicine, physics, astronomy and the like will not have a certain foundation because their fields of study involve the actions of particular things that may not correspond to our experiential opinions of them. However, there are disciplines that treat of only the most general features we have already enumerated. Thus, arithmetic and geometry are able to function even in dreams because they deal *only* with those features common to both sense-like (dream) experience and sense-derived experience. They remain 'indifferent' to whether or not anything exists to correspond to the objects of their study. Indeed, from the perspective of pure mathematics, there are no triangles or circles in reality; there are only shapes which approximate these geometrical entities.

Stage three: the deceiving God

Having consolidated his position after the dream argument, Descartes seems to have brought his method of doubt to a natural conclusion. As he declares:

For whether I am awake or asleep, 2 plus 3 makes five, and a square does not have more than 4 sides. It does not seem possible that such obvious truths should be subject to the suspicion of being false. (AT7:20)

Having sought certain foundations for a science that could supplant the Aristotelian science of his day, he has arrived at the position of Aristotle's classical rival, Plato, who contends that mathematics is the first and most certain science because only mathematics can be thought independently of the world of particular objects. At this point, it would seem that, armed with the mathematical sciences and the general features of corporeal nature, Descartes ought to set about reconstructing his belief structure. It is therefore striking that Descartes pushes on.

Descartes' certainty about mathematics amounts to the claim that, having survived the dream argument, there no longer seems to be any reasonable suspicion that would call these sorts of things into doubt. Unfortunately, Descartes suddenly becomes aware that there is still one possible reason for suspicion: 'there is fixed in my mind a certain opinion of long standing, namely that there exists a God who is able to do anything and by whom I, such as I am, have been created.' (AT7:21) Merely having this opinion is grounds for doubt of even the simplest claims, including those of mathematics. Moreover there are two aspects of this opinion about God and these lead to two separate worries. On the one hand there is the omnipotence of God and on the other there is God as creator.

The possibility of having an omnipotent being around is devastating to any claim of certainty. It is a function of omnipotence that such a being can cause anything to be the case. Not only could such a God deceive me about particular experiences at any given moment, and therefore be equivalent to the dream argument, but such a God would be able to disrupt any claims about parallels between sense experience and dream experience. Descartes' analysis of dream experience relies in large part on the assumption that whatever else might be true about dream experience it shares certain features with sense experience and therefore we ought to be able to derive certain reliable features of experience even in dreams. But an omnipotent God has the power to make dream experience and sensory experience entirely unlike. Indeed such a God has the power to guarantee that life in its entirety is a dream with no regularities of experience and thus no meaningful way to speak of reliability and certainty. Perhaps more worryingly for Descartes, such a God has the power to make me go wrong even in the performance of simple mathematical calculations.

But at the same time, Descartes introduces another worrying scenario. If an all powerful God is also my creator there need not be occasional interventions in my experience nor an entirely illusory world. Rather this God could simply have created me in such a way that I am always, in effect, deceiving myself. If God created my faculties of sense then it is at least possible that God created them such that they are always given to faulty reports. In such a scenario God can create the world one way and create me such that I never have an accurate experience of how the world is. For example, God can make it the case that from birth I am wearing rose-coloured glasses and I would then never have the visual experience of whiteness. Still, it is curious that Descartes adds this second scenario when it is clear that an interventionist omnipotent God is sufficient to wipe out any possibility of certainty thus far considered. As we will see, not only does the interventionist God prove to be incoherent, but the creator God proves to be necessary.

It is crucial at this point to remember that Descartes does not need such a God to exist for the opinion to be useful in the method of doubt. The mere possibility of such an omnipotent God existing is enough to raise doubts about the certainty of other opinions. This is important for two reasons. First, Descartes has made it clear that he will not be in a position to begin metaphysical enquiries, such as proving the existence of God, until he has established his firm foundations. And here the idea of God is being deployed within the method of doubt rather than as a certain conclusion.

Secondly, however, it is sometimes argued that Descartes never doubts the existence of God and that by failing to do so he has either undermined the entire method of doubt or smuggled God through it so that God can be 'discovered' in the third meditation. Quite apart from the fact that it is not at all incumbent upon Descartes to call *everything* into doubt for the first meditation to be successful, Descartes undertakes just such a doubt of the existence of God in this very passage. Unfortunately, what most people who urge this objection against Descartes want is not that the existence of God be called into doubt but that it be denied; and this Descartes neither can do at this point nor, given the explicit point of *Meditations*, should he.

Descartes is forced to call his opinion that there exists an omnipotent deceiving God into doubt in order for the third stage of doubt to be fully effective. As it stands, this opinion, while devastating, is far from secure itself. Moreover, as we have seen, this opinion is internally complex. Not only does it require that God be omnipotent but it also asks that God be the creator of my faculties; add to this the possibility that this

God deceives me and a powerful doubt is available to Descartes. Of course, like the madness hypothesis, this doubt is useless to anyone who denies any of the above features of Descartes' opinion. Rather than attempting to prove the existence of such a deceiving God, however, Descartes examines each of a set of alternate hypotheses.

Because of the complex structure of the opinion Descartes starts out with, there are two basic challenges to the deceiving God hypothesis: on the one hand there are those who would accept the existence of an omnipotent God but deny the deception; on the other there are those who would deny the existence of such a God altogether. Descartes takes each of these alternatives in turn to see whether the force, if not the form, of the deceiving God hypothesis holds within the framework of the method of doubt.

The first alternative admits that an omnipotent God exists but denies that this God would deceive me. If this opinion is sufficiently compelling upon meditation then the deceiving God hypothesis will be defused, for a God who will not deceive me is no use in the method of doubt. However, if this opinion is itself in some way doubtful, then the possibility of a deceiving God remains a live option and the doubt beyond the dream argument is effective.

So Descartes observes that 'it is said' that God is supremely good and it would be repugnant to this goodness to wilfully deceive me. This seems to challenge the notion of an interventionist deceiving God. But Descartes is then left with a further quandary: if such a God would not actively deceive me would it not also be incompatible with this goodness to allow me to be deceived at all? But Descartes has already determined that, at least on occasion, the senses are deceptive and even on the good God hypothesis these senses were created by God. If the appeal to God's goodness is used to deflect the force of the actively interventionist deceiving God then it cannot account for the God who creates deceptive faculties. At this point the first alternative is put aside as inconclusive because Descartes has been able to cast enough doubt on the good God hypothesis to allow the deceiving God hypothesis to stand within the first meditation. We should note that it is to just this quandary that Descartes must return in the fourth meditation.

The second alternative to the deceiving God hypothesis is its flat denial: 'Perhaps there are some who would rather deny so powerful a God, than believe everything else is uncertain.' (AT7:21) It is worth noting the formulation Descartes uses here as it reinforces the meditational aspect of the process. Although not as repugnant as the madness hypothesis, many readers would be more than willing to forego the belief in an omnipotent being because this can in fact be a disturbing idea. Hence Descartes both notes that the denial of so powerful a God is a free choice ('would rather deny') and recognises the very human reasons that might lead one to such a choice. This is important because Descartes will want to win these people back to the idea of living in the shadow of an all powerful God but will not want to do so under false pretences. It is, and ought to be, disturbing to think of such a God. Descartes' central argument for the existence of God rests on taking seriously the meaning of 'all-powerful' and so any reader needs to be prepared to take this idea in its full strength.

Whatever the motivation, however, there are those who will deny the existence of an omnipotent God. Rather than fight this objection head on, Descartes simply points out that one of the consequences of denying the existence of God in this way is the denial of God the creator. In this case, the burden of explaining how it is that I came into being shifts to them. That is, the deceiving God hypothesis may have unwelcome consequences but at least it offers a plausible account of how I was created as I am and with the faculties I have. To reject that hypothesis opens up an explanatory void that must be filled. Thus, to these objectors Descartes poses the legitimate challenge of explaining how it is that I came to be as I am.

Descartes lists several possible alternatives to the creation by an omnipotent God (fate, chance or a causal chain of events). But it is apparent that even if this list is not exhaustive, any possible origin will be inferior, by definition, to originating from an omnipotent being. Take, for example, natural selection as a modern solution to this problem. As good as natural selection is at weeding out imperfections and developing better adaptations, the product of natural selection will necessarily be inferior to the product of an omnipotent God because omnipotence does not imply very, very good or even excellent; it implies perfection. Even the most ardent supporter of evolutionary theory will only be able to argue for perfectibility, and not perfection, through natural selection. Being the product of an all powerful creator is, as we have seen, no guarantee that I will be perfect; but no other 'author of my being' can possibly do better than this God's best work.

Thus, even if Descartes were to concede some other origin for his being he would still have to admit that creation by an omnipotent God, even with the risk that this God is deceptive, is the option most likely to result in reliable faculties. As he puts it, 'the less powerful they [the objectors] take the author of my origin to be, the more probable it will be that I am so imperfect that I am always deceived.' (AT7:21) In this way, Descartes establishes that, while he might not be the creation of an omnipotent God, any other option actually puts him in a position of less certainty. Therefore, for the purposes of the method of doubt the deceiving God hypothesis holds. And then he is left with nothing from his former opinions that he can be certain of and no faculty that he can rely on. Quite tellingly, even the opinion he deploys in the third stage of doubt, that there exists an omnipotent God, has been called into doubt by the very process that lends it its persuasive force.

Bad habits and the evil genius

Perhaps the most striking image to come out of *Meditations* is that of the evil genius, or, as he is sometimes called, the evil demon (or evil deceiver). It is therefore useful to remind ourselves that the evil genius is not in fact deployed as part of the method of doubt. That method drew to a close with the deceiving God hypothesis and the evil genius can add no more force to the doubt achieved through that hypothesis. Once the possibility of a deceiving God is admitted to the method there is simply nothing more to do because there is nothing that the possible existence of an omnipotent being cannot call into question. So why introduce the evil genius?

Having completed the arduous task of purging himself of all his dubious opinions, Descartes declares that, if he wishes this method to bear fruit, he must continue to withhold assent from these opinions as if he knew them to be false. But this task is not as easy as it sounds: saying it does not make it so. And it is upon this challenge that Descartes asks us to meditate. In order not to sacrifice all he has gained through the preparatory method of doubt he must find some way to keep his mind clear of these opinions. And yet he discovers that he is the victim of long habit and finds that he assents to dubious opinions even against his will. The problem is that he has established through the method of doubt that these opinions are dubious and yet highly probable; but against the long habit of assenting to opinions, for example from the senses, this fact is not persuasive. Thus he proposes that, instead of simply withholding assent he should, for a time, turn completely away from these opinions and treat them as if completely false.

This is the language of someone who is trying to break a habit. It is not enough to tell a smoker, for example, that smoking is bad for them. They probably already know this. But put into a situation where cigarettes are available, for example at a party with smokers, and the habit will likely overpower the will. And so it is perhaps necessary to remove all cigarettes from their presence until the danger of temptation has passed. Descartes is taking similar actions with the results of his method of doubt. It is just far too tempting to believe that the world really is the way it appears to me. And so he plans to turn his will in entirely the opposite direction until either the temptation has passed or he has the results he needs from the procedure.

It is on this note that he introduces the evil genius. The purpose of the evil genius is to strengthen Descartes' will. Thus, he will suppose that he has been created by an evil genius who is supremely powerful and clever and by this means strengthen his resolve not to fall back into the habit of assenting to dubious opinions. In this regard the evil genius is like a personal trainer. In a perfect world no-one would ever need a personal trainer in order to take on a fitness regime. The information about health and fitness is available and anyone who wishes to take up a fitness regime may do so. And yet there are personal trainers. This is because just knowing what is good for you and even wanting to do it are not always enough. A personal trainer keeps you on track and refuses to let your laziness or bad habits overcome your decision to become fit. The personal trainer is like an external source of willpower for our endeavour. In the same way the evil genius is an external source of resolve in the face of habitual assent.

The role of the evil genius is fairly straightforward. Whenever he finds himself faltering in the course of the meditational exercise, Descartes will remind himself that he may be under the sway of an all-powerful and evil being who wishes to deceive him. In this way the temptation to fall back into the opinions he has strived so hard to set aside will be thwarted. But to take the evil genius as a stage in the method of doubt would be a mistake. Similarly, to believe that the evil genius hypothesis is an essential feature of Descartes' metaphysics is to miss the point of the meditational process. If *Meditations* were a discourse this device would not be necessary; but *Meditations* is a meditational text. If humans were not given to bad habits and weakness of will the evil genius would not be called upon; but then personal trainers would all be out of work.

This casts light on one of the more misunderstood features of the evil genius. As I mentioned earlier he goes by a variety of aliases and each name is misleading in its own way. By far the safest is 'evil deceiver' because it captures the basic function required by Descartes: he deceives. To adopt this title, however, is to sacrifice an important dimension of the character of the evil genius by reducing him to his function. At the same time, both 'evil genius' and 'evil demon' lend themselves to misunderstanding. While I prefer 'evil genius' for its echo of the Latin and French original, it does tend to call to mind the anachronistic image of the mad scientist and, thanks to a cottage industry in contemporary epistemology, the brain-in-a-vat scenario. Similarly, 'evil demon' calls to mind a sort of devil, or indeed the devil himself, with the religious baggage that this carries. And there is no doubt something to this image and its power in sixteenth-century Christian Europe. Both readings, however, miss a vital point and one that ties these two names together.

The modern notion of 'genius' as an artistically or intellectually gifted individual is a very late arrival in European languages. In the French of Descartes' day this meaning would not have been primary or even fully formed. More importantly, Descartes wrote the first edition of *Meditations* in Latin and so it is to this meaning that we ought to turn. The Latin 'genius' has a variety of meanings circling around a general notion of a guardian spirit. A person's genius would be the guiding spirit that accompanied them through their lives and, depending on its competence and the degree to which it was heeded by its charge, protected that person.

In this the Romans are modifying the Greek notion of *daimon* which played a similar role and which should give us pause when we consider the character of the 'evil demon'. The most famous *daimon* for philosophers is probably that of Socrates. According to Socrates this *daimon* was a negative guide insofar as it never told him what to do but only prevented him from doing certain things. Thus, we could think of Descartes' *daimon* in a similar fashion insofar as he only wants to use the image of the evil genius to keep him from falling back into bad habits. In Roman culture another key feature was added as '*daimon*' was transformed into 'genius'. In addition to being a guardian spirit, the genius would be a sort of personal tutor and it was not uncommon to refer to the genius of a youth as a sign of their intellectual capacity. Thus was resolved the mystery of learning for Roman education: a student who listened to their genius would learn while the student who paid no heed to their personal genius would not.

In light of this history we should banish all our B-Movie images of mad scientists and brains in vats when we think of the 'evil genius'. We also ought to be careful about how much weight we give to the adjective 'evil' which is much stronger in English than its roots in either French or Latin. In fact, we are put into the odd situation whereby, while we cannot deny that Descartes' genius is evil, we ought to remember that this genius is good for Descartes. Indeed, what Descartes needs at this point in the meditational process is a guiding spirit who will actively deceive him. More to the point, this sort of genius is the only one that Descartes will be able to learn from because, like a good teacher, this genius knows that what would most likely prevent Descartes from learning anything from the method of doubt would be his weakness of will. Thus, as an image, that of the evil genius, properly understood, is both appropriate and richer than it is usually given credit for being.

The Second Meditation

The traditional story of the second meditation is well known and fairly straightforward. After the doubts of the first meditation, Descartes discovers what he was looking for: an absolutely undoubtable starting point for his philosophy. The method of doubt has served its purpose and, having discovered that one truth (I exist) will survive any failure of the senses, the dream argument and even the deceiving God hypothesis, Descartes begins to reconstruct his world of opinion – but now on a firm foundation. As a first step into this new enquiry into what he can know with certainty he turns to the examination of just what he can know about himself and what he can discover about simple bodies – in this case a piece of wax.

Unfortunately, like many philosophical legends concocted through the Chinese whispers of repeated summary and commentary, this story has little bearing on what actually happens in the second meditation. Nonetheless, this account reveals three temptations readers face when approaching this meditation: to believe that the *cogito* is discovered directly by the method of doubt; to believe that the *cogito* serves as a foundation in the way Descartes had envisioned; and finally to believe that this meditation has anything to do with material bodies.

With these temptations in mind, let us step back and meditate afresh. Perhaps the first thing we should notice about the second meditation has more to do with style than content. If we were to believe the traditional account, the structure of the second meditation is fairly simple and any problems that arise have to do with the ideas that are presented there and the fact that these are presented largely without argumentation. It is unsurprising, then, that so much effort has been made to fill in the logical gaps and provide accounts of the philosophical assumptions that must be underpinning these controversial ideas.

But the second meditation is also rhetorically rich and we would do well to spend time with what goes on in the text rather than hurrying toward the conclusion of what this meditation supposedly proves. The first meditation presents its rhetoric in the service of a nearly straight narrative line that aids the reader in taking up the meditative stance. In the second meditation, however, because the reader has already passed through the process of radical doubt, the rhetoric is pressed into the service of more traditional philosophical means. Thus, especially in the first half of the meditation, Descartes uses rhetorical devices for the sorts of philosophical ends that commentators are often keen to shore up with speculative arguments and suppositions. These rhetorical moves are subtle and only a reader who is prepared to meditate through them will be able to grasp the main points of the second meditation.

The meditation falls into three parts which will serve as guideposts for this chapter. First, Descartes discovers, much to his surprise, that he exists and thus founds the philosophy of subjectivity. Next, he sets about attempting to understand better what this might mean; in the process he radically transforms the notion of soul, and presents, perhaps for the first time, the modern notion of mind. And finally, in order to keep the promise of the title, he shows that this mind is better known than body; the main point to be taken from this demonstration, however, is the way in which he manages the relation between sensation and perception.

The whirlpool effect

Descartes begins the second meditation by remarking on the effect the first meditation has had on him: 'It is as if I had suddenly fallen into a deep whirlpool; I am so tossed about that I can neither touch bottom with my foot, nor swim up to the top.' (AT7:24) While perhaps it should be obvious given the first person narrative we are caught up in, it is rarely acknowledged that this effect passes into the writing itself. In stark contrast to the methodical and controlled rhetoric of the first meditation, the style of the opening passages of the second meditation is marked by just this whirlpool effect. There is no clear line of argument to follow and the reader is tossed about along with Descartes as he grapples, like a drowning man, for some hand-hold or place to set down his foot. The first meditation has, quite unexpectedly, robbed him of the confidence with which he had started this exercise and the search for firm foundations has taken on a genuine and existential urgency.

In the first meditation it is very clear that Descartes is leading us in our meditational practice: he has the plan and lays down the steps for us to follow. What is therefore most striking about the opening of the second meditation is the degree to which this method has overwhelmed Descartes. As we enter this meditation it is no longer the case that Descartes is in control; he is struggling to hold on. This is the natural outcome of the hyperbolic doubt that Descartes has so ruthlessly deployed and, in some sense, he ought to have seen this coming. Therefore, that he is caught unawares is significant.

By allowing this loss of control to inform his writing Descartes signals an important fact about the method of doubt: as Descartes had envisioned it, the method fails to identify the *cogito* or any other certainty. Instead, in the course of his chaotic flailing he comes upon his first certainty quite unexpectedly. We will return to this accidental discovery shortly. But first, we should meditate on the loss of control evidenced in the opening of the second meditation.

It remains true that the method of doubt is necessary to the discovery of the *cogito*. However, neither this discovery nor the way in which the method of doubt supports it comes about in accordance with Descartes' plan. In effect, the first meditation makes it possible to discover the *cogito* by working *better* (and indeed differently) than Descartes intended. In the first meditation, Descartes is careful to construct the stages of doubt so that the reader is led progressively toward the total doubt at the end. That is, at each stage Descartes controls his rhetoric in order to make certain that the reader is confronted with and takes on board the full force of the doubt being presented. This is not merely an academic exercise. The meditational approach demands that the reader commit to the exercise and it is only through this commitment that the text can be fully understood. The text must be meaningful *for* the reader rather than simply convey meaning *to* the reader.

But like the evil genius who can only be helpful to Descartes by being 'evil', the method takes over from Descartes the one thing that he has stubbornly refused to surrender: control. This is indicated in the image of the drowning man that Descartes conjures for us. And it is with this groundlessness that Descartes comes to realise what is at stake. That is, having asked for a total commitment from the reader he is now forced by his own method to commit for himself. As long as the method of doubt is being controlled by Descartes, the method will not have achieved the total commitment its success requires. It is precisely the controlled deployment of the method of doubt that holds it back from success as this control of the method indicates a prejudice about how it is supposed to work.

This is not the same objection, sometimes offered, that Descartes fails to call into doubt the opinion that 'whatever survives the method of doubt will be undoubtable'. Descartes is right to hold (even implicitly) to that opinion. The method of doubt will necessarily yield the results Descartes seeks, providing Descartes commits himself to the method. It is a different prejudice that holds Descartes back. By believing uncritically that he knows how to control the method of doubt, he exposes the related prejudice that he already knows what sort of thing would count as a result. It is therefore crucial that Descartes give up this control. Only by giving up his opinions about how the method ought to work and what a positive outcome ought to look like, will the method make it possible for Descartes to find an answer. For, as we shall see, the *cogito* is neither what he thought he was looking for nor where he thought he would find it.

A roundabout way to the *cogito*

The opening passages of the second meditation are stylistically and rhetorically rich. It is difficult to fully convey the sense of wandering, of rushing headlong without clear direction, of doubling back on himself as he returns to already dismissed positions, of clutching at straws that typifies Descartes' writing in these sections but it is there if the text is attended to. It is perhaps clearest when these passages flooded with rhetorical questions and counter-questions are compared with the confident and composed rhetoric of the first meditation. Far too often the narrative effect of the text is passed over in favour of conceptual analysis and reconstruction of argument; but we should take time to meditate on the movement of these passages because these narrative features will inform our reading of the *cogito* and therefore the whole of Descartes' First Philosophy.

Beginning in a sort of despair and moving into what amounts to rhetorical panic, the writing not only exhibits loss of control but also illustrates Descartes' misunderstanding of his own method of doubt. Throughout the first meditation Descartes was under the misapprehension that whatever certainty he would discover would be outside him, other than him, an opinion among his stock of opinions, a belief like any other. The loss of footing resulting from the method of doubt induces the loss of control that allows Descartes to see what he never looked at – himself – because he was always busy looking at something else.

After admitting to the disorientation that has been induced by the first meditation Descartes puts on a brave face and vows to carry on with his search. Almost immediately, however, he is shaken by the realisation that his chosen method might very well result in the discovery that nothing whatsoever is certain. While coupled with a hope for great things if but one Archimedean point can be found, this admission marks a dramatic shift from the confidence of the previous meditation. Nowhere in the first meditation does he seriously consider the possibility that nothing is certain; it is always assumed that a final certainty will be discovered. We should make special note of this worry for it returns in a more threatening way a few lines later.

Faced for the first time with the possibility that there will be no certainty other than that there is no certainty, Descartes' first move is telling. As a sign that Descartes sees his method as a safe haven, his first attempt to regain his footing is ironically a rehearsal of the very method of doubt that brought him to this point:

Therefore I suppose that everything I see is false. I believe that none of what my deceitful memory represents ever existed. I have no senses whatever. Body, shape, extension, movement, and place are all chimeras. What then will be true? (AT7:24)

In one sense, this quick repetition of the doubt from the first meditation is methodologically appropriate to this meditational text; indeed, he starts the third and fourth meditations with similar reminders. Here, however, the rehearsal serves another narrative purpose as well.

Faced with the despair and disorientation with which he introduces the second meditation, Descartes' recourse to method signals an attempt to regain his bearings by continuing on in the same manner that had afforded him such control in the first meditation. But the method has run its course and there simply is no way to carry on in the same manner. Descartes' attempt to regain his composure and the confidence with which he started his project is dashed as soon as he begins because in answer to his own question 'what then will be true?' he discovers he has been brought around to the same worry that he had set out to escape: 'Perhaps just the single fact that nothing is certain.' (AT7:24)

Let us compare the two occurrences of this paradoxical certainty. Initially this arises as an undesirable alternative to the possible discovery of another certainty: 'I will stay on this course until I know something certain, or, if nothing else, until I at least know for certain that nothing is certain.' (AT7:24): 'at least', 'if nothing else'. This paradoxical and unwelcome certainty is not only diminished by these phrases, but it is also presented as an alternative to the explicit aim of the method of doubt: to find something certain. The weakness of this initial worry is further signalled by the immediate and confident claim that great things can be hoped for. It is significant that Descartes acknowledges this unsettling possibility at all but as we can see, he does not really take it too seriously at this point. He returns to the method of doubt hoping for (if not expecting) a more positive outcome. Yet the method insistently returns him to the unwanted result. This time, however, the paradox of the certainty of uncertainty occurs on its own and in direct response to his query; this time it is only buffered by 'perhaps'; this time it is serious.

In effect, the method of doubt has failed him for the first time. It has not failed to produce doubt but it has failed to produce a satisfying outcome. Not only does Descartes not *want* to discover that the only certainty is that there is no certainty, he has not even taken seriously that this might be the outcome until just now. And by presenting this possible outcome so forcefully, by working so successfully in the production of doubt, the method of doubt fails to satisfy Descartes' present need for control and stability. Ironically, the success of the method undermines Descartes' plan to attempt 'the same path he entered upon yesterday' and to 'stay on this course' until he has a certain resolution. Thus the initial outcome of the method of doubt is not, as Descartes had envisioned it, in securing the certainty of a particular opinion but in putting Descartes in a position to step back from this method.

At this point, bereft of even his faith in the method, Descartes presents us with a remarkable passage which is characterised by the sort of panic one brings on oneself through the sheer act of flight. As sometimes happens when walking through a dark forest alone, the ability to hold one's nerve collapses all of a sudden. Once one gives in to fear and begins to run the fear becomes compounded and flight feeds fear feeds flight. And so in this passage the sentences tumble into each other and

Descartes considers possibility after possibility with greater urgency each time, answering his own questions with still more questions. The distinction between claim, question, answer and counterclaim blurs and could not be in starker contrast with the rhetoric of the previous meditation. If the first meditation was meant to purge him of individual prejudices, in this passage we see the purging of the very possibility of method.

Within this rhetorical rush, however, there is a richness that will inform the final stopping point. For instance, Descartes opens this paragraph with the apparent disavowal of both the method that has disappointed him and the doubts that are flooding his mind. His first response is to ask the wholly illegitimate question 'how do I know there is not something else, over and above all those things I have just reviewed, concerning which there is not even the slightest occasion for doubt?' (AT7:24) This is an illegitimate question because he has already established in the first meditation how he knows this. In a fit of buyer's remorse, he abandons the method he had claimed just moments before would be his guiding principle, and lunges into pure speculation.

Like any good Christian he first alights upon God as his saviour from this dilemma; but, like many a not-so-good Christian, he turns upon God as a scapegoat in the same breath: 'Is there not some God . . . who instills these very thoughts in me?' (AT7:24) Remarkably, Descartes does not adopt the position that is open to him of positing his faith in God as the founding and certain principle. He could, of course, appeal to God in this more traditional manner; he could claim that his belief in God is dogmatically certain and in this appeal he would be able to stop the whirlpool. Give yourself over to dogmatic faith, he could tell himself, and these troubles will dissipate. In keeping with his panic, however, he glides past this opportunity and instead decides, rather bizarrely, that it would be better to blame God for the mess he is in. It is as if he were to say to himself 'it is not the result of my own method that I find myself cast adrift in a sea of doubt; it is God who has instilled these thoughts in me.'

While it is by no means certain that Descartes has this possibility in mind at this point, in such a scenario it would at least be true that God as the author of these thoughts must exist. Unfortunately, Descartes cannot even be sure that God instils these thoughts in him because it is possible that Descartes is the author of these thoughts himself. And here Descartes first turns his search inward. Up until this point, his method has focussed outward on the world, the senses, opinions, even on God.

Like a searchlight that can illuminate anything but itself, the method of doubt has been very effective in the examination of opinions other to Descartes. That is, Descartes has been examining the opinions he has about other things, and these opinions must themselves be other to Descartes. But in his initial counter to the hypothesis of God as author of his thoughts Descartes notices himself (in the guise of author of his own thoughts) for the first time.

At this point it is by no means certain whether Descartes is the author of his own thoughts but the insight into the possibility of this being the case leads inevitably to the *cogito* itself. The steps are slightly haphazard but the path is clear. If God were the author of my thoughts then it would necessarily be the case that God exists (as author). This hypothesis cannot be affirmed as certain because it may be the case that I – not God – am the author of my own thoughts. However, it would be no less certain that I would exist if I were the author of my own thoughts. As yet, of course, these arguments, while parallel, are indecisive. Thus far, Descartes is only in a position to claim that *whatever* is the cause or author of my thoughts must exist. Descartes does not yet see the full implications of this line of thinking because he has yet to examine the mind into which these thoughts are instilled, but he has finally allowed himself into the discussion.

From the question 'am I not at least something?' Descartes digresses into questions about his body. However, this digression only serves to remind him that he has already employed the method of doubt to dispel all thought of having a body or senses. This is crucial because it allows him to take up a position he had initially ascribed to God. He (re)calls to mind an occasion – the application of the method of doubt – in which he was the author of his thoughts. He is no longer employing the method of doubt but is reflecting upon it.

But I have persuaded myself that there is absolutely nothing in the world: no sky, no earth, no minds, no bodies. Is it then the case that I too do not exist? But doubtless I did exist, if I persuaded myself of something. (AT7:25)

In the act of persuading himself of these things he necessarily authored his thoughts on these topics. And to be an author of the thoughts he has to exist.

But wait. It is not yet clear who this author is. It certainly seems to Descartes that he persuaded himself of these things, that he authored these doubts. And if this is the case then all is well. But in this he must rely upon his 'deceitful memory'. Moreover, he opened the paragraph by admitting the possibility of another author. Perhaps in this case he is succumbing to a deception by his evil genius. Perhaps he is being deceived even in the memory of having persuaded himself of his doubts. Fortunately, at this point Descartes is ready to recognise the second half of the situation of having thoughts, doubts, or deceptions. Just as the act of persuasion requires the existence of both persuader and the one who is persuaded, the act of deception requires the existence of both deceiver and deceived. Thus either he really did undertake the method of doubt and persuade himself that, for example, he had no body, or in all this he is being deceived by the evil genius. In either case, he exists; either he is the persuader or he is the deceived.

And so we arrive at the famous *cogito*.

And let [the evil genius] do his best at deception, he will never bring it about that I am nothing so long as I shall think that I am something. Thus, after everything has been most carefully weighed, it must finally be established that this pronouncement 'I am, I exist' is necessarily true every time I utter it or conceive it in my mind. (AT7:25)

The unexpected discovery

Let us pause for a moment and meditate on this discovery and the path that has led to it. It is perhaps surprising to think that all this work has led to the underwhelming discovery of 'I am, I exist'. On the one hand it is difficult to see how this is the sort of claim that could be in need of discovery. How could this be the sort of thing one did not always already in some sense know? On the other hand, this claim seems to add nothing whatsoever to our knowledge. Even if for some reason I wanted to claim that I really had not known that I existed, it is not clear how this discovery would help with any other knowledge claims; or more to the point, it is not likely that such a ubiquitous and possibly empty claim is suited to serving as the foundation of all knowledge.

It is perhaps for these reasons that there is a long tradition of commentators who have assumed that something else must be going on here. Thus it is that Descartes' project is dragged into dialogue with scepticism as it is argued that this claim is necessary as a final refutation of the absolute scepticism of the first meditation. Thus it is that interpretations of *Meditations* become embroiled in questions of epistemological foundationalism. Similarly, there is a vast literature that has grown up around the nature of the supposed inference involved in 'I think, I am'. But these approaches and obsessions are not supported by the text's narrative and meditational dimensions that we have been exploring. It is rather the extraordinary fact that the mundane 'I am, I exist' has thus far escaped Descartes' notice that should capture our attention.

The objection that this ought not to count as a discovery has the same blind spot as the objection that this discovery adds nothing to our knowledge. Both objections take a third person, objectivist view of knowledge and truth. And thus, the claim 'I am, I exist' is subject to analysis in the same way that 'the morning star is the evening star' would be. But Descartes is not conducting a third person investigation and so we should not expect his discovery to be subject to an objective analysis. As odd as it sounds, it is entirely plausible to say that Descartes had never noticed that he exists. But what this brings to light is that this is probably true of most people. To notice this in an existentially meaningful way is extraordinarily difficult not least because of the habits of third person analysis to which we are given.

In the course of *Meditations* thus far, Descartes has *not* considered his own existence in a meaningful, first person way. Instead, while adopting a first person perspective, he has steadfastly looked elsewhere. All along, of course, the claim 'I am, I exist' was available to Descartes; it is not discovered as new knowledge. All along, the claim 'I am, I exist' was implicit in all of his actions and thoughts; it is not something that suddenly became true. Rather it is precisely the ubiquity of the claim 'I am, I exist' that makes it so difficult to discover by such third person means. And this is just the same ubiquity that leads some commentators to claim that 'I exist' is a 'degenerate' proposition in that 'exist' adds nothing to the use of the 'I'. And yet this is the great thing that Descartes has claimed to discover. If we follow the narrative flow of this text as a meditation then perhaps Descartes has made it possible for us to notice this for ourselves as well.

With this in mind we should review the method Descartes has thus far employed. As we have seen, the success of the method of doubt was not in the immediate discovery of the *cogito* for this it cannot achieve. Rather, as its name would imply, the method of doubt is good at raising doubts. In this case, the first success of the method was the creation of such powerful doubts that Descartes was forced to abandon the use of the method itself. The second success of the method was that it provided an opportunity, close at hand, for Descartes to take up his own practice (of doubting) as an object of investigation. Hence, by its first success the method allows Descartes to take up a perspective on what he is doing rather than simply to continue to do it. This meta-perspective is crucial to Descartes' project because it marks a shift from practice to reflection on practice. But that means that the third success of the method of doubt is that it brings into view that which had always been present but had never been seen: that Descartes is.

This has always been available to us as well but the practical needs of the everyday constantly cover it over. We spend our time looking out on the world as a satisfaction of need, a source of danger, a means of sustenance, or even an object of enquiry. When I refer to myself in the course of daily affairs it is far more likely to take the form 'I am a teacher', 'I am hungry' or even 'I am Kurt' than to take the form 'I am'. And even if the statement 'I am' were to occur it would not likely be taken in the existentially meaningful way that Descartes has brought us to. For here in *Meditations* we discover that the fact that I am is not only a certainty but it provides the basis for all our activities in the third person, objective world.

What the method of doubt does above all is purge us of the practical concerns that constantly blind us to that which underlies every claim we make about the world and every action we take in the world. The *cogito* is not something new but something newly seen and seen in a dramatically new way.

The *cogito*: handle with care

What, then, has Descartes achieved in the course of this meditation? It is easy to assume that in the *cogito* he has secured a certainty upon which to found his opinions. But this is not yet the case. As we have seen, the path to this certainty has taken Descartes away from the original course of his investigation. The *cogito* is not an opinion like other opinions. Its discovery via reflection on the process of thought itself marks it off as different in kind. Thus, it is not yet clear that the *cogito* is the sort of foundation Descartes was looking for. For all its certainty, knowing that he exists will not be immediately useful to Descartes. Because this opinion is not of the sort he was expecting, he must still learn how to use this newfound certainty as a foundation.

One thing that the discovery that he exists does provide is a way to regain the balance he had lost through the success of the first meditation.

This is reflected in the tone of the passages immediately following the discovery of the *cogito*. Descartes may have regained his balance but the brash confidence of the first meditation has been replaced by the need for caution as he moves forward.

He has seen in a flash the certainty of the *cogito* but now urges a cautious return to the method in order to flesh out the details of this insight. Having arrived at the *cogito* in a rush and quite unexpectedly he realises that he is in danger of misunderstanding the one thing that ought to be most certain. While he knows with certainty that he exists he does not yet know what this means; knowing *that* he is, he does not yet know *what* he is. Thus we have this curious warning:

> And so from this point on, I must be careful lest I unwittingly mistake something else for myself, and thus err in that very item of knowledge that I claim to be the most certain and evident of all. (AT7:25)

This certainly would be a grave error and one that ought to be avoided; as errors go, this one would appear more serious than mistaking a round tower for a square one or even, as in Oliver Sacks' famous study, of mistaking one's wife for a hat. At the same time, however, we have to ask just how such a misidentification could be possible in the first place.

The naïve observer, or Descartes himself prior to the method of doubt, could be forgiven for thinking that he has now entered the realm of delusion and paranoia. How in the world could one mistake something else for oneself? But we are no longer the naïve observers of *Meditations* and Descartes has already passed through the method of doubt. As fellow meditators we are ready to acknowledge that Descartes' worry is genuine for, even without recourse to the fiction of the evil genius, we have sufficient reason to doubt our ability to examine even the simplest and closest things. To ask what we are likely to mistake ourselves for is simply to ask what we are likely to say of ourselves. Put this way, the worry behind the question comes into focus.

Many of our answers to the question 'who are you?' are entirely contingent and situational. Thus, sometimes I am likely to say 'I am a philosopher' and other times I am likely to say 'I am a tourist' and on still others I am likely to say 'I am his brother'. But on some occasions I might use entirely different locutions as the need arises. I might say to a doctor 'I hurt my hand' or to a waiter 'I'll have the lasagne' because for a doctor or a waiter I just am 'someone who has hurt his hand' or 'the person having the lasagne'; and so in these situations I am happy to go along with the reduction of my being to these descriptors. But if I am willing to be complicit in these sorts of ascriptions, titles and names in certain situations how can I be certain that I will not succumb to the transient security of a similar ascription in my current situation? After all, the situation of radical doubt is a fairly extreme situation. And, as we have seen in the case of Descartes, there is pressure on someone caught in this state of groundlessness to grasp at any security that presents itself.

Thus Descartes redeploys the method of doubt on the field of opinions he might ordinarily have about himself. By subjecting the answers to the question 'who did I think I was?' to the method of doubt he hopes to avoid settling too quickly on an answer to the question 'who am I?'. In this way Descartes also reminds us that we are not accustomed to answering this latter question without a contextual frame; and unfortunately these frames have all been called into doubt.

Descartes' return to the method of doubt is now focused on the opinions he once had about himself. The first thing to note is that this entire discussion is framed in terms of 'what I used to believe'. Thus he is reflecting on the position and opinions he held before the radical doubt of the first meditation. These opinions about himself had never been properly subjected to the method of doubt because in the first meditation he was focussed on things other than himself. So in these passages we see Descartes recalling what his naïve opinions were so that he can subject them to the test of doubt.

Having already arrived at the initial formulation 'I am, I exist', there is a temptation to skip over the question 'what did I formerly think I was?' to arrive at the answer to the question 'what am I?'. 'After all,' we might say, '*this* is the real question. Any return to the naïve standpoint we have already discredited is an admirable caution on Descartes' part, but having been reminded of the danger of misidentification, there is no reason to rehearse these previous opinions; let us not dally with these intervening steps when we already know the form of the question we need to be asking.' Indeed, there seems to be little philosophical meat to be had in the passages linking 'I am, I exist' to 'I am a thing that thinks'. But the answer is not the point of the exercise. Not only is the process essential to the text as meditational, but upon meditation, it becomes clear that an enormous amount of philosophy is going on in the transition from the initial question (what did I formerly think I was?) to the final answer (I am a thing that thinks).

Rethinking the question 'What am I?'

It is worth remembering that the title of the second meditation is 'concerning the nature of the human mind (*mens*) and that it is better known than the body'. This is worth remembering because thus far we have yet to encounter any treatment of mind whatsoever. In fact, the Latin word '*mens*' does not even occur in Descartes' initial treatment of the nature of his being. Instead, in this naïve account of what will become mind-body dualism, Descartes contrasts the body with *anima* (soul) rather than *mens*. And it is within this frame that he introduces the naïve belief that he knows more fully the nature of body than that of soul (*anima*).

The relation in Latin between '*mens*' and '*anima*' is complicated on its own; Descartes' treatment of the transition between *anima* and *mens*, however, adds a layer of complexity that is often glossed over by commentators. Thus we will pay particular attention to how this transition from *anima* to *mens* unfolds in the course of the meditation. Marking both the language and the rhetoric of this unfolding is important because the way in which Descartes manages the transition from *anima* to *mens* here is essential to the final sense that Descartes ascribes to 'mind' and bequeaths to the tradition of modern philosophy.

Having determined to apply his method to the opinions he once held about himself, Descartes begins his enquiry in a halting manner: 'What then did I formerly think I was? A man, of course. But what is a man? Might I not say a "rational animal"? No, because then I would have to inquire what "animal" and "rational" mean.' (AT7:25) It is no accident that Descartes rejects this initial answer out of hand for it is Aristotle who famously defined man as a rational animal and Descartes has positioned himself against this tradition in important ways. At the same time, however, we must note that it is the method of Aristotelian taxonomy rather than the terms of the definition that Descartes is rejecting here. As we shall see, in the passages that follow on from this dismissal of 'man is a rational animal', Descartes reinstates the key terms in his own account.

Part of the problem, of course, is the inappropriateness of the answer for the question at hand. Descartes is concerned with answers to questions of the family 'what am I?' Aristotle's taxonomy, however, is based on the principle relation of genus to species. Thus, in answer to any question of the form 'what is x?' Aristotle's first answer will be to identify the genus (general category) to which the species (particular x) belongs. For Descartes this Aristotelian approach misses the particularity of the question 'what am I?' by pretending that the 'I' can be subsumed under general categories. Indeed this pretension allows the tradition to subsume humans of both genders under the general category 'man'. From the position of subjective philosophy this pretension even misses what it means to be a particular man (such as Descartes).

Hence, the initial answer, 'I am a man' leads to yet further categories (in this case 'animal' and 'rational') without giving a satisfactory answer to the original question. In this movement away from the Aristotelian taxonomy by category, we see most clearly Descartes' commitment to the philosophy of subjectivity. In short, this problem arises because it is clear that no answer that appeals to the genus-species relation will satisfy the demands of thinking the subject itself.

Descartes initially moves away from the Aristotelian categorical approach by insisting on taking seriously the particular that he has before him: himself. In order to short circuit the 'chain of subtleties' involved in the categorical approach he also appeals to a naïve state: 'Instead, permit me here to focus on what came spontaneously and naturally into my thinking whenever I considered what I was' (AT7:25–6, translation altered). While this approach both blocks the Scholastic tendency toward definition and is attractive to a philosophy that wants to take seriously the question of subjectivity, an appeal to 'spontaneous' or 'natural' intuition of self sounds alarms in many philosophical circles. Worries about immediate intuition are often only surpassed by the mistrust of the very possibility of intuitive self-reflection.

Suspicions about self-reflection

At first sight the question of self-reflection might not seem problematic. After all, what object of enquiry could be more readily available to me than myself? Here, of course, is the problem: the naïve approach to self-reflection must treat the subject as an object. *Meditations*, however, has been pursuing a line in subjective philosophy; indeed, the most hard-won result thus far has been the pure subjectivity of the *cogito*. Having just been warned of the danger of mistaking something else for myself, I ought to handle the question of self-reflection with caution. Otherwise, I might find that I have substituted an object for my own subject.

For many contemporary thinkers this initial problem is compounded by the implausibility of any such self-reflection being genuinely spontaneous. Indeed, even the spontaneity of the task at hand seems suspicious as Descartes was driven to undertake this project by the unexpected and sudden discovery of the *cogito*. In other words, projects such as that of self-reflection always happen against a background of motives and intentions, they have a history and thus there is no way to begin with a clean slate.

While I think these sorts of worries are appropriate for the sort of Cartesian subjectivity inherited by the tradition, there is, as always, the temptation to confuse this tradition with the text of *Meditations*. Insofar as Descartes makes an appeal to naïve intuition, this sort of objection bites – and it seems clear that some such appeal is in play. However, to be fair to Descartes, we should also acknowledge that his method goes some way toward deflecting the main thrust of these worries. Rushing to judgement here covers over certain oft-neglected subtleties of Descartes' own position.

It is significant that Descartes poses his question in the past tense. That is, his approach to the question 'what am I?' is via the question 'what did I formerly think I was?' This shift throws the entire meditation back into the naïve position prior to the radical doubt of the first meditation. Thus, Descartes' naïve position is not an artificial construct but is drawn from his (and our) own past; as a recollected belief, his initial answer does not involve the sort of pure immediacy that would be expected from the question 'what do I think I am?' Thus, rather than turning his current subjectivity into an object he turns to his prior (pre-meditative) state as an object. In so doing he avoids the first pitfall.

In effect, Descartes starts the quest for subjectivity by turning his own naïve self-reflection into an object. It is no accident that Descartes does not address the question of his being directly. Rather, by shifting to the past tense form of the question he provides himself with an object to examine. And by shifting us back into the position prior to the radical doubt, he can begin his investigation in keeping with the meditational process thus far.

Moreover, by examining what he once took to be 'spontaneous' and 'natural' in the self-reflections of his naïve self, Descartes disarms the second worry. Not only am I no longer the naïve self who began the first meditation, but I am also able to acknowledge the background and history that informed the self-reflection of that naïve self. The meditational practice thus far has been geared exclusively toward exposing this background and quarantining it so that I am in a better position to begin the proper enquiry into myself. Descartes may not be able to achieve the sort of position that would allow pure self-reflection but we should acknowledge that at this point in *Meditations* he is not trying for this.

Soul-body dualism

The first formulation of what will become mind-body dualism arises from this reflection on Descartes' past naïve position. In the naïve formulation, however, it is not yet the mind (*mens*) that accompanies the body but the soul (*anima*). Simply put, what Descartes recalls from the naïve attitude about himself is that he believed that he had a body and that he did things. The former ascription straightforwardly leads to the body half of the dualism: he would have been likely to say of himself that he was composed of various bodily members such as hands, arms or face. The link between believing of himself that he did things and the second half of the dualistic position relies on the meaning of the word '*anima*'.

The Latin term '*anima*' (from which we get 'animation' and 'animal'), originally indicating air or breath, signals an active force: that which animates animate beings and is therefore lacking in inanimate objects. Philosophically, this word can be traced back to the first Latin translations of Classical Greek philosophy and in neither the Greek nor the Latin traditions does it have a specifically cognitive meaning. Rather, in the pre-Christian tradition the term is used to differentiate living things from non-living things and so ranges in usage from 'life-force' to 'active nature'; in the Latin Christian tradition the term comes to indicate the human soul and hence the seat of the true human nature that will survive the death of the body.

With this in mind it is easy to see how the belief that he did things would lead to the belief that he was also soul (*anima*). This is a crucial addition because, as Descartes points out, to be a body alone is not readily distinguishable from being a corpse. Moreover, the examples Descartes gives for the activities he would attribute to the soul are themselves telling: 'It next occurred to me that I took in food, that I walked about, and that I sensed and thought various things'. (AT7:26) These activities are hardly accidental as they represent the hierarchy of living things in the established Aristotelian science of the day. Animate objects (plants, animals, man) are distinguished from inanimate objects (rocks and corpses) by the addition of an active soul. But within this second category, plants are distinguishable from animals (including man) because while they exhibit the activity of taking in nutrients they do not (for the most part) move themselves as animals have the power to do. But non-human animals, while taking in nutrients and moving themselves, do not think as humans have the power to do. Hence, for Aristotle, man is a rational animal.

In the space of a few lines, Descartes has dismissed the Aristotelian definition of man and then reinstituted the main points by his own method. The difference, of course, is that Aristotle's method operates in generalities and will explain what 'man' is rather than what I am. Descartes' method gets to the same place by starting with and sticking to the particularity of his own being. Descartes' subject will not be a species of a genus or a particular instantiation of a category; Descartes' method insists on the subjective perspective on the subject itself. This subjective focus is entirely in keeping with the meditational text we are reading and must at all times be differentiated from the universalist and objective claims one finds in treatises and essays. In effect, Descartes is making claims exclusively about what he subjectively discovers about his subjective experience and asks if perhaps we discover the same things. The refusal of the Aristotelian method in this passage is an example of how to go about this process.

Having presented the position of soul-body dualism as implicit in our naïve position prior to radical doubt, Descartes is not yet in a position to give a full account of what soul (*anima*) and body are. However, his initial assumption is that he has a clearer understanding of what a body is than he does of the soul.

> But as to what this soul might be, I either did not think about it or else I imagined it a rarefied I-know-not-what, like a wind, or a fire, or ether, which had been infused into my coarser parts. But as to the body I was not in any doubt. On the contrary, I was under the impression that I knew its nature distinctly. (AT7:26)

Given that this assumption runs counter to the title of this meditation (that mind is better known than the body) we ought to be prepared for a major revision of the naïve account.

The account Descartes gives of soul here is probably more or less in keeping with the unreflective answer most of us would give if asked what the nature of the soul was. In popular culture we have ethereal ghosts, and see-through spirits that seem to be composed of smoke; in the popular iconography of the middle ages, paintings of saints (those blessed by the Holy Spirit) are shown with small flames on their heads;

in the very etymology of '*anima*' we encounter the notion of breath and air. These are the ways we naively imagine the soul to be. And it is this naïve account that will be put under scrutiny. But Descartes is involved in three projects here. First, he will analyse this naïve notion of *anima* in order to determine what he can really know about it. Secondly, he will show that what we really know about *anima* we know more clearly than anything we can know about body. But thirdly, in the process, Descartes shows that what we *really* know about *anima* is that it is *mens*.

From *anima* to *animus*

In keeping with his method, Descartes' examination of his naïve opinion of himself as soul and body invokes the test of doubt. Using a shortened version of the full method of the first meditation, Descartes deploys a version of the deceiving God hypothesis straight away. In the case of such divine deception, the attributes of the body fall away as uncertain. That is, because in this position of radical doubt he cannot even be certain that he *has* a body, he is in no position to affirm that he *is* in any sense a body. This is discouraging because, as we have seen, he was more certain about the nature of body than he was of the nature of the soul. Now, however, while he is certain that he knows what body is he cannot be certain that any such body exists, let alone that he is in any sense body. Thus he is forced to turn to the nature of the soul about which he was already less than certain.

On Descartes' naïve account, we recall, the soul maps perfectly onto the Aristotelian hierarchy. Thus, the attributes of the soul he mentions are the powers of nutrition, self-movement, sensation and thinking. That this hierarchy is in play is important because upon examination we find that these peel away in order as they are more or less dependent on there being a body. Thus, the nutritive dimension of the soul serves only in the feeding of the body; similarly, the attribute of movement turns out on examination to involve the movement of the body. These lower attributes of *anima*, those that the human is meant to have in common with all living (animate) things, are so closely linked to the body that once the existence of a body is in doubt they become meaningless.

At first sight it would appear that sensation would be in the same boat as these attributes of soul. After all, it is difficult to conceive of the sensation of colour or sound without implicating the bodily sense organs. And while Descartes does dismiss sensation on these lines, this case is treated separately and slightly incongruously: 'What about sensing? Surely this too does not take place without a body; and I seemed to have sensed in my dreams many things that I later realized that I did not sense.' (AT7:27). The first observation is enough to dismiss sensation in the same way that walking about has been dismissed and it is not immediately clear what the addition of the occasion of dreaming is in service of; after all, it is no less true that I have had dreams in which I seemed to walk and eat.

Moreover, at first glance this supplement seems in some way to diminish the argument thus presented: does the fact that I have seemed to have sensations in dreams not suggest that the link between sensation and the body is not as strong as Descartes needs it to be? That Descartes applies this argument to sensation alone and not to the other body-related attributes of soul should give us pause. As we shall see, this moment is significant because Descartes' project involves not only a rethinking of *anima* but of sensation as well. Sensation differs from these other body-related attributes because it is a sort of cusp attribute that, like *anima* itself, needs to be refined. In the end, the short detour through dreaming lays the groundwork for loosening the bonds between sensation and the body in important ways.

Nonetheless, sensation is put aside for the moment and it is with thinking that Descartes comes to a final certainty about the soul. Of all the attributes of the soul, only thought is not disqualified by its ties to the body. Thus from the naïve starting point 'I am body and soul', Descartes has arrived at the claim that 'thought alone cannot be separated from me'. The discovery that thought exists (or that thought alone is essential to the soul) is immediately coupled with the previously discovered 'I am, I exist' to yield the claim 'I am a thinking thing'.

In this way Descartes is brought around to a version of 'I am a rational animal' but on his own terms. That is, where Aristotle would assume that for something to be a rational animal it would need to bear the essential attributes of both a rational being and an animal, Descartes has by-passed this assumption entirely. As we have seen, the ordinary assumption that an animal (animate being) is composed of soul (animating force) and body (that which is animated) is undermined by the method of radical doubt. The further assumption that all animals (including man) share certain characteristic features with only rationality setting man apart from the rest, has been set aside by Descartes' analysis of *anima*. And thus Descartes, operating in the frame of radical doubt, is able to say of the soul of man not only that it is rational but that it is exclusively rational: thought remains as the only essential feature of *anima* when considered under Descartes' method. Put another way, for Aristotle it would be meaningless to say of man as a rational animal that he is any less a body, an animate body, or a sentient body than he is rational. By starting from the subjective position and employing radical doubt, however, Descartes transforms 'man is a rational animal' into 'I am a thinking *anima*'.

This is reflected almost immediately in Descartes' first characterisation of his discovery (here presented partially untranslated): 'I am therefore precisely nothing but a thinking thing; that is *mens*, or *animus*, or *intellectus*, or *ratio* – words of whose meaning I was previously ignorant.' (AT7:27) Thus, the first occurrence of *mens* (mind) since the title sits alongside *anima* transformed. That is, '*anima*', which we have been referring to as 'soul', has become *animus* in the course of Descartes' analysis. This transformation is often lost in translation but the difference between the terms is both subtle and significant.

As we have seen '*anima*' has the broader meaning insofar as it will be applied to anything animate. In keeping with the general gender bias of language and philosophy, this life-giving force is also a feminine noun in Latin. In contrast, the masculine '*animus*' has a much more specific meaning; in general '*animus*' refers to the rational part of the soul. Thus, while these terms are clearly related to each other, their meanings are significantly different. Even a hamster has *anima*; but only a man (so the gendering suggests) has *animus*. As we can see, therefore, Descartes, in the space of two pages has transformed the naïve account of *anima* into the refined *animus* and equated this new term with mind (*mens*) by grammatical association. The ultimate formulation, that I am a thinking thing (*res cogitans*), is a foregone conclusion. No longer an animal (*anima*) who happens to be rational, I am now *animus*.

Worries about the thinking thing

Once again Descartes has come around to the fundamental certainty of his subjectivity. Rather than a simple return to the same, however, Descartes' method has developed his initial discovery 'I am, I exist' into the richer 'I am a thinking thing (*res cogitans*)'. This difference is significant primarily because it specifies the nature of the 'I' of the initial discovery. However, this new formulation in terms of *res cogitans* has aroused suspicion from many different quarters. Philosophers who are happy to grant the 'I am, I exist' as long as it remains empty and does no metaphysical work reject the move to the fuller claim 'I am a thinking thing' as an illicit introduction of the sort of metaphysical speculation we ought to avoid. From another perspective, those who take the *cogito* as a metaphysical starting point are often still suspicious of the substantialisation of the 'I' that this process involves. And still others query the sudden appearance of the 'thinking thing' out of the subjective experience of thought. In short, these worries share one common question: where did this 'thing' come from?

On the surface, this question seems legitimate. Descartes does not offer any clear line of argument for the shift from 'I am, I exist' to 'I am a thinking thing' and so it is quite reasonable to ask how he got there. Descartes seems to be using the intermediary discovery that thought exists (or that thought is the only feature essential to the soul) to do the heavy lifting here. That is, by combining 'I exist' with 'thought exists' he seems to draw the conclusion 'I am a thinking thing'. That this is not a plausible line of argument (let alone a valid one) hardly needs to be pointed out. Perhaps then, there is something else going on here. The discovery that thought exists is crucial to the conclusion but does not serve as a premise in any way.

Keep in mind that this discovery is the result of an examination of 'what I once thought I was'. Thus, within the hypothetical framework of the enquiry into the naïve soul-body dualism, Descartes discovers that the only feature of either soul or body that survives radical doubt is thinking. Because this discovery is the result of a hypothetical enquiry (if I am body and soul, what can be certain of me?) it cannot now be used straightforwardly in the argument. What it can do, and indeed what it does do, is remind Descartes of his initial discovery: that he exists. After this initial discovery, Descartes had urged caution upon himself so that he did not too quickly ascribe any details to his being. Now however, he is in a position to see clearly that what brought him to the discovery 'I am, I exist' was nothing other than thought (in the form of doubt or persuasion). Thus, the initial claim 'I am' can be augmented as 'I am thinking'. What the discovery that thought exists accomplishes is nothing more than a clarification of that which was already available to him at the outset; the intervening stages merely show a prudent caution in this regard. This still leaves us short of the final position 'I am a thinking thing' and so the worries we began with remain. The question is still: why does Descartes introduce a thing (that thinks) here?

A thing that thinks?

Perhaps the most famous objection to the 'thing' that thinks concerns the status of the 'I' and the subsequent reification of the subject by the introduction of *res cogitans*. In its purist form this objection can be attributed to the German aphorist and scientist Georg Christoph Lichtenberg (1742–1799):

> We should say *it thinks*, just as we say *it lightens* [or 'it is raining']. To say *cogito* is already to say too much as soon as we translate it *I think*. To assume, to postulate the *I* is a practical requirement. (Lichtenberg, *The Waste Books*; see Note on Texts Cited)

Now before we begin, we should note that in this form Lichtenberg's observation has no direct application to *Meditations* wherein '*cogito*' does not occur. That is, Lichtenberg is attacking a form of the *cogito* (I think therefore I am) that has no place in the course of our text. This being said, the objection can be modified to fit *Meditations*.

The radicality of this objection for the traditional '*cogito ergo sum*' is that it denies Descartes the right to say that *anything* thinks and would therefore call into question the whole of Descartes' philosophy of subjectivity. Lichtenberg suggests that Descartes is only entitled to the claim 'it thinks' the way we say in English 'it is raining'. In the case of 'it is raining' the 'it' is a grammatical rather than a real requirement; no one makes the mistake of believing that *anything in particular* rains and so Descartes ought not to suppose too quickly that *anything in particular* thinks. Perhaps, it will be argued in many quarters, Descartes has been bewitched by the grammar of his own language. Within the frame of radical doubt, Descartes ought to remain as agnostic about the 'I' as he has been about everything else. To be clear, in fact, Descartes ought to say something like 'thinking happens'.

Lichtenberg's objection can also be made to fit the later developments in the second meditation. There is a legitimate worry that, even if we allow the intermediary claim 'I am thinking' to stand only as long as the 'I' remains a mere placeholder of no more meaning or substance than the 'it' of 'it is raining', the imposition of 'thing' in the final formulation undermines this agnosticism toward the subject; 'I am a thinking thing', it could be argued, reveals Descartes' true colours and denies him recourse to the agnostic position he ought to have maintained. The worry here is that Descartes has smuggled in a prejudicial notion of the subject as independent of the thought. And this is not a small worry, as some would argue that the history of modern western philosophy has been an attempt to accommodate or overcome this prejudice about the subject.

Put another way, the prejudice that seems to plague Cartesian metaphysics is that an action requires an actor – a doer for every deed. While this supposition might seem commonsensical, we must remember that at this point in the second meditation the commonsensical is precisely what is being held in doubt. More worrisome is the possibility that Descartes has never noticed this potential prejudice and that he will be unable to prevent this from contaminating the rest of his project. A close reading of the second meditation, however, reveals not only that Descartes does not succumb to this prejudice about the subject but also that the sort of objection levelled by Lichtenberg suffers from its own prejudice about language.

A thing that thinks: Descartes' reply

Descartes does declare that he is a thinking thing. But if we have learned anything from our reading of *Meditations* thus far, it is that we should beware of taking even the most direct statements unequivocally. That is, already in the second meditation we have encountered several apparent stopping points only to discover that the dialectical process of the meditation is unready to pause. This occasion is no exception and Descartes follows the declaration that he is a thinking thing by embarking immediately on a further enquiry: 'What else am I?' The course of this next investigation deposits us seemingly in the same position that we have just left: 'But what then am I? A thing that thinks. What is that? A thing that doubts, understands, affirms, denies, wills, refuses, and that also imagines and senses.' (AT7:28) What then has been accomplished?

On the surface this seems to be nothing more than an aborted excursion through the faculty of imagination that is perhaps undertaken to show that, like the senses, the imagination is not to be trusted. This is no doubt going on here and we will have occasion to return to this theme later. However, perhaps the most remarkable thing that Descartes reveals in the course of this 'excursion' is that he too is suspicious of the *res cogitans*. Descartes' caution in the second meditation is profound. Not only does he pause after the discovery 'I am, I exist' so that he does not mistake something else for himself, but here he finds cause to worry that by employing the imagination he might take the 'thing' of the 'thinking thing' in the wrong way.

Cautious not to suppose that he is in any way what we call the human body or the material aspects he had once ascribed to *anima*, Descartes asserts that nevertheless he is something. At this point he deploys his imagination to better know what this 'something' might be. He quickly rejects this as a way forward because this involves a manifest misuse of the faculty of imagination: imagination cannot be the source of knowledge! While the absurdity of claiming to know by imagining does not escape Descartes, it seems to have escaped the notice of many of his critics.

Upon meditation it becomes clear that many of the worries about *res cogitans* are grounded in the misuse of the imagination. In order to worry that Descartes has overreached in describing the subject as a thinking thing, in order to object to the thing of *res cogitans*, one must believe that 'thing' is not the kind of thing that can be neutrally ascribed to the 'I'. But to have this belief is already to give content to the word 'thing'. Whence this content? As Descartes becomes aware in his aborted attempt to employ the imagination to know this 'thing' better, there is a deep temptation to derive our prejudicial beliefs from what we imagine to be the case.

At least tacitly, then, the critics of *res cogitans* imagine 'thing' as it is used here to be akin to other things they think they know. Alas, as Descartes shows, this imagined comparison is out of bounds both because we ought not derive our knowledge claims from imagination but also because within the radical doubt we do not have access to 'ordinary things' upon which to base the comparison. Hence Descartes' warning to himself:

Thus I realize that none of what I can grasp by means of the imagination pertains to this knowledge that I have of myself. Moreover, I realize that I must be most diligent about withdrawing my mind from these things so that it can perceive its nature as distinctly as possible. (AT7:28)

As his excursion through imagination illustrates, Descartes is fully aware of the temptation to take 'thing' in this way. Thus, when he returns to the position of declaring that he is a thinking thing he has insulated himself against this temptation. Instead he explicitly limits his account of this thing to the enumeration of its functions. Indeed, among these functions is the imagination that he had recently been tempted to employ. By means of the implication that 'I am a thing that imagines' Descartes recentres the enquiry on the subject – that which imagines. Thus in a repetition of the initial discovery of the *cogito*, Descartes finds that even in the functioning of a faculty he does not trust (the imagination), he has further proof that it is indeed he who imagines. Therefore, neither the content nor the process is the focus of the investigation. As we will see, while he has been tempted to commit himself to more, in describing the subject as a thing that thinks he has said nothing more than that he is.

What might be called a 'prejudice of the philosophers' with regard to *res cogitans* involves a prejudice about the nature of substance. As we have seen, Lichtenberg is suspicious of any derivation of the 'thing which acts' from the action itself. But underlying this objection is the notion of the subject as *cause* inferred from supposed *effect*. In later thinkers, the Cartesian subject is taken to be the cause of actions in just this way but at this point in *Meditations* a different relation between the 'thing that thinks' (subject) and 'the thinking' (action) is in play.

This specific notion of causality is derived from the laws of physics and is grafted onto Descartes' metaphysics by later generations. It is often forgotten that Descartes, while an advocate of modern physics, is still a Scholastic philosopher by training. Thus, when he refers to thinking substance as a thing that thinks, he does not imagine that the thing *causes* the thinking; rather, in substance metaphysics, the language of expression rather than causation holds. There are a variety of technical distinctions of the relation between substance and expression (property, attribute, mode, etc.) which we need not go into here. But these technical distinctions aside, thought is an expression of substance; and the substance of which thought is a proper expression is a thinking substance.

This non-causal relation is largely purged from metaphysics by the Empiricist tradition and post-Kantian philosophy before resurfacing (transformed) in such thinkers as Nietzsche and Deleuze. Nonetheless, this expressivist metaphysics is essential to understanding the philosophies of Spinoza, Leibniz and, indeed, Descartes. The advantage of the expressivist metaphysics for the problem of *res cogitans* is that it allows just the sort of subject-agnosticism Lichtenberg thinks is required. To say 'I am a thing that thinks' and 'I am thinking' is not to make two different claims but to make the same claim in two different ways. That is, Descartes does not imagine that he both has a property (a mind) and that he is involved in an activity (thinking). Rather, to be involved in the activity of thought is to be a mind. Lichtenberg's worry that a subject separate from the thought has been introduced illicitly is allayed: in this substance metaphysics to be a thinking substance just is to think. Thus, I am a substance of a particular type (thinking) and thinking is essential to the expression of the 'I' that thinks – or, to satisfy Lichtenberg, thinking happens. The danger, as we have seen, is to suppose that there is more to the substance than the thinking but Descartes is under no obligation to make this supposition.

The power of 'I think'

At each return to the certainty of his subjectivity, Descartes is able to add a layer of detail. Thus from 'I am, I exist' we arrive at 'I am a thinking thing'. Now, however, having cautioned himself against taking this thing too casually, Descartes is confident in saying: 'But what then am I? A thing that thinks. What is that? A thing that doubts, under-stands, affirms, denies, wills, refuses, and that also imagines and senses.' (AT7:28) The ground for this extension is not a preconceived notion of what comes under the heading 'thinking'. Rather, Descartes is able to review each of these activities within the process of meditation itself: these are the activities of thought that he is now involved in. Moreover, he takes care to remind himself that these activities are not themselves the focus of this meditation. These activities are pressed into service as answers to the question 'what am I?'

Thus Descartes notes that it is the same 'I' who doubts many things but understands some things, the same 'I' who affirms some things and denies others, the same 'I' who desires to know more and wishes not to be deceived. But, and this is crucial, it is also the same 'I' who imagines and senses. The inclusion of imagining and sensing here at first seems curious. After all, he has just censured himself for the misuse of imagi-nation and, when considering the activities of *anima*, sensing seems to be on the wrong side of the thought/non-thought divide. However, upon reflection we see that sensing and imagining are no less activities of thinking than are doubting and affirming. What sets imagining and sensing apart from the other activities of thinking is that they also have a part in corporeality.

Sensing, as it has thus far been treated, involves the bodily sense organs and 'imagining is merely the contemplating of the shape or image of a corporeal thing.' (AT7:28) In this sense, we might call those activities that have no part in corporeality 'pure' and these others 'impure' activities of thinking. This is not to devalue sensing and imagin-ing but simply to note the distinction currently in play. As we shall see, Descartes will need both the purity of thought and the impurity of these other 'hybrid' activities in the course of meditating. Here in the second meditation, the focus is on the purity of thinking as necessary for the investigation of the subject within the frame of radical doubt. As a result both sensing and imagining will be brought into line with this require-ment and their impure aspects will be suppressed. Later in *Meditations*, however, the hybrid nature of both sensing and imagining will become crucial to Descartes' project.

In the course of this investigation of the distinction between pure and impure thinking, Descartes comes upon one of his most important insights: that when properly considered from the perspective of the thinking subject, sensing is an activity of pure thinking. This is a crucial insight as it allows Descartes to show that, even in the case of sensing, the content of thought is entirely irrelevant for the thought to be existentially meaningful. This, of course, calls for a rethinking of the naïve account of sensing that he has been working with that will ultimately lead to a distinction between sensing and perceiving. First, however, we need to examine the way in which he secures the purity of sensing as a reliable indicator of the certainty of subjectivity.

Each of the pure activities of thought further solidifies the sense of certainty that 'I exist'. That is, each act of doubting, affirming, denying or willing testifies to the subjective existence of the 'I' that acts. Each of these acts of thinking is true as an act of the thinking subject even in the most deceptive environments, for example that under the sway of a deceiving God. These pure activities are existentially meaning-ful without reference to any of the parameters that the deceiving God could alter in a deceptive way. Put another way, the content of an act of willing, for example, has no effect on its value in affirming the truth of subjectivity. At first glance, however, sensing seems to be in a different boat as a result of its relation to the suspicious realm of corporeality.

This difference can be thought of in terms of the truth of a claim based in sensing, as compared to that of a claim based in a pure activity of thought such as doubting. For instance, it remains true that I doubt something even if it turns out that I was wrong to do so: if I don't believe you when you tell me that you are ill, it remains true that I don't believe you even if you are in fact ill when you tell me this. For sensing, however, the case seems to be different: the truth of the claim 'I see a ship on the horizon' seems to be dependent upon there actually being a ship on the horizon. Descartes treats imagining similarly. Drawing us back to his own misuse of the power of imagination in the attempt to better know what this thing is that thinks, Descartes writes: 'for although perhaps, as I supposed before, absolutely nothing that I imagined is true, still the very power of imagining really does exist, and constitutes a part of my thought.' (AT7:29) Here the truth of the 'imagining' seems to be dependent upon there being something (even if only corporeal extension) existing in the world that could correspond to the images I have the power to call forth. At the same time, however, that I have this power to call forth images is independent of any corresponding reality. It is thus true that I have this power and it remains existentially meaningful and subjectively true for imagining regardless of the truth of the content of that imagining. This treatment of imagining should give us pause to reconsider the case of sensing.

By examining the case of sensing, Descartes comes to perhaps his greatest insight. Following the lead of imagining and the model of the pure activities of thought, Descartes discovers that from the perspective of subjectivity sensing is properly a function of thinking and not of the body at all. Let us examine how this might work. While in one sense the truth of a claim of sensation is dependent upon a correspondent reality, in another sense it is independent of this reality in the same way as the 'pure' activities of thought. Descartes' insight is that all the claims of sensation, for instance 'I see a cow', can be made reliable by ensconcing them in a frame of thought. In effect, it is within the power of the subject under the threat of radical doubt to withhold the material half of the claim of sensation by simply adding a disclaimer of the form 'I think'. It remains true even in the depths of dreams or divine deception that 'I think I see a cow' as long as I do think it. Even if there are no cows, the claim 'I think I see a cow' is secure as long as I think I see a cow. At this juncture Descartes uses 'it seems to me' but practically any other activity of pure thought would work here; commentators often use 'I believe' as the neutral operator but I prefer 'I think' because it is the most general operator.

Let us pause to meditate on this insight for a moment because it is tempting to read this as little more than a clever manoeuvre deployed by Descartes to get himself out of a jam. After all, it does look like the sort of childish game one might encounter in a six year old who has just learned the power of modal operators. But this insight is the key to Descartes' philosophy of subjectivity and the first tentative step back from the brink of radical doubt. In this passage, Descartes moves from the claim that all the activities of thinking properly belong to him, to the discovery that the content of these activities is not entirely out of bounds. This is crucial because without this insight Descartes will forever be trapped with the certainty that he thinks but, because of the frame of radical doubt, he will never be able to examine *what* he thinks. The unrefined radical doubt of the first meditation has reduced him to the pure activity of thinking but without the capacity to discriminate between the various thoughts that he may have. In effect, the method of doubt he deployed to get to this point is too blunt an instrument.

When Descartes discovered the certainty of 'I am, I exist' we noted that, because this opinion is not of the type he had expected, he would need to learn how to use it as a foundation for his thinking. With the insight into the buffering power of 'I think. . .' Descartes has secured the method he needs to move forward. Rather than treating 'I am, I exist' (or even 'I am a thinking thing') as a foundational opinion, Descartes uses this certainty to secure the status of *all* of his opinions as foundations within thought. In effect he can build an entirely secure structure of opinions behind the veil of 'I think' before tackling the task of linking this structure of opinions to thought-independent reality. The 'I think' shields his initial investigation from the persistent doubt that has thus far led to such a halting and frustrating meditation. Thus Descartes divides his task into two parts: first he will sort out the content of his thinking in order to better understand the structuring of opinions; then he will attempt to bridge the gap between this world of thought and the external world currently under the suspicion of radical doubt.

The possibility of taking seriously the content of his thought is crucial for the investigation because this content is as yet the only evidence, however dubious it might be, that anything other than his subjectivity exists at all. As we shall see, in the third meditation the possibility of examining the content of thought will become vital to Descartes' entire project. However, at this point, Descartes turns to something closer to hand: a piece of wax. Through the examination of the claims he has from the senses, Descartes further refines his account of purified sensing, or perception, and presents a model for the proper use of this new-found faculty.

The wax example

In his famous wax example, Descartes conducts a mini-experiment on a piece of wax ostensibly in order to better understand the nature of the wax. In the process, however, he also discovers the limitations of both sensing and imagining as they apply to understanding bodies. In the course of this experiment, perhaps because it approximates the familiar form of basic empiricism, it is easy to forget that we are still operating under radical doubt. What makes this experiment possible at all is that we are able to operate freely within the shielding cocoon of the 'I think' that Descartes has discovered. Rhetorically, Descartes frames the wax example by saying that he will give free rein to his thoughts and even succumb to the temptation to believe that he can examine corporeal things. Of course, he now can do precisely this because this temptation still only gives rise to beliefs which remain subjectively true of his thinking. Moreover, all of his claims about the wax arise with the frame of 'I think' attached. Thus, while Descartes does not repeat the operational frame 'I think' at every turn we must remember that this entire experiment takes place under its auspices.

Descartes' naive conviction was that he knew the body much better than he knew the soul (*anima*). He abandoned the examination of the body because with the threat of radical doubt in play there seemed no reliable way to know anything about the body. Instead he reluctantly turned to an examination of *anima* and to his surprise he discovered not only the certainty 'thought exists' and the subjective truth of each of the acts of thinking, but also a way forward in the investigation of bodies. With 'I think' shielding the investigation from the threat of radical doubt, he returns to the examination of body he had set aside earlier. Unsurprisingly, however, the examination has changed in subtle ways.

Originally he had proposed to investigate body as a part of the question 'what am I?' and therefore the body in question would presumably have been his own. Now however, he has returned to the question 'what is body?' from *within* the position of subjectivity. Instead of attempting to understand himself as body, he now hopes to examine what body can mean to a thinking subject; for the moment he has abandoned the naïve belief that he is body. No longer shackled to the attempt to prove that he is himself a body, he is free to choose a simpler object of study. In this case he chooses to focus on a particular piece of wax. We must remember, however, that operating as he is behind the shield of 'I think', anything he learns about the nature of body will be held in suspension until he finds a way to drop the 'I think' without succumbing to radical doubt. Thus what he 'discovers' about the body from the wax example will properly extend only to his *thought* about the wax and only provisionally apply to the wax in itself.

It is no accident that he chooses to examine a piece of wax fresh from the honeycomb. Indeed, in the history of philosophy there has probably never been a more apt example, for the wax will appeal to each of the five senses and yet none of these sensory markers proves stable. That is, when he begins the experiment the wax is hard and cold, yellow, tastes of honey, makes a sound when rapped, and smells of flowers; and yet by the end of the experiment all of these properties will have changed dramatically. The experiment is simple: hold the wax near a fire and watch how each of these properties literally melts away. While it is difficult to imagine the taste of hot wax being tested, it is easy to see how each of the properties of the wax is transformed: the puddle of wax that results is soft and hot, colourless (or at least not as yellow), unlikely to emit the same (if any) sound when rapped, and the smell of flowers has fled. And yet, Descartes notes, we are likely to insist that it is the same wax both before and after.

What this experiment reveals is that sensing is able to provide an account of the wax at any given time but is unable to account for the change of the wax over time. Put in the form of a question: what is it that allows us to say of the wax before and after the experiment that it is the same wax? Of course, were this an experiment on an object in the world, it would remain possible that the wax is not really the same wax solid and melted; perhaps the change was complete. Here the experiment is helped by operating within the frame of 'I think' for it is no less certain that I think this is the same wax as it is that I think it is solid before the experiment and melted after the experiment.

Thus, Descartes is forced to address his belief that something about the wax remains the same through change. As he puts it:

So what was there in the wax that was so distinctly grasped? Certainly none of the aspects that I reached by means of the senses. For whatever came under the senses of taste, smell, sight, touch, or hearing has now changed; and yet the wax remains. (AT7:30)

Descartes' method here follows a familiar pattern. Having employed the activity of sensing in the investigation of the wax, Descartes identifies the limits of this approach and hence the limits of sensing in general: sensing can only report on the sensible properties of an object but not what makes that object persist through time, through changes of those sensible properties.

This leads Descartes to suppose that the wax, whatever it might be, is not equivalent to its sensible properties and that there must be some other way to think of the wax in itself. To this end he employs his imagination to attempt to think the wax without any of its sensible properties. Recalling Descartes' reaction to his own misuse of imagining to better understand himself, we might think that this use of imagining is not legitimate. Like sensing, however, that he has the power to imagine remains true even within the frame of radical doubt. Within this shielded experiment, therefore, imagining is a tool at his disposal. Still, like all tools, its use will have limits.

Having decided that the wax is other than its sensible qualities, and determined that the senses are not adequate to the task of showing him what this 'other' might be, Descartes calls upon imagining in order to peel away the various sensible properties of the wax. In this way Descartes hopes to discover the nature of the body that expresses itself to the senses in one way at one time and another way at another time. As a result of this imaginative exercise, the wax is found to consist of general features such that the wax in itself is said to be something extended, flexible and mutable. Without these general features the sensible properties would not be possible as, for example, it is impossible to think of the wax being coloured without an extended surface of some description. Similarly, the one thing that he is certain of from his experiment is that this extended something changes and so it must be both mutable and flexible. The attempt to understand flexibility and mutability, however, soon reveals the limits of imagining in this investigation.

For Descartes, imagination is the process by which images are produced and manipulated in thought. Thus, in the exercise we have just undertaken, imagination is used to remove sensible properties such as colour from the image of the wax. In the case of shape and size, however, the imagination would be limited to the power of showing Descartes that no particular shape or size is essential to the wax. This would be accomplished by the power of showing the wax in a variety of shapes and sizes and thus emphasising the mutability and flexibility of the wax as it is thought. At no point, however, would the imagination be able to produce an image of the wax with no size or shape. Hence, Descartes is able to assert that being extended (in some way) is an essential feature of the wax – a feature without which the wax cannot be thought even in imagination. Thus far the power of imagining is both useful and reliable. Upon reflection, however, this is as far as the imagination can take us in understanding the wax.

It is clear that Descartes comes to his understanding of the wax as extended, mutable and flexible through the use of imagination. However, he soon realises that he does not understand mutability and flexibility by means of the imagination; imagination simply provides the occasion for this discovery by presenting the mind's eye with examples. This is demonstrated by the simple fact that he knows the wax to be capable of innumerable changes in shape and yet the power of imagining has not, and indeed cannot, present all of these to the mind's eye. Instead, the imagination provides images of the wax in a variety of shapes and sizes as a prompt for the recognition that the wax is capable of far more (indeed innumerable) mutations. The examination of the nature of extension provides similar evidence of the limits of imagination. In short, just as Descartes has established that the proper use of sensing is restricted to sensible properties, he here establishes that the imagination is a tool that can aid understanding but is itself neither necessary for, nor capable of, understanding.

An act of the mind

In the course of the wax example, Descartes has exposed the limits of both sensing and imagining. In this way he has started to learn how to use these faculties in a reliable, albeit limited, way. In the process, however, the naïve account of sensing has been transformed. In place of the naïve notion of sensing having primarily to do with the body, Descartes has introduced a distinction between perception and sensation that marks the boundary between mind and body. While this distinction has played various roles in philosophy since *Meditations*, it must be emphasised that here, in the second meditation, the division between sensation and perception is absolute. Keeping this in mind will help to avoid some of the more common misreadings of Descartes' project.

Descartes manages the transition from naïve sensation to the introduction of perception by means of the use of an intermediary term: 'grasp' or 'comprehend'. At the outset of the investigation into his being, Descartes asks about sensing as one of the activities of *anima* and later as a kind of thinking. When he begins the wax example, however, he shifts his language to the more neutral 'comprehend' so that he can begin to speak of what he knows of sensible properties without having to speak of sensing. Thus, the wax example opens: 'Let us consider those things which are commonly believed to be the most distinctly grasped [*comprehendi*] of all: namely the bodies we touch and see.' (AT7:30) And again, after the experiment: 'So what was there in the wax that was so distinctly grasped [*comprehendebatur*]? Certainly none of the aspects that I reached by means of the senses.' (AT7:30) In this way, Descartes initiates the split between sensation and a general act of the mind.

The use of 'comprehend' also plays a role in disqualifying imagination as the activity of thinking by which we know the wax itself. The use of 'grasp' in some translations is highly appropriate because this exposes the often suppressed literal meaning of 'comprehend' that is much more evident in Latin usage. Literally, the Latin word '*comprehendo*' means to hold together and for this reason commonly indicates holding in a closed hand or fist. The transference of this word to the life of the mind has a rich heritage in Ancient philosophy, with the Stoics placing particular weight on the link to the closed hand in their theory of knowledge; thus, to know something is for the mind to hold it in a firm grip, to hold it together and give it unity.

Descartes' treatment of the power of imagining in the second meditation implicitly draws upon this sense of 'comprehend'. Imagination, as a power to present images, is capable of grasping particular shapes of the wax but is unable to 'hold as a unity for itself' the notion of the wax being capable of innumerable shapes; the power of imagination does not grasp what we comprehend about the wax. Thus, Descartes is able to move straight to the claim that this comprehension must be some power of thinking other than imagination. It is only after the disqualification of both sensing and imagining, therefore, that Descartes is able to replace the placeholder 'comprehend' with 'perceive'.

Both in common parlance and in certain philosophical circles, sensation and perception are often treated as interchangeable synonyms. We must avoid this sort of assumption as Descartes makes it very clear in this meditation that perception is an act of the mind alone; he sometimes indicates this by referring to intellectual perception. Moreover, while the dual aspect of sensing will play a central role later in *Meditations*, it is important to recognise that perception and sensation are not simply two sides of the same coin. It bears repeating: perception is an act of the mind.

But I need to realize that the perception of the wax is neither a seeing, nor a touching, nor an imagining. Nor has it ever been, even though it previously seemed so; rather it is an inspection on the part of the mind alone. (AT7:31)

On the one hand this absolute distinction is a necessary result of operating within the frame of 'I think'. On the other hand, however, the insistence that perception is an act of the mind alone is not something that will resolve itself back into sensation once the 'I think' is dropped.

Descartes emphasises this by means of a particularly dramatic example that fixes our attention on a particular prejudice that must be overcome if we are to recognise the full import of perception being an act of the mind alone. In a manner befitting Wittgenstein's warnings about the bewitchments of language, Descartes points out that he has been in danger of being deceived by the very language he has used in the wax experiment:

> For we say that we see the wax itself, if it is present, and not that we judge it to be present from its color or shape. Whence I might conclude straightaway that I know the wax through the vision had by the eye, and not through an inspection on the part of the mind alone. But then were I to perchance look out my window and observe men crossing the square, I would ordinarily say I see the men themselves just as I say I see the wax. But what do I see aside from hats and clothes, which could conceal automata? Yet I judge them to be men. Thus what I thought I had seen with my eyes, I actually grasped solely with the faculty of judgment, which is in my mind. (AT7:32)

It is important to note that in this example Descartes is not suggesting that we are always or automatically wrong in judging that these are men covered up in coats and hats; nor is he arguing for the likelihood of a world filled with robots. Rather, he is drawing to our attention a certain prejudice about judgement. That is, we are predisposed to forget that we judge objects to be present to us from the particular reports of the senses. Given that the proper objects of sight are colour, shape and size, it is no more possible to see the wax than it is to see the sound of songbirds; the complex object 'wax' is simply not the sort of object fitted to visual sensation. In our way of talking we forget that to say that an object *has* a particular colour is not the same as saying that it *is* that colour. The wax is not a colour (nor a shape, nor an odour, nor a smoothness, etc.) and therefore is in no way available to the senses. That we shorthand our way of talking and speak of 'seeing the wax' is entirely appropriate for communication but we must guard against forgetting that we have created this shorthand.

In this way Descartes links perception with judgement and thereby further differentiates it from sensation. Judgement, whatever else it involves, is an active power of the mind; it is something we do rather than something that happens to us. As such, it can be under our control;

what we judge to be the case is not something that is imposed upon us from without. The danger of the shorthanded way of talking is that this power, this autonomy of mind, is obscured if we believe that when presented with an object, such as a piece of wax, we are compelled to see it. If we are compelled to see anything then it is no more than the objects of sight (and similarly for the other senses). What we judge to be the case as a result of these sensory objects is something entirely in our power. That we generally surrender this autonomy has effects and we will examine these when we turn to the fourth meditation.

Results of the inward turn

Descartes finally arrives at the point that he had signalled in the title of the second meditation. In the course of this meditation he has discovered that, quite against his expectations, he knows the mind better than he does the body. As in the first meditation, this process has involved challenging and overcoming certain prejudices. Where the second meditation differs, however, is in the turn inward. No longer challenging prejudices about the experience of the outside world, Descartes has turned his method upon himself and challenged prejudices about his own being. But he has also accomplished a great deal more.

He has discovered the limits of the method of doubt and in doing so stumbled upon his first certainty: the *cogito*. He has shifted our default notions of both soul and sensation by introducing the corresponding notions of mind and perception. Along the way, he has established the limits and proper use of the faculty of imagination. And perhaps most importantly, he has discovered the autonomy of the activities of thought through the power of judgement and the use of the 'I think'.

At the outset Descartes had promised great things if he could find but one Archimedean point. And now we are in a position to see just how literally he has fulfilled this promise. Archimedes claimed to be able to move the world itself if he could find but one solid and stable point in space. It would not be too much to say that Descartes has accomplished the same thing via the *cogito*. However provisionally, in the course of the second meditation, the world itself has moved from the realm of matter to the realm of thought; it has shifted from outside to inside; once other to me it has now become, through the power of judgement, part of me. And, while Descartes does treat this shift as provisional, the world once moved will never be the same again.

The Third Meditation

Several paragraphs into the meditation 'Concerning God: That He Exists' Descartes announces in no uncertain terms that we 'should at the first opportunity inquire whether there is a God, and, if there is, whether or not he can be a deceiver.' (AT7:36). Given Descartes' habit of rehearsing the steps leading up to each new meditation before beginning the main enquiry, it is not at all surprising that this declaration is delayed as it is. What is surprising, however, is how the language of this declaration appears to betray its own import, for it might seem that Descartes delays this 'first opportunity' for several more pages.

More than a stylistic curiosity, this further delay highlights several problems of interpretation embedded in the seemingly straightforward title of the third meditation. Too often commentators overlook this delay and reduce the third meditation to the (in)famous exercise of proving the existence of God; too often readers take the title to indicate a scholastic prejudice that simply does not speak to modern ears; and too often students of meditations commit the very sin that Descartes repeatedly warns against throughout his meditations: accepting prejudices as starting points. Meditation takes time and as readers we would do well to pause before assuming we have the slightest idea what it would mean to 'enquire whether there is a God' – Descartes does pause.

For us this task is further complicated by a set of prejudices that Descartes cannot have known we would have. For all the fanfare that goes along with *Meditations* as the foundation of modern philosophy, it is a text that is very unmodern. Too easily we forget that Descartes is writing before the cognitive turn in philosophy – a turn that he helped initiate – and that, as a result, his philosophy of mind is very different from what we might expect. Post-Lockean and Post-Kantian philosophies have given us a default way of talking about 'minds', 'thoughts' and 'ideas' that is alien to *Meditations*. These prejudices will make it difficult to understand the degree to which *Meditations* – and in particular the third meditation – is shot through with a generic version of Aristotelian substance metaphysics. In addition to the pause that Descartes urges upon us, in order to consider what it might mean to enquire into God, we must take the time to pause and consider our own prejudices about words (such as 'thought', 'real', and 'cause') that we think we understand.

Thus, alongside Descartes, we will rehearse the steps that have brought us to this point, for the manner in which we have arrived here clarifies the question of both God and the necessity of his existence. We will also dally in the space Descartes opens for us between the declaration of the necessity of the enquiry into God's existence and the proofs that are all too often taken to constitute the heart of this enquiry, for here we can discover what distinguishes this enquiry from the formal proofs that follow. And finally, once we have examined our prejudices and thus cleansed ourselves in preparation for meditation, we will be ready to explore the proofs themselves.

What we will discover when we finally turn to the formal proofs, however, is that they are not really proofs at all. The enquiry into the existence of an other leads to the inevitable conclusion that God exists. The subsequent passages commonly identified with the two famous proofs of the existence of God in fact constitute neither proofs nor arguments for the existence of God. A careful reading of the meditation reveals that these passages ought properly to be read as elaborations of the idea of God itself. And yet, despite the fact that these passages prove nothing, as elaborations they reveal a great deal about Descartes' first philosophy.

The search for an other

The third meditation opens by reminding us that we must withdraw from the senses, insofar as this is possible, by actively treating as empty and false those images we presume to be derived from the senses. As has been shown in the course of the first two meditations, the senses are prejudicially coercive of my opinions and so must be suppressed long enough to allow me to form unprejudiced opinions on my own. Thus, building upon the second meditation, Descartes sets out to 'converse with myself alone and look more deeply into myself, I will attempt to render myself gradually better known and more familiar to myself.' (AT7:34) As we have seen, the first manner in which information from the senses can be safely and unprejudicially handled is by recognising that within this 'conversation with myself', such sensory information can be reduced to modes of thinking. Every opinion that I suppose to be derived from the senses arrives on the scene making two claims and it is the first duty of the meditator to disentangle these claims. On one hand, each such opinion reports its content: to adopt a mild anachronism, a relation between a grammatical subject and predicate. On the other hand, each such opinion makes an existential claim: that the content it reports is the case. It is the latter claim – smuggled in alongside the content claim – that is prejudicially coercive. And it is prejudicial precisely because it is smuggled in alongside the innocuous content of the opinion.

While the senses attempt to coerce me into believing that they report a state of affairs that exists independently of me, it is always within my power to treat their reports as contentful without granting their existential claims. Whether or not the content of the opinions of the senses corresponds to anything outside my mind – whether in addition to their content claims these opinions also make true existential claims – is open to doubt. What is not open to doubt is that I have these opinions, entertain these thoughts, think the content of these opinions. By withholding assent to the potentially illicit existential claims that come along with these thoughts I remain on safe ground. And, as a result, a space is opened up within which I can continue my investigation of these thoughts.

At this point Descartes takes a further step which our post-Cartesian cognitive ears may not register: in addition to granting truth status to the content of these opinions (insofar as 'I think' them) he also grants these opinions limited existential status.

> even though these things that I sense or imagine may perhaps be nothing at all outside me, nevertheless I am certain that these modes of thinking, which are cases of what I call sensing and imagining, insofar as they are merely modes of thinking, do exist within me. (AT7:34–5)

That is, while the truth of the reference to existing objects outside me remains suspended, as modes of thinking these thoughts exist. This is a crucial point in the third meditation because it signals a break with our default notions of mind, thought and thinking.

As we have seen the question of the 'thing' that thinks in the second meditation has caused a good deal of controversy. Perhaps because we no longer hear the above claim as involving reification in the same way, very little attention has been paid to the *existence* of thoughts. For post-Cartesian philosophy of mind, thoughts are something that the mind *has* (or perhaps could be described as something the mind *does*); rarely is the question of the *being* of thought considered beyond these sorts of issues. But just as the question of the nature of the mind is central to the second meditation, in the substance metaphysics of Descartes and his contemporaries, the being of thought is inextricably linked to its existence.

We can get a sense of the different mindset involved from heeding the fact that most English translations resort to 'exist' in order to approximate the Latin word '*esse*' in this passage. The evolution of the language has rendered the etymological descendents of '*esse*' ('essence', 'essential', etc.) inadequate to the task. However, as in the case of any translation that diverges from etymology in order better to capture concept, something is lost. In this case what is lost is the link between the *essence* of thought and its existence. In the context of the third meditation Descartes' usage of '*esse*' has more in common with its Greek root '*ousia*' than it does with the English 'exist'. Indeed, it is a central feature of Aristotelian metaphysics – which we must recall is the default metaphysics of the day – that to exist is to have an essence.

The starting point: ontological solipsism

Before we can properly begin the enquiry into the existence of God we will need to be clear on the ontological relation between mind and thought, between substance and mode. This also clarifies the impasse that necessitates the third meditation in the first place. If the second meditation supplies us with a way to stop the freefall of the first meditation, the solution it provides is not entirely satisfactory. True, I discover the certainty that I am; that what I am is thinking substance; and that the content of my thoughts can be safely handled if properly insulated from doubt by the 'I think'. But this gives rise to a new worry: that the retreat from the senses and the power of doubt lands me firmly in a solipsistic position: a position in which only I exist with certainty. This is a complex worry insofar as it admits of both epistemological and ontological solipsism. The two worries are related but distinct. On the one hand there is the question of whether I will ever be able to *know* anything other than myself with certainty; on the other hand there is the worry that nothing other than myself *exists* – that I am alone in the world.

Traditionally, the greater weight has been placed on the epistemological question for two reasons. First, the third meditation seems to be offering God's existence as a guarantor of knowledge and certainty. Secondly, and more insidiously, determining whether I can know whether something else exists would seem to be a necessary first step to determining whether something else exists. As a result, too little attention has been paid to the ontological side of the question. Given the emphasis on ontology in the opening of the third meditation, this is problematic. In fact, while it is clear that addressing the epistemological side of the question is necessary to answering the ontological question of God's existence, it is also clear that the position from which this enquiry begins is grounded in the ontology of thinking substance.

Put another way, we put the cart before the horse if we start asking what we can know from an ontologically neutral position. The enquiry of the third meditation both starts from the ontologically rich position of thinking substance and is also driven by ontological concerns. Throughout the third meditation Descartes draws upon the ontological commitments and implications of substance metaphysics. Moreover, to make sense of the third meditation at all we must take seriously the ontological (not merely epistemological) solipsism that we find ourselves in. Descartes asks us to start not only with the assumption that I cannot *know* whether anything else exists but also with the real possibility that there *is* nothing else. Despite the title, then, the first real question concerns the possibility of the existence of an other to me: is there something other than me (that exists)? Only incidentally does it turn out that this other is God; or, more to the point, one of the things we discover in the process is what God is.

Clearness and distinctness: a false start

There is of course an epistemological storyline in the third meditation. In this story Descartes introduces the criteria of clearness and distinctness as a means of determining what it is possible to know. Advocates of the epistemological reading of *Meditations* give the doctrine of clear and distinct perceptions a central role in the story that follows. In addition to developing a Cartesian epistemology out of the notions of clearness and distinctness, this reading insists that the necessity of 'enquiring whether there is a God' arises out of the defence of this doctrine. That this reading ultimately leads to the infamous Cartesian Circle should give us pause. Nonetheless, as we shall see, there are textual reasons beyond this unfortunate outcome to de-emphasise this storyline in the third meditation. First, however, a brief outline of this reading is necessary.

In broad strokes, it runs as follows: having run the gauntlet of the first meditation I have come to doubt all of my previous opinions. I now doubt: that there is an external world reported to me by the senses, that I have a body, and that the laws of mathematics are reliable. Having navigated the second meditation I now review those things that I can reliably know: that I exist; that I am a thinking substance; that my thoughts, insofar as they are merely thoughts, are reliable. From these observations I draw the conclusion that what sets these cases of reliable knowledge apart is 'a certain clear and distinct perception of what I affirm.' (AT7:35) Therefore, I posit a general rule: 'everything I very clearly and distinctly perceive is true.' (AT7:35)

This rule seems adequate to account for the doubtfulness of the majority of my opinions (i.e. those that would be challenged by the dream argument). Moreover, this rule seems to capture the manner in which these opinions can be safely handled by the proper use of 'I think'. There is the sticky problem of mathematical truths, however. These opinions survived the dream argument and seem to carry with them the highest degree of clearness and distinctness. Indeed, they seem so clear and distinct that I am compelled to admit them even in dreams. In the first meditation even these opinions were called into question by the possibility of a deceiving God. Once admitted, however, the deceiving God hypothesis is sufficient to undermine all the security I had gained through the doctrine of clearness and distinctness. Therefore,

I should at the first opportunity inquire whether there is a God, and, if there is, whether or not he can be a deceiver. For if I am ignorant of this, it appears I am never capable of being completely certain about anything else. (AT7:36)

So the story goes.

Among the problems that inevitably arise from this epistemological story is the Cartesian Circle. If the reason we need to prove the existence of God is in order to guarantee the reliability of the criteria of clearness and distinctness then it seems problematic to employ the criteria of clearness and distinctness in the proof(s) of the existence of God. And yet, Descartes calls upon the notions of clearness and distinctness in the first proof of the existence of God. Alas. In other words, if God is brought into the equation in order to guarantee the epistemological ground of clearness and distinctness then Descartes appears to argue in a circle. While I do not think that this problem is as insoluble as is sometimes assumed, the entire problem can be avoided if we do not fixate on the epistemological story set out above.

Fortunately, there is good reason not to give this story too much weight. In addition to the explicit emphasis Descartes puts on the ontological questions we have already discussed, the epistemological story relies on a certain amount of rhetorical blindness. Not least, putting so much weight on the doctrine of clearness and distinctness at this point demands that we fail to notice that these passages mark a hopeful yet abortive attempt to short-circuit the meditative process. We have seen this pattern before and have been cautioned against it. As in the second meditation, we should worry that we risk sacrificing everything we have gained if we succumb to this easy temptation. This is not to say that clearness and distinctness do not play a role in what follows, but we should not give them disproportionate weight.

We recall that in the second meditation Descartes momentarily succumbs to the temptation to reject the outcome of the first meditation because he finds the result uncomfortable and unsatisfying. So it is that he asks the illegitimate question: 'how do I know that there is not something else, over and above all those things that I have just reviewed, concerning which there is not even the slightest occasion for doubt?' (AT7:24) So it is that he comes to blame God for the mess in which he finds himself. It is of course Descartes' own method, not God, which has created this mess; it is of course not God who can serve as the 'something else that is certain'. In the course of the second meditation, however, the rejection of this digression leads, by twists and turns, to the certainty of the *cogito*.

In the third meditation we see a similar pattern. Descartes, though in less of a panic, is tempted to reject the outcome of the second meditation; in this case, the uncomfortable and unsatisfying outcome is ontological solipsism. Just as he once refused to face the possibility of absolute scepticism he now refuses to face the possibility of solipsism. Instead he decides to investigate everything once again, just in case he missed something: 'Now I will ponder more carefully to see whether perhaps there may be other things belonging to me that up until now I have failed to notice.' (AT7:35) It is as if, before he can go on, he needs to convince himself that the previous meditation has well and truly run its course. This approach bears the same sort of accidental yield that blaming God does in the second meditation.

In this case the 'rule that everything I very clearly and distinctly perceive is true' plays the role reserved for the blameworthy God in the second meditation. Descartes claims to derive this rule from the certainty of the *cogito*:

I am certain that I am a thinking thing. But do I not therefore also know what is required for me to be certain of anything? Surely in this first instance of knowledge, there is nothing but a certain clear and distinct perception of what I affirm. (AT7:35)

In other words, Descartes claims to be able to derive a general rule for certain knowledge from the one instance that he has thus far encountered: that it involves a clear and distinct perception. The legitimacy of such a claim is at best questionable and it would indeed be troubling if Descartes did not immediately set about calling that legitimacy into question.

At first blush the addition of the notions of clearness and distinctness does not seem to add much to the unadorned 'I perceive'. At best, this gets us past the initial hurdles of the first meditation. That is, if we insist on clear and distinct perceptions then at least we are not likely to succumb to circumstantial error. However, once we remember that perception is an act of the mind, the insistence on clearness and distinctness seems redundant. On the one hand, the confusion that led me to affirm that there exists something other than the perception itself corresponding to the content of the perception is born out of the failure to recognise that perception is an act of the mind rather than of the senses.

On the other hand, in the second meditation, we already established that *all* my perceptions are true insofar as they are acts of my mind (i.e. can be prefaced with 'I think'. In what way then do clearness and distinctness allow me to differentiate between equally true perceptions? In other words, it is not at all clear that the notions of clearness and distinctness add anything that we had not already secured by the addition of the 'I think'.

Descartes immediately sets about discovering these limitations to the 'rule' he has just posited. He goes so far as to conclude that in these cases 'if my judgment [that there exists a corresponding reality] was a true one, it was not the result of the force of my perception.' (AT7:35) The case for the rule of clearness and distinctness is rendered all but useless when he considers the case of mathematics for what could be a more compelling case for clear and distinct perception than the belief that 2 plus 3 makes 5? He has to admit that he may have a nature that leads him to 'see' clearness and distinctness when there is none. It is important to note that we are not at this point required to make an appeal to a deceiving God because in the first meditation the deceiving God hypothesis was only one of the possible sources of a defective faculty. The crux of the problem is not whence this potentially faulty faculty but whether this faculty is reliably known not to be faulty. In other words, I am led back to the brute fact that I simply do not know enough about myself to be positing such rules at all.

Thus far, then, Descartes has merely forced himself to rehearse the first two meditations in light of the rule of clear and distinct perceptions. As a result he is forced to admit that he managed the first meditation without recourse to this rule; using the proposed criteria of clearness and distinctness does not change the outcome. Once he enters the dream argument and restricts himself to the field of 'it seems to me' the most this rule proposes is that the most clear and distinct of perceptions left to me are those of mathematics. But here this rule founders on the already admitted possibility of error even in these opinions. In other words, he discovers in the third meditation that he had already in the first meditation disproved the effectiveness of clearness and distinctness as reliable criteria. Moreover, the proposed rule does nothing to ease the solipsistic bind of the second meditation. This little excursion has brought him back to the point he thought to escape: that he is only able to know the contents of his own thoughts. Beyond this he cannot proceed until he better knows *himself*.

At this point, however, Descartes does something remarkable. Having been brought to the point where he ought to abandon (at least for the time being) his fanciful digression through the 'rule' of clear and distinct perceptions, he instead asserts his belief that the truths of mathematics are as certain as the *cogito*. More remarkable still is the manner in which he declares this:

On the other hand, whenever I turn my attention to those very things that I think I perceive with such great clarity, I am so completely persuaded by them that I spontaneously blurt out these words: 'let him who can deceive me; so long as I think that I am something, he will never bring it about that I am nothing. Nor will he one day make it true that I never existed, for it is true now that I do exist. Nor will he even bring it about that perhaps 2 plus 3 might equal more or less than 5 or similar items in which I recognize an obvious contradiction.' (AT7:36)

Instead of describing clearness and distinctness he reports the experience of clearness and distinctness. It is this recourse to reported speech that realigns Descartes' relation to his supposed 'rule', for it is a rule no more.

In this exclamation Descartes acknowledges that the rule he had hopefully posited has failed to be a rule that could be applied objectively. What he had taken to be a rule, the criteria that he thought he could abstract from the certainty of the *cogito*, turns out to be nothing more than the subjective experience of certainty he had met with in the discovery of the *cogito*. The marker of certainty is not something that can be abstracted from the experience and applied elsewhere; the true marker of this certainty is the 'blurting out' that arises from the encounter. In other words, the experience that he has characterised as one of clearness and distinctness is coercive. The *a posteriori* description fails to provide a rule for further investigation precisely because it cannot replicate the coercive nature of the experience of certainty itself.

Nonetheless, we would be wrong to discard the notion of clearness and distinctness entirely. What has failed is the *rule* that Descartes had hoped to secure. That is, as a rule the criteria of clearness and distinctness would have alleviated the stress of subjectivity. There would in fact be something other than my own subjective existence against which to measure my judgement. What remains intact is the coercive experience. And while at this point I have no way to think of this experience except within the subjective realm of my thoughts, it is crucial to the meditative project that I have identified this fact. When we return to the coercive experience that makes me blurt out 'but something so clear and distinct must be true!' it will no longer be marked by a rule. Clearness and distinctness remain as markers of the experience that allow me to differentiate amongst my opinions, but for the time being they have been supplanted by what Descartes will later call the natural light of reason. We will return to this notion, but for now suffice it to say that the coercive experience of a clear and distinct opinion is based in the fact that, as a solipsistic subject, I have exposed this opinion to the greatest scrutiny at my disposal – pure reason – and can find no fault in it. If there is any fault in the opinion it can only be because my faculty of reason is impaired.

Therefore, much as the attempt to blame God in the second meditation reinforces the subjective responsibility of the *cogito*, the attempt to formulate an objective rule reinforces the subjective experience of certainty. This lands Descartes back in the middle of his solipsistic fortress. The criteria of clearness and distinctness are entirely reliable when they report what Descartes already experiences as certain (i.e. the subjective experiences of thought) and not at all helpful beyond this. If the Archimedean point of the *cogito* allows me to move the entire world into the subjective realm of thought then there remains the need for a second point beyond this subjective realm that I can use as a point of reference. In order to validate the experience of certainty that I 'blurt out', it is necessary to establish an other to my solipsistic universe. It is for this reason, and not to guarantee the 'rule' of clearness and distinctness, that Descartes turns to the enquiry into the existence of God. The 'rule' always comes after the experience of certainty anyway.

Thoughts: modes of my being

Descartes had opened the third meditation with the promise to 'converse with myself alone and look more deeply into myself [in order to] render myself gradually better known and more familiar to myself.' (AT7:34) And while the possibility of the objective 'rule' temporarily distracted him from his promise, this digression in fact brings him back to himself even more fully. Having given up on the escape through clearness and distinctness, he is able to affirm the ontological solipsism of the second meditation as a necessary starting point for the enquiry into the existence of God. It may, therefore, seem strange that Descartes immediately sets out to examine and categorise his thoughts. At first blush, this project seems to have little to do with either the promise to better understand himself or the enquiry into the existence of an other. That is, it might seem that Descartes is once again deferring on his promises. Nonetheless, from within the situation of ontological solipsism and given the parameters of substance metaphysics this move is both necessary and appropriate.

Descartes has taken great pains to remind himself of the limitations imposed by the second meditation and we would do well to take the resulting ontological solipsism seriously. That is, while it might very well be imperative that we enquire into the existence of God, any such enquiry must begin with the resources we have at our disposal. In this case, all I have to work with is my own existence (as thinking substance) and my thoughts. We must recall that within the solipsistic position *everything* has been reduced to the status of my thought; it is only within the frame of 'I think' that I am able to deal with the reports of the senses, the products of imagination, experiences, judgements, or other acts of thinking. It is this condition of ontological solipsism, in fact, that has just undermined the attempt to posit an objective rule: within this frame there is simply no way to distinguish a clear and distinct perception from a perception that *seems to me* to be clear and distinct. Therefore, any enquiry (even one into the existence of God) must begin by examining my own thoughts.

Even if we grant this condition, however, it might still be objected that this betrays the promise with which Descartes opened this meditation:

to converse with himself alone in order to better know himself. Such an objection simply brings to light a prejudice of post-Cartesian philosophy of mind: that my thoughts are not me. This objection, however, relies on a philosophy of mind that is incompatible with the substance metaphysics Descartes deploys.

In post-Cartesian philosophies of mind it is commonplace to treat thoughts as products of thinking (created by acts of thinking) or properties of mind (things had by minds). In such cases it is easy to see how thought is distinct from thinker. Thoughts can have an origin, cause, or author but they are in no way the same as that cause or author. For Descartes, however, each thought is a mode of thinking and it is this relation between substance and mode that allows Descartes to remain true to the strictures of ontological solipsism while fulfilling his promise to better know himself.

We will return to the question of substance more fully later, for now it is sufficient to illustrate the ontological relation between substance and mode by drawing upon the wax from the second meditation as an example of material substance. According to Descartes, any material substance has three basic features: extension, shape, and motion. As a mode is primarily a modification of substance we will take up the example of shape as this best illustrates the notion of mode as modification. Our wax will have a particular shape (say that of a cube) but we can change (modify) that shape (say into that of a sphere). That is, we are able to change the mode of the wax but we are still entitled to call it the same wax because we have not changed the substance.

For the wax (substance) to exist at all, however, it must have some shape (mode) or other. If the wax were to cease to have any shape at all – even an ill-defined fluid shape – we would not be able to say that it was still wax. Therefore, it is a necessary feature of substance (wax) that it have some mode (shape) or other at any given time. Because this relation between substance (wax) and mode (shape) is ontologically necessary – necessary for the wax to *be* wax – we can see that the relation is more intimate than that between a substance and a mere property that is had or possessed. Rather, a mode is a particular kind of property insofar as it is an expression of the being of substance. The wax in our example may take on innumerable shapes – its substance may have innumerable such expressions – but what cannot happen is for the wax to have no shape. Similarly, it is impossible for substance to exist without a mode of expression.

With this in mind we may return to the promise with which Descartes opens the meditation: to converse with himself about himself. In the second meditation I learned that I exist as thinking substance (mind). As (thinking) substance, my being must have some mode of expression or other. Unlike the material substance of our example, however, the mode appropriate to thinking substance will not be shape. Rather, the mode appropriate to thinking substance is thought. That is, at any given time, a thinking substance must express itself in some way or other as thought. We speak loosely, however, when we speak of a mind 'having' thoughts because, just as in the case of the wax, to reduce a mode to a property that is 'had' is to miss the intimacy of the ontological relation between substance and mode. In other words, my mind is expressed at any given moment by a particular thought; it would not be too much to say that I am my thoughts. Therefore, we can see that in examining my thoughts I am examining myself; in conversing with myself about these thoughts I do not violate the strictures of ontological solipsism by positing entities other than me. Moreover, understanding my thoughts as expressions of my being (as thinking thing, substance) will bring me to a better understanding of myself.

The existential need for an other

At this point we are in a position to understand the delay between the imperative to 'enquire at the first opportunity into existence of God' and the proofs that have dominated discussions of the third meditation. On the one hand, any enquiry starting from the position of ontological solipsism must begin with the resources at hand, namely, those of the self. On the other hand, and as a result, the enquiry into the self that Descartes does undertake 'at the first opportunity' constitutes the beginning of the enquiry into the existence of God. It is true that the proofs (such as they are) must wait but, far from incidental preliminaries, my examinations of my own thoughts are essential to the enquiry into any possible other (even God), precisely because it is only in my thoughts – as expressions of substance – that a sign of that other can be found.

Like Robinson Crusoe, the ontological solipsist is trapped in the island of his own mind. Robinson is of course always free to speculate about the possibility that there is an other on the island. However, any search for this possible other must involve the exploration of the island itself. Thus it is that the first sign of the other for Robinson is the set of footprints in the sand: footprints that must have been made by someone, but were not made by Robinson. This, in a nutshell, is Descartes' first proof of the existence of God to which we will return in greater detail soon. First, however, Descartes the ontological solipsist must explore his own thoughts for it is here and here alone that such a sign might be discovered.

This approach to the question of God's existence sets the project of *Meditations* apart from traditional approaches to proving the existence of God. For many in the Scholastic tradition the existence of God was never in doubt. As a result, for these thinkers the notion of proof carries a different valence than we might ordinarily expect. In some of the most celebrated cases such as Anselm, the proof of the existence of God is almost entirely heuristic; that is, the proof serves as a support for faith rather than as a cause for belief. In other cases, the proof of the existence of God serves the greater Scholastic project of harmonising reason and revelation. In these cases, the question is not whether or not there exists a God but rather whether the existence of God can be brought into line with the demands of reason. Despite the fact that Descartes will adopt strands from the Scholastic tradition in his own proofs, the manner in which he sets out on this enquiry is markedly different from that of his predecessors.

It is sometimes argued that Descartes is operating in bad faith with regard to the existence of God. That is, like the scholastic philosopher, he never seriously entertains the possibility that God does not exist but, unlike the scholastic philosopher, he is not honest about this. While I find such an objection to be a particularly pernicious form of *ad hominem* argument, little can be said in opposition. Once we admit the possibility that Descartes is dishonest in what he writes, the declarations from the first meditation (that there is no reason to believe that there is a God) and the second meditation (that recourse to God's existence is illicit) will fall on deaf ears. Nonetheless, in the third meditation, the overall form of the enquiry goes some way to disarming this 'bad faith' objection.

The third meditation starts from a situation (ontological solipsism) and a perspective (subjectivity) that both necessitates the enquiry into the existence of God and dictates its form. Unlike that of the scholastic philosopher this is neither an academic nor an entirely heuristic exercise. The first two meditations have brought the meditator to the position of ontological solipsism which precludes the possibility of admitting *a priori* the existence of God. Similarly, the perspective of subjectivity reduces any faith in the existence of God to the form 'I think that God exists'.

Together, these two conditions serve to prevent the meditator from succumbing even to the sorts of prejudices that the scholastic philosopher
would happily use as axioms.

Instead, Descartes has brought us to a point where the enquiry into
the existence of God is an existential necessity. Without evidence that
there is some other to my existence, the condition of ontological solipsism is final. Unlike the scholastic philosopher who thinks of a proof
of the existence of God as a comfort in the face of worldly doubt or as
evidence that human reason is not incompatible with faith, for Descartes
the proof is of the utmost personal urgency: failing in this leads back not
to the comfort of naïve faith but to the torture of existential despair.

At the same time, however, the twin conditions of ontological solipsism and subjectivity set the course for this enquiry. Like Robinson
Crusoe, Descartes' enquiry is an exploration rather than a speculation.
The project to better know himself (the world of his being) is the only
course left open to him. But this means that he is involved in a genuine
search that pushes back against the claim that Descartes is operating in
bad faith. Of course, even this can be seen as an elaborate ruse or self-
deception. But if it is a ruse it is so elaborate that it begins to make more
sense to take Descartes at his word. After all, he has gone to great lengths
to secure himself against the sorts of prejudices he knows he is given to.
If his enquiry is genuinely grounded in the condition of solipsism and
is conducted from the perspective of subjectivity then we ought to give
Descartes the benefit of the doubt and see what comes of it.

Inventory of ideas

With this background in place, the details of the enquiry into the existence of God are fairly straightforward. Having accepted the limitations
imposed upon him by the second meditation Descartes sets out to
examine the resources of his being. In doing so he hopes to come across
some sign – some footprints in the sand – that will assure him that he is
not alone in the world. The metaphysical details of the so-called proofs
follow directly from the subjective perspective, the solipsistic position
and the conditions of substance-mode relations. Moreover, in the inventory of thoughts that opens the enquiry there is little that is not directly
derived from the discussion of the second meditation. In other words, if
one has taken the time to meditate along with Descartes up to this point,
the proofs will follow as a matter of course.

The first step in this process is the specification of what is meant by the word 'idea'. At the outset we must note that Descartes has thus far restricted himself to the use of 'opinion', 'thought' and 'perception' so when he takes the time to introduce a new term with a specific range of meanings we should take heed. The manner in which he initially defines the term is of less interest than the list of examples he appends to his definition. He begins by noting that 'Some of these thoughts are like images of things; to these alone does the word "idea" properly apply, as when I think of a man, or a chimera, or the sky, or an angel, or God.' (AT7:37) In effect Descartes uses these five extraordinary examples of ideas to override the narrow definition he has just given, for were it not for these examples, one might easily draw the conclusion that ideas are entirely imagistic or visual.

One thing that becomes clear in the course of these examples is that ideas are, in some sense or other, representatives of objects. Here, however, we must recall that by 'object' we cannot (at least initially) mean something existing external to us; we cannot mean 'thing in the world'. We cannot use 'object' in this way because we are operating within the subjective frame of 'I think'. Thus by 'object' we simply mean the object of thought or that about which I am thinking. In this way, we must resist the temptation to think that the first example (man) indicates a relation between a material thing in the world and thought. Rather, within the world of thoughts the idea 'man' represents an object taken to be of sensation. Similarly, the idea 'chimera' represents an object taken to be of imagination. In each case the naïve belief that we can be certain of the origin of these ideas must be suppressed.

For our purposes it is incidental that these two examples serve to distinguish two potential sources of ideas. However, because from our naïve perspective 'man' and 'chimera' represent two different fields of ideas, Descartes is able to illustrate a more important distinction: each of these ideas represents an object that is individuated according to different rules. That is, there are different ways in which such objects come to be treated as individuals. The object 'man' is individuated according to the rules of material objects: it is bounded in space and acts as a unit. The object 'chimera' on the other hand cannot be individuated in the same way. Because we assume 'chimera' to be a product of the imagination this example ought to call to mind the painter's analogy of the first meditation. While a painter is free to depict likenesses of things that will never be met in experience, they are still constrained by rules that govern likenesses (spatial orientation, colour, and so on). What these initial examples have in common, however, is that the idea I call to mind when I think of either a man or a chimera is a likeness of that object.

The example of 'sky', however, problematises this initial understanding of idea in terms of likeness. Like the object 'man', the presumption about the object 'sky' is that it is delivered to us by the senses. However, unlike man, sky is excessive. Because the sky cannot be encompassed by the senses – cannot be taken in at once – because it exceeds the capacity of the senses, the idea of sky cannot represent in the same way as the idea of man (or for that matter chimera). Just as my experience of the sky is always as that which exceeds my sensory field, my idea of the sky must include markers of such excess. When I think of the sky I can call to mind only a partial image (for example, a blue field) that is meant to represent something far greater than I can encompass in thought. Just as the whole of the sky exceeds my senses, the whole of the sky is merely indicated by my idea of sky.

More importantly, however, the object 'sky' is individuated differently than either 'man' or 'chimera'. Because my idea of sky indicates an excess, I must recognise that my notion of 'sky' as an individual cannot be derived from either the senses or the imagination. Indeed, the idea of sky surpasses any sensory report about the object 'sky'. In this case, therefore, the individuation of the object 'sky' (that I treat it as an individual) must be based on my idea of sky and the markers of excess that this idea bears. Unlike the objects 'man' or 'chimera' which present themselves to me as wholes already individuated, the individuation of the object 'sky' is dependent on the nature of the idea of sky. Within the subjective frame of 'I think' none of these is a hard and fast distinction for the naïve distinction between 'of the senses' and 'of the imagination' is suspicious. Nonetheless, what the example of sky brings to the table is a certain richness in the nature of ideas which exceeds simple likeness.

If the example of sky shows us that ideas can include markers that indicate that which exceeds likeness, the next example eliminates likeness altogether. Angels have a long and eventful history as examples in scholastic philosophy, a history that threatens to take us too far afield at this point. However, Descartes is certainly drawing upon this history and would expect his readers to be familiar with it. In short, angels are ideal examples for metaphysics because they are finite but neither material nor imaginary. Thus, in our list, an angel stands as an example of an individual whose individuation is neither dependent upon materiality (man) nor the rules of depiction (chimera). Moreover, unlike the idea of the sky which invokes a representation of a part to indicate a whole, the idea of an angel is entirely present to thought. Thus the idea of an angel does not involve a likeness, nor does it represent by means of part to whole; the idea of an angel is entire and individual without being material or visual. The idea of angel must include enough markers to indicate these special features when I call it to mind.

Descartes closes the list of examples with the idea of God. Like the sky, God exceeds thought and so must be representative rather than a mere reproduction of a likeness. However, like an angel, God is immaterial and so the idea of God cannot be representational in the same way as the idea of the sky. In addition, however, because God is infinite he exceeds individuation. It is this final excess that sets the idea of God apart from the other examples in the list. God is not simply big like the sky and immaterial like an angel. God is excessive. God explodes the notion of individuation itself. By including God on this list, Descartes extends the notion of idea to include that which can only be thought of in the most abstract terms. Thus Descartes introduces a key feature of the idea of God at the outset.

Will and judgement

In this same passage Descartes further specifies the key notion 'idea' by differentiating ideas from other types of thoughts. These thoughts, which we might call actions of the mind, include volition, affect and judgement. In the case of these thoughts *I* add something to the object of the thought. Thus, as an example of affect, I might say that I *fear* the tiger: my thought still includes the idea 'tiger' but in addition to this there is an affective dimension which reports how I relate to this object. Similarly with judgement, I might affirm (judge in the affirmative) that a tiger is dangerous. In this case the idea 'tiger' is further elaborated in terms of my beliefs about the object 'tiger'. And finally, of course, we have the complex case of volition which we have been tacitly deploying throughout *Meditations* thus far.

Every time Descartes reminds himself to withhold judgement about something (for example, the reports of the senses), he is relying on volition to carry the day. The key here is that volition has the power to override judgement and thus reveal the difference between judgements and affects. An affect involves an immediate response to an object; however, many judgements pretend to such immediacy. As a result of this pretence, certain judgements can appear coercive. For example, the judgement 'this table exists external to me' appears to be a simple idea because of the ease with which we append the notion of external existence to ideas we believe to be delivered to us by the senses. In the meditative practice where we actively will not to make such a judgement, the complexity of this idea is revealed. In other words, we had been passively willing to believe the reports of the senses all along but this only comes to light in the active use of the will. Active volition deployed in this way reveals that such judgements are never immediate in the way affects are. Rather they always admit of a gap which must be filled, either passively or actively, by the will to affirm or deny.

The passive use of the will in such cases, then, is what gives rise to the habits and prejudices (pre-judgements) that we have been trying to overcome throughout the meditations thus far. But this also reveals something else extraordinary about volitions: they do not apply themselves directly to ideas. Affects and judgements require an idea as an object. That is, it is the idea 'tiger' to which the affect 'fear' is applied. Volitions, however, do not apply to ideas in the same way: it is meaningless to say 'I will tiger'. Even in the fanciful realm of magic where the mantra 'I will tiger' might result in the appearance of a tiger, the mantra is concealing the more elaborate volition 'I will that a tiger exist'. In this case we see what sets volition apart from other operative thoughts. Volition takes as its object, not ideas, but judgements and occasionally (but perhaps less effectively) affects: one can *choose* not to fear a tiger but the immediacy of affect may overpower will.

While the relation between judgement and volition will be central to the fourth meditation, at this point in the enquiry into my thoughts the crucial point is the relation between judgement and error. Because judgements take ideas as their objects, because they make claims about the status of ideas, it is with judgement that the possibility of truth and falsity first arises. That is, as Descartes points out 'if [ideas] are considered alone and in their own right, without being referred to something else, they cannot, properly speaking, be false.' (AT7:37) This discovery, though now couched in the discussion of ideas and judgement, is nothing more than an elaboration of the claim from the second meditation that the frame of 'I think' insulates me from doubt. That is, the claim 'I think this is a tiger' differs from the judgement 'this is a tiger' insofar as the former case does not attempt to refer the idea 'tiger' to anything outside the field of my thoughts, while the latter case implicitly links the idea 'tiger' to an existing tiger. And once again it is worth noting that it is the implicit nature of most of our judgements that makes them so insidiously coercive.

Thus, judgements introduce the notions of truth or falsity into our thoughts and were we satisfied to remain forever within the solipsistic frame 'I think', we could never err. For it remains certain when I think I see a square tower that I think I see a square tower, regardless of whether the tower is square or round. Even in the case of the most extreme hallucination or deception it remains certain that I think I see what I think I see. And, as a summation of the first two meditations, Descartes reminds us that the most common error introduced by judgement involves the claim that my ideas conform to something external to my thoughts – that the world conforms to my thoughts about the world. Of course, alongside this error is the possibility not yet overcome that there is nothing other than my thoughts, nothing other than me.

Innate ideas

Having redescribed the protective frame of 'I think' in terms of the purity of ideas prior to judgement, Descartes carries on his categorisation of ideas. It is worth noting that this project is carried out with extreme caution in light of the recent worries about judgement introducing error. Thus he begins by declaring that '[among my] ideas, some appear to me to be innate, some adventitious, and some produced by me.' (AT7:38) Where we have been careful when describing those ideas that we take to be delivered by the senses (or imagination), Descartes deploys the equally cautious 'it appears to me'. However we choose to describe it, the fact remains that ideas do seem to carry a mark of their origin; it only remains in doubt whether or not we are correct in our interpretation of these marks. The marks themselves, however, provide a useful way to distinguish types of ideas.

Thus, when I examine my ideas I am able to sort them according to the origin they appear to have. For Descartes there seem to be three distinct kinds of ideas: those derived from my own nature (innate), those that I take to be produced by something other than me (adventitious), and those that I have produced by my own power (fabrications). As we shall see, these categories correspond to the three faculties of reason, sensation and imagination. It is easy to see how the last category relates to the imagination because, recalling the painter's analogy, we understand how it is that the imagination is able to produce things never encountered in sensation (for example, hippogriffs). Similarly, as we have seen, the most common judgement we make about certain ideas is that, because we believe them to be reports of the senses, their source must exist outside us. It is the category of innate ideas, however, that has proven the most controversial. Nonetheless, the examples Descartes gives here provide a sense of what he means by innate.

According to Descartes 'I understand what a thing is, what truth is, what thought is, and I appear to have derived this exclusively from my very own nature.' (AT7:38) Here we must recall that what I know about 'my very own nature' includes only those things that were discovered in the second meditation. Thus, I am certain: that I am; that I am a thinking thing; that I am thinking substance; that thoughts exist. I could not be certain of any of these things if I did not also know what it is to think, to be a substance, to be a thing, and so on. Thus, from my knowledge of my nature (as revealed in the second meditation), I am able to derive the corresponding ideas of 'thing', 'truth' (from the notion of certainty) and 'thought'. It is tempting to suppose that this derivation involves some sort of logical analysis of the *cogito*. Indeed, something like this may be going on in Descartes' reasoning. However, this opens the door to just the sort of objective rules that we have seen Descartes reject in the case of clearness and distinctness. In order to maintain the integrity of the derivation 'exclusively from my nature' it is best to avoid such rules. Thus while he may not have the resources to make this entirely explicit, perhaps the best way to read the derivation of innate ideas is by means of a rudimentary transcendental deduction.

While we must await Kant's critical philosophy for the introduction of a fully specified transcendental deduction to philosophical discourse, partial versions of it have been deployed by thinkers through the ages. In broad outlines, a transcendental philosophy asks: what is necessary for X to be the case. A transcendental deduction then begins with the assumption of X being the case and attempts to derive what must therefore necessarily be the case (despite the lack of direct evidence) for this to be possible at all. In the case of innate ideas, then, the derivation seems to involve a transcendental deduction of the following form: I am certain that I exist as a thinking thing; it would be impossible for me to be certain of this were I not also aware of what it means to think, to be certain, to be a thing; therefore, I must have had the idea of 'thought', 'truth' (from certainty), and 'thing' prior to the certainty that I am a thinking thing; therefore, these ideas pre-exist my most fundamental certainty insofar as they make this certainty possible. In this way, Descartes does not rely upon the imposition of logical rules and instead draws upon the resources of pure reason. The results may be the same but only in the transcendental argument does the derivation rely 'exclusively' on his own nature.

While in the history of philosophy innate ideas have proven to be the most controversial, adventitious ideas are those that are central to the current discussion. We must recall that the point of the third meditation is to establish that there exists an other to me. In this light, neither those ideas derived from me nor those produced by me would seem to be of much use. Moreover, the standard line of argument for the existence of a world independent of my thoughts runs through those ideas that at least seem to indicate the existence of something else. It should be noted, however, that this entire examination is still provisional because 'I can even think of all these ideas as being adventitious, or as being innate, or as fabrications, for I have not yet clearly ascertained their true origin.' (AT7:38)

Adventitious ideas

Thus Descartes turns to an examination of those ideas which appear to have been delivered by the senses in order to determine whether or not this will allow him to escape his solipsistic position. Of course, the first two meditations seem to have already answered this question. Therefore, in these passages we should pay special attention to the detail Descartes chooses to add to the already devastating analysis that has led him to this point.

The first such detail to note is that one of the most compelling cases for the judgement that the senses report things other than me is that these reports can happen against my will. This is indeed a compelling argument for I have come to believe that my will is powerful enough to override most judgements. Nonetheless, it remains true that there appear to be situations where my will is insufficient to bring it about that I do not entertain certain ideas. For example, when seated by a fire I tend to entertain the idea of heat regardless of whether I choose to or not. This fact adds a level of detail to what we have been calling the coercive nature of sensation. That is, those ideas we take to be delivered by the senses are coercive in more than one way. In addition to being coercive in terms of judgement they also seem to be coercive in the very production of ideas. In the presence of fire the idea of heat is coercively present – and this presence overpowers my will.

Descartes describes this coercive association of fire and heat – that the presence of fire causes the feeling of heat – as being 'taught by nature'. Given our experience of the first meditation, we should expect this association to collapse under analysis; what we gain from analysis this time, however, is a detailed account of the distinction between 'taught by nature' and 'by the light of nature'. It is no doubt valuable that nature teaches the association between heat and fire; it is no less valuable that this association has the hallmarks of immediacy and coercion; however, this practical value falls short of the certainty we require to overcome doubt. Thus, Descartes acknowledges that those things taught by nature involve a spontaneous impulse, but this is hardly the same as saying that these things are not open to doubt.

Against those things that I have come to believe through the coercive power of nature's conditioning, Descartes places the certainty that is revealed by the natural light of reason. The example of the *cogito* illustrates this point. The *cogito* once seen cannot in any way be doubted; the situation wherein the fact that I doubt necessitates my own existence renders the doubt of that existence impossible. *This* certainty is more than simply coercive. The *cogito* represents a truth that once seen simply cannot be denied. It is revealed in the clear light of reason that leaves no shadow of doubt. The coercive power of 'taught by nature', however, is always open to the radical doubts of the first meditation (the dream argument, deceiving God) and even circumstantial error (sometimes very cold water seems to cause the feeling of heat). The practical value of what I am 'taught by nature' is never in doubt, but it is based on likelihood and probability rather than the sort of certainty Descartes needs in order to escape the solipsistic position.

At this point we can see how the introduction of 'by the light of nature' replaces the rule of clear and distinct perceptions. As we have seen, the possibility of such a rule is deeply problematic given the situation at the outset of the third meditation. What the rule ends up reporting, however, is the experience of certainty that 'by the light of nature' describes in a more immediate way. It is the immediacy of 'once you see it you cannot but acknowledge it' that Descartes had tried (but failed) to distil into a rule. In these passages he settles upon the descriptive 'by the light of nature' instead of the prescriptive rule of clear and distinct perceptions.

Nonetheless, the fact that certain of the experiences *taught* by nature are coercive remains. To finally rebut this coerciveness as indicative of things existing outside me, Descartes falls back on a version of the dream argument. To break the association between coerced feelings (heat) and the supposition of an external cause (fire) Descartes reminds himself that he dreams. The very fact of dreaming indicates that there might be some faculty (not sufficiently known to me) which produces these ideas. In other words, once again he is forced to admit that he does not yet sufficiently know himself well enough to trust even the most coercive of the associations taught by nature. *Something* other than an external thing produces ideas in dreams; could it not also be at work in my waking life? With this inconclusive suggestion, Descartes temporarily exhausts the exploration of those ideas that appear to be adventitious and must try another way forward.

The Other is God

Having finally disposed of the basic empirical evidence for an external other, Descartes turns to the metaphysics of ideas. That is, having attempted to sort ideas in terms of their empirical (even if only seeming) origins, he now turns to the question of how ideas stand in a substance metaphysics. The first thing to note is that ideas cannot be differentiated in terms of their own ontology. This is because each idea is a mode of thought and therefore has identical ontological status. However, as *representations* these ideas differ from each other greatly. And here is where things get complicated.

At this point it is best to deviate from the ordinal reading of *Meditations* because Descartes is about to introduce a number of key technical claims that, while familiar in some form or other to his contemporaries, are almost entirely alien to today's readers. Moreover, some of these terms will be used in a manner that seems counterintuitive to our ears. Therefore, it will be worth taking some time to sort out this background.

Degrees of reality

The first point to be made is that reality admits of degrees: some things are more real than others. At first glance this seems puzzling; surely if something is real it is no more or less real than anything else that is real; surely this is a black and white issue: something is real or unreal. Not so for Descartes or for the long tradition of metaphysics that informs his work. As far back as Plato we find philosophers committed to the notion of degrees of reality. For Plato only the forms are entirely real; particular entities in the world of experience derive their reality in greater or lesser degrees from their degree of participation in the corresponding form. We see a crude version of this basic idea at work in the judging at dog shows. While it might appear that schnauzers are being judged against each other, for example, each schnauzer is actually being judged against an ideal form of schnauzer determined beforehand (*a priori*) by the official keepers of such things. While in the dog show the title 'best in breed' simply denotes the dog that best approximates this standard, in Plato's metaphysics this would denote the most real schnauzer where only the ideal form is fully real.

In broad outlines, this example shows us what Descartes might mean by saying that reality admits of degrees. Of course, Descartes is not wedded to the particulars of Plato's metaphysics. Rather he is drawing on an Aristotelian metaphysics that rejects the notion of an ideal form standing outside the world. For Aristotle, understanding degrees of reality requires an understanding of the relation between being, reality and substance. Substance is that which is capable of independent being (or of existing without the support of an other). Thus, for example, because the shape of a piece of wax is dependent upon the being of the wax we would not call shape substance. Indeed, shape is precisely the sort of thing that *never* occurs on its own; for shape to be, something else (namely, whatever is shaped) must be. It would be folly, however, to deny that shape is: we still say of the wax's shape that it *is* spherical. Thus, the reality (being) we ascribe to shape will be less than that we would ascribe to something that is capable of being on its own (independently of another).

But what of the wax? Certainly it would be impossible for the wax to be without some shape or other. So why would we say that it is capable of independent existence? The key here is realising that the higher degree of reality of the wax is based on the fact that it is not dependent on any particular shape. Were it a requirement for the being of the wax that it always have one particular shape we would have to admit that this particular shape was essential to the being of the wax. Recall that, for Aristotle, to be is to have an essence ('*esse*', '*ousia*'). Therefore, whatever is necessary for the *esse* of something will be (have a degree of reality) at the same level as that something – they are co-dependent.

While neither Descartes nor Aristotle would be likely to extend the analysis of substance metaphysics to particulars in this way, we can see this sort of co-dependency in the case of a key to a particular lock. The key may be made of steel and steel does not necessarily require any particular shape. However, *as a key*, this particular piece of steel does require a particular shape. It is essential to the being of this key that it have this shape. Moreover, this key *as a key* is dependent upon the relation between this shape and the shape of the lock which it fits. When we say of a key that it is broken, at least part of what we mean is that it has ceased to *be* a key. But, drawing once again on Plato, we can imagine a situation where a key becomes worn over time such that it fits the lock less and less well. In this case we can see that the complex being of the key *as a key* loses its being (reality) over time.

A key, of course, is not a substance for Descartes because its being is dependent upon the material (steel) it is made of. But then neither is steel a substance. Even though it has a greater independence of being than the key, and therefore is more real, steel is dependent for its being upon matter. We can see this in that the particular properties that steel has (size, hardness, weight) are made possible by the more basic properties of matter (extension, shape, motion).

Types of reality
In addition to allowing reality to admit of degrees, however, Descartes also invokes two different types of reality. Again, to understand what this might mean we must recall that reality has to do with being: whatever *is* must admit of some reality or other. In this case, Descartes is specifically interested in the sort of reality (being) that ideas have. This ought to be unsurprising for the simple reason that at this point the only things Descartes knows to be are his thoughts and the most pure form of thought (unadulterated by affect, will or judgement) that he has thus far encountered is the idea. Thus he introduces the distinction between formal and objective reality.

Warning! These terms do not mean what you think they mean!

In fact, they mean almost precisely the opposite of what they would mean in contemporary discourse.

In order to appreciate the distinction we must recall that in this enquiry 'object' does not mean 'thing in the world'. Nor does 'objective' here mean the opposite of 'subjective'. Rather, 'object' refers to that which something is about and 'objective' is simply an adjective derived from this sense of 'object'. While this use of the word has largely exited philosophical discourse, we are familiar with this use of 'object' from the field of grammar: as when we say that something is the object of the sentence or of a preposition. Thus in the phrase 'for the cat', 'the cat' is not an object in the world (because that would be the cat); rather 'the cat' is the object of the preposition 'for'. In this distinction between the cat (in the world) and 'the cat' (in a sentence) we see a basic outline of the distinction between formal and objective reality.

A better illustration of this distinction comes from the field of painting. Imagine you would like to have your portrait painted. No matter how well this portrait turns out, no one who understands the rules of artistic representation would confuse you with your image in the portrait. And yet, there *is* (exists) an image of you *in the painting*. We cannot deny that the image has being because it really is there (in the painting). This reality, however, is obviously of a different sort than the reality we would attribute to you *in the world*. The key to the distinction here is that we understand the *objective* reality of the representation but the *formal* reality of the sitter (you). Of course, the painting also has its formal reality because the wood of the frame, the canvas and even the paint are real in the same way as you are: the painting is there in the world. It is the image in the painting (the likeness, the representation) that has objective reality because it is the object of the painting just as 'the cat' is the object of the preposition.

Now, an interesting feature of objectively real things is that there need not necessarily be any corresponding formal reality. Take our painting example. In the case outlined above, you sat for the painter and the resulting painting was your portrait (likeness, representation). But we know there to be paintings for which there was no sitter. We know it to be possible for a painter to create an image (likeness, representation) of something they have never seen or even something that does not exist in the world: a painting of a unicorn or the painting of a man who happens to exist only in the artist's imagination. The images in these paintings do not fail to have objective reality simply because there is no corresponding formal reality. The images still are; they still exist as objects of the painting.

Conservation of being

The next principle that Descartes invokes is a metaphysical version of a law we might recognise from laws governing energy in a system.

According to Descartes the reality of an effect cannot be greater than that of its cause. Put another way, in a relationship of ontological dependence, the dependent being cannot be greater than the being of that upon which it relies. In a relationship of ontological dependence we recognise that one member of the pair depends upon the other for its being (shape depends upon the being of the wax). Therefore, it is not too much of a stretch to think being (reality) is a transferable commodity.

To illustrate this point let us examine a parallel with another transferable commodity: energy. As a consequence of the law of conservation of energy, in the transference of energy from one point (say, a battery) to another (say, a light bulb) to a third (light) one thing is certain: the energy of the light will be less than (or equal to) that of the light bulb which will be less than (or equal to) that of the battery. That the form of the energy changes from point to point does not affect the overall level of energy involved in the system. For this reason, no system can create more energy than is put into it; but also no energy comes from nothing.

Descartes, therefore, is simply invoking a law of conservation with regard to being (reality). In any system of ontological dependence nothing that derives its being from something else can have a greater level of being than that source. Similarly, no being can come into being from nothing. Crucially, just as in the case of energy, that the form of reality (being) changes in the course of the dependence relation does not affect the rules governing the conservation of reality (being). Thus, the transference of being from a substance to a mode 'runs downhill': it is lesser (or at most equal) at the end than at the beginning. But just as importantly, the transference of being from formal reality to objective reality also 'runs downhill': simply in virtue of having formal reality you are guaranteed to have more being than even the most realistic portrait of you.

In this last case, of course, the question of representation comes into play. By using the formally real you as a model, the painter will be drawing a degree of being from you to inform the objective reality of the image (likeness, representation). But of course we must remember that not all paintings require such a formally real model. No being (not even objective being) can come from nothing and so there must be some source somewhere. *Something* must have enough formal reality to inform the objective reality of the image (for example, of a unicorn). In such cases of painting, the answer lies in the fact that the image in the mind of the painter (as mode of the painter's being) has enough formal reality to create such an objective being. But of course painting is always only an analogy and Descartes is interested in that other form of representative objects: ideas.

The source of my ideas: a clue

Ideas, of course, are primarily (or formally) modes of thinking substance. That is, each thought is a modal expression of my being (as thinking substance). But this only accounts for the formal reality of ideas. In addition, we recall, ideas are representative objects that therefore have objective reality. In other words, just as our painting has formal reality in the canvas and paint and objective reality insofar as it represents, ideas have both formal reality (as modes of thinking substance) and objective reality (as representational objects). As such there must be something or other that has as much formal reality as these ideas have objective reality. Put another way, the objective content of these ideas must be 'caused' by something formally real. In saying this, however, it is important that we remember that 'cause' has a wider meaning than it does in contemporary discourse. While Descartes has recourse to the Aristotelian metaphysics of causes, here all that need be indicated by 'cause' is a source of being.

Therefore, we can return to the content of the various ideas I have at my disposal in order to determine what might stand as cause of these ideas. To twist our earlier analogy, the footprints on Robinson Crusoe's beach are both things in the world (formally real) and also representative of a formal cause (objectively real). Of course we must recall that Descartes is looking for evidence that something other than his being exists. Therefore, any idea whose representational content could even possibly have been caused by himself is of no use. What he needs is an idea whose representational content demands a formally real cause that could not be accounted for from his own being.

Returning to our inventory of ideas we find a slightly modified version of the list that introduced the notion of idea: 'Among my ideas, in addition to the one that displays me to myself . . . are others that represent God, corporeal and inanimate things, angels, animals, and finally other men like myself.' (AT7:42–3). It is the representational content of these ideas that will now be examined:

If the objective reality of any of [these] ideas is found to be so great that I am certain that the same reality is not in me formally or eminently, and that therefore I myself cannot be the cause of the idea, then it necessarily follows that I am not alone in the world, but that something else, which is the cause of this idea, also exists. (AT7:42)

In other words, if the footprints on the beach are too big to have been made by Robinson then Robinson knows he is not alone on the island.

There are several well-worn complications in the analysis that follows. The basic outline of the analysis of the objective reality of these ideas involves the general claim that for the vast majority of the ideas under consideration – those of corporeal things, other men, and so on – Descartes does find it possible that he is the formal reality that stands behind the objective reality of his ideas. That is, Descartes knows that he has formal reality (exists) and claims that the formal reality of his being as thinking substance is sufficient to have caused the representational content of these ideas. The details of these various claims and arguments have come under a great deal of scrutiny – a scrutiny, however, that is misplaced.

Many commentators have been puzzled by the claim that Descartes can account for the objective reality of his ideas of corporeal being out of the resources of his entirely incorporeal being. Others have been unconvinced by arguments that seem to involve a fair amount of metaphysical gymnastics in these sections. For example, distinguishing what will come to be known as secondary properties from the idea of material substance seems a little convenient given the sparse resources at his disposal. Fortunately for Descartes, however, nothing of any significance hangs on any of these points. As in the method of doubt, Descartes need only deploy a plausible account of the manner in which the objective reality of these ideas may be derived from the certainty of his being. These accounts need not be airtight or capable of sustained scrutiny; the force of his argument here requires only a *prima facie* case.

We must recall that the purpose of the enquiry is not to disprove the reality of the external world but to ascertain whether something other than me exists at all. We must also keep in mind that the purpose of the enquiry is not to establish the true relation between my mind and my ideas, but to ascertain whether there is any idea which cannot under any circumstances be thought of as effect to my mind's cause. So long as we remember this, the parallel with the method of doubt is clear. I need only make a *prima facie* case against the idea of corporeal things, for example, being the sort of idea that cannot have been caused by me. This is so because what I am looking for is an idea that cannot, under any circumstances whatsoever, be thought of as having been caused by me. Thus, as in the method of doubt, in this investigation too, the slightest suspicion that I may be the possible cause of the objective reality of the idea is enough to disqualify it.

The *prima facie* case, therefore, is fairly simple. I exist as a thinking thing and have the formal reality of an existing substance. Moreover, I have the power of imagination as well as whatever faculty it is that gives rise to dream experience. I have no reason to believe that I am not the formal reality standing behind the ideas of imagination or dreams. Therefore, however the technical details and subtle arguments in these passages fare, the *prima facie* case is sound. As a result, the vast majority of my ideas fail to provide conclusive evidence for the existence of an other to me. It is possible, just possible, that all of life is a hugely complicated dream or a coherent illusion that I am unknowingly presenting to myself. This leaves only the idea of God.

Descartes' idea of God

It is necessary to consider what it might mean to say that the idea of God does not fall into the same category as the ideas Descartes has just dismissed as possible candidates for the evidence of an other formal existence. At the outset we note that any idea of God that has features in common with those of corporeal nature, other men, animals or even angels is out of bounds. This is a point that is often overlooked by students of *Meditations* who are convinced by the story that Descartes only included the proofs of the existence of God in order to appease the politico-religious authorities of his day; after all, Descartes' horrified response to the trial and imprisonment of Galileo is well documented. Upon examination, however, the details of Descartes' idea of God are extraordinarily radical if not straightforwardly heretical.

In the process of testing the representational content of his ideas Descartes has claimed that it is at least possible to account for their objective reality out of the formal reality of his own being as thinking substance – except in the case of God. Thus, the idea of God that Descartes is invoking must be entirely different from the other ideas he has just examined: the representational content of the idea of God must be free of the sorts of features that disqualified those other ideas. But this means, among other things, that Descartes cannot be invoking the idea of a personal God: he cannot have in mind the sorts of personal attributes that one would ascribe, for example, to Thor, Apollo or Isis; his idea of God cannot involve such features as bodily appearance, spatial location or individuated acts. More worryingly for a writer in Christendom is the fact that Descartes' idea of God precludes such items of faith as the incarnation. Whatever else the idea of God might encompass, the notion of his embodiment in the person of Christ who had corporeal existence, spatial location and bodily appearance is excluded here. Where Galileo faced non-specific charges of writing about things he had been told not to write about, Descartes' position runs very close to the specific heresy of Arianism.

What then can be affirmed of the idea of God Descartes invokes? Descartes laid the groundwork for understanding the idea of God in his initial inventory of ideas. That the idea of God is distinct from the idea of sense (exemplified by the idea of man) should be obvious. The idea of God, however, also exceeds the idea of imagination (chimera) because it is neither bound nor bounded by the rules of depiction: any depiction of God would fail to capture the excess that is essential to the idea of God. However, while the idea of the sky involves a notion of excess, this is not the proper way to think of God. Even if the idea of the sky includes markers of excess, the representation of the object 'sky' is by means of a part: an image of a patch of blue (along with the indication of sensory excess) represents the object 'sky' to me in my thoughts. Not only does the idea of God not involve *sensory* excess, but neither does it involve the mode of representation by means of part to whole. The idea of an angel provides an example of an idea that does not rely on either sensory or imaginary parameters. Like God, the idea of an angel (as immaterial being) is present to pure intellect. Thus, as a start, the idea of God involves the notion of excess (like that of the sky) but is present to pure intellect (like an angel).

When Descartes returns to the idea of God in his examination of objective reality he is more explicit: 'I understand by the name "God" a certain substance that is infinite, independent, supremely intelligent and supremely powerful, and that created me along with everything else that exists – if anything else exists.' (AT7:45) This formulation of the idea of God bears a complexity that leads to the two (so-called) proofs that follow, and determines that there are two. However, at this point it is worth noting that Descartes short-circuits the process by drawing a conclusion directly from this very formulation:

Indeed all these are such that, the more carefully I focus my attention on them, the less possible it seems they could have arisen from myself alone. Thus, from what has been said, I must conclude that God necessarily exists. (AT7:45)

This is not an insignificant moment. In effect, Descartes has declared that the proofs themselves are of no account. Moreover, this is entirely in keeping with the nature of the meditative exercise as it is the intuitive clarity of this certainty that is compelling for the provisionally solipsistic meditator. This, then, constitutes the genuine end of the enquiry into the existence of an other: Descartes now knows that he is not alone in the world. The idea of God (as formulated) constitutes the set of footprints on the beach that leads immediately to the conclusion: there is an other. As with Robinson Crusoe, of course, there will follow the further question concerning the nature of this other. But from the point of view of the solipsistic subject, from the point of view that necessitated the third meditation, these further questions are mere details.

Proofs as elaborations

Why then does Descartes supply the so-called proofs of the third meditation? Part of the answer of course lies in the nature of the meditative process. While it is clear that the meditator who has strictly followed *Meditations* thus far ought at this point to be able to see the necessity of God's existence intuitively, Descartes has not forgotten his heuristic principles. Not all meditators will have been as successful as Descartes in the suppression of prejudice and the acceptance of the solipsistic bind. As Descartes writes at the end of the first 'proof',

Indeed there is nothing in all these things that is not manifest by the light of nature to one who is conscientious and attentive. But when I am less attentive, and the images of sensible things blind the mind's eye, I do not so easily recall why the idea of a more perfect being than me necessarily proceeds from a being that really is more perfect. (AT7:47–8)

For these 'less conscientious and attentive' readers, the initial declaration that God necessarily exists serves as a measure of what can have been achieved by this point. What follows are *a posteriori* elaborations of the reasoning involved in this intuition. Even Robinson Crusoe *could* go to the trouble of explaining to himself: these are footprints in the sand; they indicate that someone has walked here; they are bigger than my footprints; therefore someone who is not me must have walked here. But why would he need to?

That there are apparently two proofs of the existence of God in the third meditation does seem odd. It is sometimes suggested that this superfluity indicates a lack of faith in either of the proofs: 'if one does not work at least I have a backup'. But this is not the case and, insofar as any proof is required, both are necessary. As mentioned above, the complexity of the formulation of the idea of God justifies the two proofs of the third meditation. To simplify the formulation, God is both an infinite substance and is the creator of my being. Thus, the first proof addresses the question of the being of God and the second tackles the notion of God as creator. The fact that the proof is thus divided, however, both reinforces the case for the intuitive conclusion Descartes starts with and reflects a further complexity that has been running through *Meditations*.

Any proof of the existence of a single being that requires two separate proofs of two separate aspects of that being is suspicious at the outset. Could it not be that the first proof proves the existence of an infinite substance while the second proves that something has created me? Would this not necessitate a further proof that these two beings are one and the same? Of course, if these two proofs are thought of as heuristic elaborations, this problem evaporates. There is no reason why one cannot be shown two different aspects of what has already been intuitively established. Indeed, it might be more effective to break the lesson up in this way.

More importantly, however, the two proofs address the twin concerns that drive the third meditation. We have already dealt at some length with the need to establish that there is an other. However, there is the further concern with the reliability of my faculties. Recall that the abortive attempt to posit as a rule that clear and distinct perceptions are reliably certain foundered on the fact that I have no way of knowing whether or not my faculty of perception is reliable in reporting clearness and distinctness in the first place. Indeed, this faculty claims to present clear and distinct perceptions of mathematics and yet I must admit that this faculty may be inherently unreliable. The proof of the existence of a supreme being is in itself insufficient to address this concern. In addition I need to know that this supreme being created me and my faculties. This is the necessary first step in recovering a faith in the reliability of my faculties. Thus the first 'proof' establishes that there exists a God while the second 'proof' establishes that this God is my creator.

God, infinity, infinite substance

The basic form of the first 'proof' is clear from the preceding discussion and rests almost entirely on the fact that the idea of God involves the notion of infinity. Indeed, it would not be too much to say that the idea of God could be functionally reduced to the idea of infinity itself. In the context of this proof, Descartes understands 'God' to be a substance that is infinite, independent, supremely intelligent and supremely powerful. Of these, 'independent' is ironically the least autonomous feature as independence is included in the notion of substance itself. By separating this out, however, Descartes may be highlighting the fact that this independence is itself supreme, infinite or total. That substance which is supremely independent draws attention to the relative use of 'substance'. In other words, Descartes would have to admit that in a non-solipsistic universe his being as thinking substance is not absolute. As 'relative substance' he would be admitting a degree of dependence – in this case on God – which will inform the second proof. Nonetheless, the notion of independence involved in the idea of God seems capable of reduction to the notion of infinite substance.

Similarly, the twin notions of 'supremely intelligent' and 'supremely powerful' seem to already involve the notion of infinity. By specifically referencing intelligence and power here Descartes is specifying the nature of the infinite substance he has already named. That God is intelligent indicates that God is not an infinite material substance but an infinite intellectual substance (or a supreme version of thinking substance). As we shall see, this is necessary to understand the relationship between my being as finite thinking substance and the formal existence of the idea of God – a relationship that has come to be known as the trademark argument.

That God is also powerful is necessary to guarantee his activity. The Latin root '*potentia*' (from which we get words such as 'potent' and 'potentate') indicates an active power. Thus Descartes' God cannot be reduced either to the Deist 'Watchmaker God' or to a teleological principle such as Hegel's Absolute. Instead, because Descartes' God is *infinitely* powerful he is of necessity constantly acting; it is essential to the being of an infinitely powerful God that this God never be passive. This feature of the idea of God will play a crucial role in the second 'proof' and will give rise to the philosophical doctrine of Occasionalism.

While the secondary specifications of the idea of God add important features to the idea of infinite substance, for the purposes of the first proof only the notion of infinity is essential. In short, the argument runs: I have the idea of infinity; the objective reality of an idea requires a cause of at least as high a degree of formal reality as the idea contains objective reality; the objective reality of the idea of infinity is infinite; therefore the formal reality of the cause of this objective reality must be infinite; therefore an infinite being (a being with an infinite formal reality) must exist formally. Thus Descartes proves the existence of infinite substance, though everything spelled out in this 'proof' is already available to those who meditate on the idea of God.

The first elaboration of the idea of God

The passages that constitute this first 'proof' involve the treatment of three likely objections that target the joints of the intuitive proof we have thus far outlined. I have an idea of infinity that I can only account for by the positing of a formally real being which is also infinite. Because this proof takes as its starting point that I do in fact have such an idea, the possible objections Descartes treats focus on the link between the objective reality of the idea and the corresponding formal reality, and the possibility that in fact I may be the formal being that stands as the formal cause. Nonetheless, many subsequent objections to the first proof rest on the tacit denial that I have the idea of infinity or, which amounts to the same thing, that I have an idea of infinity insufficient to get the proof off the ground. Therefore, it is essential to understand just what Descartes means by 'infinity' and what it might mean to have an idea of this infinity. What is involved in this idea can be drawn out of the objections Descartes now sets out to disarm.

Descartes identifies two possible ways to understand the possibility that my own formal being is sufficient to account for the objective idea of infinity. The first of these is to think of the derivation of the infinite out of the finitude of my being. That is, it is certain that I have ideas of finite things and that I am in fact finite so perhaps my understanding of the infinite is derived by negation from these facts. As we know, it is possible that I am the cause of the idea of finite things; therefore, can it not be the case that I derive my understanding of the infinite in the same way that I can derive the idea of darkness from the idea of light? This is an apt example as, technically, I have no visual experience of darkness, and yet I have an idea of darkness which I understand in terms of the absence (negation) of light.

In response to this worry, Descartes argues that we would be wrong to think of the finite as the default term and the infinite as derivative. This argument has two parts. First, Descartes appeals to our intuitive sense that an infinite substance would have to have more reality than a finite one. This is rather compelling once you accept that reality admits of degrees. Thus, Descartes argues that the analogy with darkness is misplaced because it is the finite (rather than the infinite) that is the privation. Secondly, however, Descartes argues that our perception of the infinite must be prior to our understanding of the finite in order for us to understand our own finitude at all.

Descartes starts with two basic facts which, as meditators, we ought to admit: that we doubt and that we desire. That I doubt has been amply established by my meditative practice; that I desire underlies the whole of the enterprise insofar as it explains why I am bothering to do any of this at all. But doubt and desire are indicative of lack. If I did not lack certainty I would not be able to doubt and I can only desire what I do not have. However, if I am to understand that I lack then I must have something more perfect with which to compare myself; without an idea of that which is more perfect than me I could not have an understanding of lack. Thus, the understanding of my own finitude requires a prior understanding of the infinite – otherwise I would (perhaps wrongly) understand *myself* to be infinite.

The importance of an adequate idea of infinity

But this leads us to the other possible way in which I could understand my own being as the formal cause of the objective idea of infinity. Perhaps, Descartes suggests, all of the perfections that I am so quick to attribute to God are really in me potentially. After all, I can imagine what it would be like to be faster than I am based on the swiftness I actually do possess. Perhaps, therefore, my idea of God is really nothing more than a version of 'super-me'. Moreover, even though I am certainly not perfect I can think of myself as perfectible. Therefore, perhaps in thinking of God I am merely projecting a perfect endpoint of the progression that could be derived from my current imperfect being. This objection has found favour especially in humanist and empiricist circles but unfortunately merely reveals the inadequacy of these philosophies in relation to the infinite.

Humanist philosophies find this objection appealing because its force rests on the implicit assumption that 'man is the measure'. Therefore, 'God' can be reduced to the manageable 'projection of me'. We recognise a version of this supposition in both Hume and Feuerbach. Hume, of course, will couple his position with an empiricism that denies the possibility of an original conception of that which cannot be encountered in experience. While this derivation of infinity from a finite progression and the notion of God as psychological projection coheres with the humanist and empiricist positions, it is forced to deny *a priori* the possibility of the notion of infinity that Descartes is invoking. While Descartes does not foresee this misunderstanding of infinity, his response to the 'potentiality' objection does reveal the nature of his own understanding of infinity and how this runs counter to what might be called the additive notion of infinity.

Descartes formulates the objection as follows:

For I now observe that my knowledge is gradually being increased, and I see nothing standing in the way of its being increased more and more to infinity. Moreover, I see no reason why, with my knowledge thus increased, I could not acquire all the remaining perfections of God. And, finally, if the potential for these perfections is in me already, I see no reason why this potential would not suffice to produce the idea of these perfections. (AT7:47)

The idea of God that Descartes is invoking, however, is entirely actual and does not involve any potentiality whatsoever. Moreover, the very notion of gradual increase – as it necessarily involves actual lack – indicates the sort of imperfection that cannot generate the idea of perfection. At best, *actual* imperfection can generate a notion of *potential* perfection, but this always and necessarily falls short of actual perfection. And finally, the notion that infinity can be achieved by a process of gradual increase is incoherent because this process, by its very nature, can never reach a point where it is incapable of greater increase; and yet, the idea of infinity involves the incapacity of greater increase. From this we see that Descartes' notion of infinity – and that notion that informs the idea of God being invoked – is an absolute infinity. The greatest mistake that can be made in understanding the first proof of the existence of God, therefore, is to think of infinity as 'very very big', for the 'very very big' always and necessarily involves the possibility of the bigger. For Descartes, 'infinity' is entirely positive, actual, total and complete and therefore does not involve any possibility of the bigger.

Returning to the humanist/empiricist objection, then, we can draw two conclusions. First, these thinkers are invoking an inadequate notion of infinity at the start and therefore their objections rest on the conclusiveness of their own proofs that the idea of absolute infinity is impossible. But secondly, this reveals that Descartes is not in fact committed to his own proof being universalisable. As we have seen, the real proof is properly intuitive and the formal passages serve as mere elaborations. In this case the elaboration is a reminder to the meditator that a particular idea of infinity is necessary to for the proof to 'work'. However, because *Meditations* is both subjectivist and meditational, Descartes can reply to those who insist on invoking inadequate ideas of infinity, either that they do not have an idea of absolute infinity, or that they have not meditated properly on the ideas that they have.

The former response is less likely because of the 'trademark argument' Descartes will deploy at the close of the third meditation; however, because this meditative journey starts from a position of subjective solipsism, Descartes can offer little more than the hopeful expectation that anyone who follows this meditative practice fully will come to see that they have the idea of absolute infinity. Of course, it remains possible that some people, Hume for example, simply do not have this idea. It is the latter response that is more generous and yet more demanding. That is, because one can only come to the point of seeing the idea of absolute infinity once one has suppressed all the coercive ideas of sense and stripped away all the prejudicial features of the idea of God, the second response to Hume is that he has not yet tried hard enough. After all, no one said this meditational journey was going to be easy.

The (so-called) Cartesian Circle

The other possible objection that Descartes foresees to the first 'proof' is more involved, not least because of the fact that his response to this objection appears to open onto the infamous Cartesian Circle. The basic thrust of the objection is to sever the link between the objective reality of the idea of infinity and the necessity of a corresponding formal being as cause. As Descartes envisions it, this objection relies on the claim that the idea of God (infinity) involves material falsity. This technical term basically implies that the idea of God is more like the idea of cold than the idea of a chair.

The idea of cold *seems* to have objective reality, but this is in fact a trick played on the mind by various scalar qualities. Instead, what I really have is an idea of temperature to which I apply the label 'cold' or 'hot' depending upon how any particular instance sits upon the scale of temperatures. That this labelling is also influenced by relative circumstances is equally damning because what I might describe as 'hot' on one occasion I would insist is 'cold' on another. In the case of 'God', therefore, this objection suggests that there is no fixed and regular referent for the term. As in the case of 'cold', we have mistakenly taken a term that has only nominal reality to have objective reality. Indeed, as the idea of God can be functionally reduced to the idea of infinity, this objection is initially appealing because infinity *seems* like a number on a scale.

In responding to this objection, Descartes does not do as well as we might hope but neither does he do as poorly as some would suggest. Descartes' formal response to this objection involves an appeal to the already discredited rule of clear and distinct perceptions:

> On the contrary, because it is the most clear and distinct and because it contains more objective reality than any other idea, no idea is in and of itself truer and has less of a basis for being suspected of falsehood. . . . It is indeed an idea that is utterly clear and distinct; for whatever I clearly and distinctly perceive to be real and true and to involve some perfection is wholly contained in that idea. (AT7:46)

Even without the problem of the Cartesian Circle that this would open onto, this response is most clearly and distinctly a matter of refutation by assertion: the idea of God is not materially false because it is most certainly true. This is not Descartes' proudest moment.

Still, there are the resources to rehabilitate this response. First, it is clear that Descartes' appeal to the rule of clearness and distinctness adds nothing to his argument and so the problem of the Cartesian Circle is readily defused. This fact, however, hardly makes this a good argument. Nonetheless, the manner in which this argument can be turned away from the Cartesian Circle reveals the manner in which Descartes' 'proof' here never actually relies on a good *argument* at all.

The basic form of the Cartesian Circle involves two claims: (1) that Descartes needs to prove the existence of God in order to establish the reliability of the criteria of clearness and distinctness; and (2) that the proof of the existence of God depends on the reliability of the criteria of clearness and distinctness. The *prima facie* case for the inevitability of the Cartesian Circle is solid as Descartes most certainly does posit a 'rule' of clear and distinct perceptions and does appeal to this rule in this passage from the proof. Upon examination of the text, however, this *prima facie* case collapses rather swiftly.

Our examination of the 'rule' of clear and distinct perceptions has already called (1) into question. Instead, it would appear that the 'rule' does little more than indicate something that we already experienced as certain and so fails to be a rule that can be applied to new cases. Establishing the reliability of clearness and distinctness as a marker of the experience of certainty may need a certain amount of work; but clearness and distinctness do not add anything to that experience. Instead, it is the coercive experience of certainty (as in the case of the *cogito*) that underwrites the validity of clearness and distinctness. In the case at hand, then, it is important to note that the appeal to clearness and distinctness is accompanied by the sort of coercive experience of certainty that causes Descartes to 'blurt out'.

Thus, Descartes 'blurts out': 'I maintain that this idea of a being that is supremely perfect and infinite is true in the highest degree' (AT7:46). This is not an accident; Descartes is here being coerced by the experience of certainty that results from the examination of the idea of God. That he then draws attention to the markers of this experience (clearness and distinctness) is incidental. Once again, as in the *cogito*, it is the experience of certainty that is doing the work. To further indicate the coercion of the idea of God, Descartes adds: 'For although I could perhaps pretend that such a being does not exist, nevertheless I could not pretend that the idea of such a being discloses to me nothing real . . .' (AT7:46) – the idea itself discloses this to Descartes and it is impossible to pretend otherwise.

But this merely brings us back to our initial point: the proof of the existence of God is intuitive and immediately arises from the contemplation of the idea of God (of infinity). In other words, here at the point that Descartes seems destined to fall into the Cartesian Circle, we see that Descartes is not offering a proof at all. Not only does he not need to invoke the 'rule' of clear and distinct perceptions, he does not need to do anything more than offer (or blurt out) assertions. The proof has already been accomplished and this passage is a mere elaboration of that proof in terms of a possible objection. But the objection in question becomes an impossibility once one sees the idea of God clearly and distinctly.

The Cartesian Circle is inevitable once one assumes that the clearness and distinctness constitute criteria rather than the descriptive markers they are. In the parallel case of the *cogito* – from which Descartes had initially hoped to derive such criteria – the objection 'but perhaps you are being deceived' dissolves totally and immediately once one sees the *cogito* clearly and distinctly. There is no question of arguing in a circle in either case because there is no question of arguing in either case. And thus, while there is no doubt that Descartes could have been clearer on this point, the second condition necessary to establish the Cartesian Circle also fails: the proof of the existence of God does not depend on the reliability of the criteria of clearness and distinctness.

The second elaboration: God as creator

The second so-called proof that occurs in the third meditation arises in answer to the question of my own origin. As a proof of the existence of God this is surprisingly dependent upon what has come before. In other words, it is not the case that Descartes offers two independent and self-contained proofs for the existence of God. As I have argued, the only 'proof' is intuitive proof that arises immediately out of the contemplation of the idea of God. Nonetheless, the passages usually associated with the first 'proof' are primary in the sense that, as elaborations of this intuition, they are not dependent upon any other proof. The manner in which the second 'proof' addresses the question of the creator God is dependent upon the prior elaboration of the existence of an infinite God in important ways.

As we noted earlier, Descartes' definition of God is in two parts. First Descartes addresses the question of the necessary existence of infinite substance; then he tackles the question of whether this infinite substance is related to me as creator. The credentials for this second enquiry being a proof of the existence of God rest on the manner in which Descartes introduces the topic: 'it is appropriate to ask further whether I myself who have this idea could exist, if such a being did not exist.' (AT7:48) That this would constitute a proof is clear; however, it is equally clear that such a proof is superfluous. In the second meditation, Descartes has already established that he really does exist, while in the preceding passages of the third meditation he has also established that 'such a being' exists. Therefore, what is at stake here is not the proof of the existence of God but the proof of the dependency relation between myself and God. Thankfully such a reading also coheres with what Descartes writes insofar as the subsequent passages deal almost exclusively with this relationship.

Recalling the content of Descartes' idea of God we note that Descartes is already committed to the claim that God created him. That this God necessarily exists is clear from the contemplation of the idea of God itself. What follows then is Descartes' attempt to secure the claim that this necessarily existing infinite substance is necessarily responsible for the creation of his being. In light of what has come before, however, we should not be surprised to discover that this claim will be secured by a proper understanding of the idea of God rather than by any direct argumentation.

Given the idea of God in play, I am predisposed to the belief that God did create me. The obvious alternative to this scenario is that I created myself. After all, apart from God I am the only being that I know to exist. Descartes' initial response to this possibility draws upon the fact that he is imperfect and the claim that if he were to have had the power to create himself he would have made himself perfect. This initial formulation is mildly compelling but remains largely speculative; after all, it is a supposition that one would want to be perfect. However, the case becomes much stronger when we remember that one's understanding of what it means to be perfect is tied to one's understanding of desire and lack. If we are aware of our imperfection because of desire for what we lack, is it not also true that we desire our perfection?

The only remaining obstacle would be the supposition that, while I desire perfection, I lack the power to achieve it. Here, however, Descartes reminds us that the one part of our being that we can be certain of is our being as thinking substance. If it is supposed that I have the power to create myself as substance then certainly I would have the power to create in myself the various attributes that I currently desire to be perfect. After all, substance has a higher degree of being than even the most perfect attribute. Therefore, the brute fact that I exist, coupled with my desire to be better than I am, leads to the conclusion that I could not have created myself.

The necessity of creation: the law of preservation

I could, of course, argue that I have always existed and in this way it would seem possible to avoid the metaphysical entanglements of self-creation. Descartes only entertains this possibility in order to reject it but the manner in which he goes about this is revealing of the sort of creator God he has in mind. His first objection draws upon a principle of preservation that might usefully be compared to the Newtonian laws of conservation. As Descartes characterises his principle:

it does not follow from the fact that I existed a short time ago that I must exist now, unless some cause, as it were, creates me all over again at this moment, that is to say, which preserves me. (AT7:49)

By comparing this principle to its Newtonian cousin we can better see where Descartes' metaphysical commitments lie.

The greatest difference between this law of preservation and the physical law of conservation lies in the perspective each takes on time. For Descartes the force (or cause) of an object (being) attaches at each discrete moment; there is no continuous system within which we can say that the object and its force operate together through time. For Newtonian Physics the whole of the system is always in question; the force attaches to an object once and then the two are coupled in the system. However, at any given time the Newtonian system can be described in terms that are amenable to the Cartesian perspective. For Descartes: at any given moment in time a ball in motion will 'require' a certain force to continue in motion; for Newtonian physics: at any given moment in time a ball in motion 'possesses' a certain force (momentum) that allows it to stay in motion. The law of *preservation*, therefore, is related to the law of *conservation* by just this limited perspective. This limitation on the law of preservation, however, is a consequence of its status as a metaphysical (rather than physical) principle.

While Descartes might well want to redescribe physical laws in terms of the system-based perspective, this is not an option in the subjectivist metaphysics in which he is currently operating. Newtonian physics takes a third-person (or god's eye) view of the system in question and is therefore able to say of a force that because it had attached in the past and nothing has interfered with it in the interim it must still be attached; it is therefore possible to describe this force as a property of the object in motion. But the self that Descartes discovered in the second meditation does not have such a perspective on itself; or better, I do not have such a perspective on myself. Unlike a ball in a physical system that I can observe from outside the system, my being as thinking substance does not have an outside and there is no way for me to take up such a 'god's eye' perspective.

Thus we can see that the metaphysical principle of preservation, as it applies to my own being, is the best I can do. There is no real way for me to understand my creation as the sort of thing that could have happened in the past such that my current existence is the result of existential momentum. I cannot understand this about myself because as a *subject* I have only subjective experience and each moment constitutes a new moment of 'I think'. Of course, the fact that I cannot think of my being in this way is not sufficient to establish that I am not this way.

Fortunately, the nature of infinite substance serves as the final guarantor of the principle of preservation.

Divine creation as preservation

Here more than at any other point in the second 'proof' we see the subsidiary nature of this second elaboration of the idea of God. It is often argued that Descartes illicitly imports the metaphysical principle of preservation in order to solve the problem of the creator God. However, the basis of this principle is already present in the idea of God that has already been established to correspond to a formal reality. In other words, the principle can be derived directly from the idea of God and this derivation is legitimised by the first elaboration.

We have already established that I am not my own creator; therefore, unless I am essentially uncreated then something must be the cause of my being. From the second meditation I have come to think of my being as thinking substance. Being substance at all is compatible with being uncreated because to be substance is to have independent existence. However, because I desire (and thus lack) I also know that I am finite substance. This finitude complicates the situation because it poses a limit on my being. If this limit is not to become a dependence – and therefore call into question my status as substance – there cannot be an unlimited (infinite) substance. But alas, as we have seen, the existence of such an infinite substance is necessary. As a result, I am forced to re-evaluate my claim to be a thinking substance.

As Spinoza will make clear in his interpretation of Cartesian metaphysics, once infinite substance exists, all other claimants to the title 'substance' can be substance in name only. My existence as thinking 'substance' was based on the solipsistic results of the second meditation. But those results were only ever provisional and with the proof of the existence of infinite substance and the proof that I am not self-created I realise that I properly exist only as relative substance. My being as limited substance clears the way for understanding the dependence relation between finite and infinite substance; and this dependence relation is necessitated by the nature of infinite substance itself.

God is not only infinite substance but infinitely active substance. Because infinite being is not ever passive there is no possibility that God would just 'let me be'. Still, it would be too much to say that God meddles in my being, because this kind of activity is incompatible with the idea of God that has had all finite features and personal attributes stripped out. Thus, God does not intervene in the world by discrete act because such an act would be finite and God's activity must be infinite. The activity proper to infinite substance, therefore, must be continuous and in-discrete. It is this notion of activity, derived from the feature of supreme *potentia* that guarantees the principle of preservation. It is in the nature of substance to support the being of attributes or lesser beings; therefore it is in the nature of infinite substance to support the being of finite substance(s). Thus, the very existence of a supremely powerful God dissolves the distinction between creation and preservation: at every moment my being as finite thinking substance is preserved (supported by) the activity of infinite substance.

Descartes versus Spinoza

Here we can see most clearly the point of contact with Spinoza (1632–1677). While Descartes does not explicitly draw the conclusion of the exclusivity of infinite substance, the basic outlines of Spinoza's meta-physics are implicit in these very passages. For Descartes *res cogitans* is a relative substance which is existentially dependent upon the being of infinite substance which is substance *par excellence* by virtue of its being entirely independent. Spinoza simply denies the title 'substance' to any but this infinite substance (God). For Spinoza *res cogitans* is only an attribute of God and is therefore wholly dependent upon the being of infinite substance.

While Spinoza sees his position on this point as a more consistent development of Descartes' basic position, Descartes' own insistence that *res cogitans* is substantial in nature – despite this dependence relation – can be explained in either of two ways. On the one hand, Descartes comes to the understanding of the relationship between finite and infi-nite substance via the solipsistic, subjectivist perspective of the second meditation. Thus there is a genuine sense in which it is necessary to have thought of *res cogitans* as substantial. That he continues to refer to himself as thinking substance, therefore, can be seen as a holdover from – or even a reminder of – this earlier stage. On the other hand, Descartes is in many ways a two-world philosopher in the spirit of Plato and Augustine, and Spinoza's metaphysical monism will not sit well with this.

This two-world system is already implicit in the very project of exam-ining first philosophy that Descartes has undertaken. That is, Descartes sees metaphysics (first philosophy) as an essential precursor to the under-standing of physics (natural or second philosophy). Already at the outset, then, this project has been a two-world philosophy. That *res cogitans* is, properly speaking, not a substance from a metaphysical perspective does not change the fact that thinking of *res cogitans* as a substance will be invaluable to physical descriptions. Part of what is going on in Descartes is a rethinking of the Aristotelian notion of substance in line with this two-world framework. As a result, Descartes is happy to implicitly rely upon the notion of a relatively independent substance – a notion that Spinoza finds absurd.

But this is exciting because it places thinking substance at the centre of Descartes' philosophy. By passing through the first and second meditations Descartes rejects the objectivist perspective that Spinoza's rational metaphysics demands. The starting point for Descartes' philosophy is the thinking subject, and the fact that *res cogitans* straddles both the physical and metaphysical worlds is essential to that position. Thus, as a relative substance I owe my existence to God at every moment; at the same time, I can understand my being in relation to the physical world as thinking substance. While I stand in both perspectives, however, Descartes is clear that any understanding of my being, beyond the bare metaphysical claim that I exist, rests on a proper understanding of this metaphysical relation of dependence upon God.

The trademark argument

Descartes closes the third meditation with a recap that has come to be known as the trademark argument. In keeping with the rest of the meditation, these passages are best read as further elucidations of the idea of God rather than as arguments *per se*. The main points to be made herein are: that the idea of God is innate; that my being is like God's in important ways; and that God is not a deceiver. The first of these has already been more or less established by the first 'proof'; the second lays the groundwork for the argument of the fourth meditation; and the third point, that God is not a deceiver, is a direct consequence of the proper understanding of God.

On the question of the origin of the idea of God, Descartes adds little that we have not already covered elsewhere. The difference here is that Descartes, for the first time, specifies the sorts of markers that normally accompany ideas I take to be ideas of sense:

For I did not draw it from the senses; [the idea of God] never came upon me unexpectedly, as is usually the case with ideas of sensible things when these things present themselves (or seem to present themselves) to the external sense organs. (AT7:51)

Instead, Descartes proposes that the idea of God is 'innate in me, just as the idea of myself is innate in me.' (AT7:51)

By making this comparison between the idea of God and the idea of myself, Descartes draws out an important parallel between the two great proofs we have encountered thus far: the *cogito* and the proof of God's necessary existence. Like the *cogito*, the real proof of the existence of God is intuitive and relies exclusively on the proper understanding of this idea. With this, Descartes puts to rest the notion that the formal proofs of the existence of God do any work other than elucidation and elaboration. Once the meditator has cleared the mind of prejudices, the truth and certainty of the *cogito* is absolutely clear; in the same way, if the idea of God is seen clearly and distinctly then there is no longer any doubt that God exists. The whole point of *Meditations* thus far has been to bring the meditator to the point where such clear and distinct perception is possible. However, we must recall that this is not the same as claiming that it is the clearness and distinctness that does the work here; rather it is the idea (that I am or of God's being) that does the work once seen clearly and distinctly.

The trademark itself is suggested as a way to understand how it is that something as extraordinary as the idea of God should be a part of my being. And the idea of God is extraordinary. We have spent a great deal of time exploring the objective reality of ideas (or the reality of the representational content of ideas). However, we must recall that ideas also have formal reality. I have been operating under the assumption that my thoughts are modal expressions of my being as thinking substance and therefore that I am the cause of their formal reality. But if the objective reality of my idea of God is so extraordinary that I could not be the cause of it, why should I think that I can be the cause of the formal reality of this idea? Thus it is that Descartes suggests that – unlike my other thoughts which are modes supported by my being – the idea of God is a mode supported by God's being: hence the analogy with the trademark of a craftsman.

This is a significant development, however, as it suggests that the idea of God is actually an expression of God's being attached to my being. Just as the potter is responsible for both the creation of a piece of pottery and the trademark they affix to it, God is responsible for both my creation and the creation of my idea of God. The key distinction is that the trademark and the pot's other attributes are not on a par. Unlike the trademark, the other attributes derive their being directly from the being of the pot while the trademark is entirely incidental to that being. The trademark, therefore, is an expression of the being, not of the pot, but of the craftsman. Thus, while my other thoughts are expressions of my being, the idea of God is a direct expression of God's being. But this in turn suggests that like me God is thinking substance for thought is only properly an expression of such a substance. For this reason Descartes declares that it is 'highly plausible that I have somehow been made in [God's] image and likeness . . .' (AT7:51) This will play a crucial role in the fourth meditation.

The most controversial conclusion of the third meditation, however, is the declaration that God is not a deceiver. Part of what makes it so controversial is the fact that Descartes apparently does little more than declare it; that is, while he goes to great lengths to elucidate the existence of infinite substance and that this substance supports his being, he offers a scant one sentence announcement concerning this crucial aspect of God's being: 'From these considerations it is quite obvious that he cannot be a deceiver, for it is manifest by the light of nature that all fraud and deception depend on some defect.' (AT7:52) Were this not a meditation, one could be forgiven for denying that this is quite obvious. It is, however, a meditation, and thus a proper consideration of this point is in order.

God is not a deceiver

That God not be a deceiver is essential to the project of *Meditations* for obvious reasons. Without this, we would never be able to get beyond the deceiving God hypothesis of the first meditation and would therefore never be able to overcome a certain degree of doubt. Put another way, the existence of God is sufficient to overcome the solipsism of the second meditation but only the non-deceiving God will allow us to escape the pure subjectivism of 'I think'. The fact, therefore, that Descartes spends so little ink on this point should lead us to believe that it is available to us as meditators rather than simply readers. And indeed, upon meditation it is clear that the impossibility of God being a deceiver is a direct consequence of our understanding of God and that he has no defects.

It is crucial at this point to understand what can possibly be meant by 'defect' and 'deception' in the case of God. In the case of finite human existence, deception is fairly straightforward: say one thing and mean another. In other words, deception always involves a gap between appearance and reality. But what could deception possibly mean for an infinite being? As infinite, active substance, God is directly responsible for the being of all created beings (that is, the whole world). However, we also know that it is not in the nature of God to act in discrete ways; God's acts are always infinite and never finite. How then would it be possible for God to introduce a gap between appearance and reality such that he could be deceptive? Even were such a God inclined to change things (say making all red things appear green) the change, because it was total (infinite and not discrete) would never introduce a gap between appearance and reality. It simply would be the case that all these things really are green now.

Nor does it help us if we think of God affecting our faculties in such a way as to introduce a gap. That is, we might want to say that God need not affect a change in the world as it is but can, in a manner of speaking, force us to wear tinted glasses. But this example overlooks the fact that my being and my faculties are also part of the world. Thus, the fittedness of my faculties to the world is as God creates it: if the world is such that my faculties report things as green then it is true that my faculties report things as green. But neither is God capable of 'point' deception whereby I am deceived *for now*, but come to see that I was deceived later: God makes this particular being appear to me to be (now) red and then (later) green. Not only would this constitute a discrete act but we could also rightly ask: where is the deception in this? If God makes it appear to be red then at that time it is red. We must recall that, based on the principle of preservation God is creating the world again at every moment.

But this reveals the strongest case against the deceiving God. Here Descartes is affirming an ontological version of the adage that 'it is good because God says so' rather than 'God says so because it is good'. This follows as a matter of course from the idea of an infinite creator God. God is the direct cause and support for the being of the world and therefore the world is the way God makes it. With this in mind, it is inconceivable that God would be able to make the world in any way deceptive: however the world is, is the way the world is; there is no possible gap. Or put another way, the only way such a gap could arise in such a situation is if we were to assume some sort of defect in God's creative power. But the possibility of such a defect is precluded by God's infinite power. In other words, it is obvious to those who understand the idea of God that God cannot be a deceiver; those who do not see this as obvious continue to understand deception in finite terms.

The Fourth Meditation

The end of the third meditation marks a dramatic transition in *Meditations on First Philosophy*. Not only have we done with first philosophy, but we must also change the nature of our meditation. In the course of the second and third meditations, all those features that properly belong to first philosophy have been established by the proper understanding of the twin pillars of Descartes' philosophy: the *cogito* and the existence of infinite substance. Neither can be proven but likewise neither can be denied; these are properly axiomatic and therefore proper to first philosophy. As a result, with the fourth meditation we enter into a new project and, accordingly, a new rhetoric, a new sort of meditation.

In another time, the second and third meditations might constitute a critical project: the ontology has been sorted out: I know that I am finite thinking substance; I know that there exists infinite thinking substance; I know that I am the creation of this infinite substance (that my being is entirely dependent on its being). In short, the second and third meditations have brought us to the point where we can begin the metaphysical project of properly understanding ourselves. The way forward, therefore, is to better understand this thinking substance that I am in light of the truth of the existence of infinite substance. And, as all that I understand my self to be is thinking, the only way forward is to meditate upon the various faculties of thought that I exhibit – that are expressions of my being as thinking substance. In this way I will better understand myself and how best to properly deploy my thoughts.

The final three meditations, therefore, do not uncover any new principles of first philosophy. Instead, here we see Descartes setting about to understand how to make use of the discoveries of first philosophy. In this sense, the fourth, fifth and sixth meditations can be read as enquiries into practical metaphysics. And indeed, while the meditative form remains, these meditations have much more in common with formal enquiries. In each case I am asked to explore the proper use of my faculties, where by proper use is meant a use that will not betray the hard won principles of first philosophy. Thus, these meditations take it in turn to understand how the faculties of will and judgement (fourth), reasoning or intellect (fifth), and finally the senses and imagination (sixth) can be harmonised with the twin truths of the *cogito* and the existence of infinite substance.

What remains of the meditative practice is the constant reminder that without having gone through the previous meditations none of this would be possible. What the meditative form gives us is the discipline to resist old habits and hold true to the discoveries we have already made. There is more at stake here than the simple question of thinking clearly, however. On the one hand, Descartes turns to the examination of the metaphysical foundations of psychology insofar as he is exploring the functioning of the faculties of thinking. On the other hand, however, this psychology is ontological insofar as the faculties of thinking are expressions of my very being. Thinking badly, therefore, does not merely lead to error: it leads to sin. For thinking substance to think badly is for that substance to be bad. With this in mind it is no accident that the fourth meditation is also a meditation on morals.

We will have to take seriously this moral dimension of the fourth meditation. In other words, we would be wrong to divorce questions of knowledge (epistemology) from questions of morality. It is not enough to think of 'the right use of the faculties' in terms of using the faculties to get the right answer. Rather I must always remember that, insofar as I am *thinking* substance, the use of my cognitive faculties is my only mode of activity. Moreover, as thinking *substance*, this activity is an expression of my being. The 'right use of the faculties' is imbued with a moral character at the outset. Put another way, getting the correct answer ought not to be my goal; instead, I will get the correct answer as a result of using my faculties properly. This propriety, however, has to do with the harmony of these faculties with the truths of first philosophy.

Thus Descartes opens the fourth meditation by noting an apparent tension between my being as finite creation and God's being as infinite creator. If I am to understand how to use my faculties, how best to express my own being, then I ought first to understand my relation to God. At first glance, however, this relationship is marked by an apparent paradox. Of course, as we have seen in previous meditations, Descartes tends to open with a red herring and so we should not be surprised to discover that this paradox is merely apparent. In light of the previous meditations, however, we should expect this red herring to be productive and its resolution illustrative.

A false paradox

Much like the second and third meditations, the fourth meditation begins by pursuing a wrong turn. In this case the meditation is set off by an apparent paradox – an irritant – that forces me to continue to meditate when, by all accounts, I have discovered all that I set out to discover about first philosophy. The basic form of the paradox confronting the meditator involves the tension involved in being the imperfect creation of a perfect creator. That this is a false paradox is fairly easy to see and Descartes wastes no time defusing it. Still, we have seen this pattern before: the resolution of an initial error leads to a greater discovery. Unlike the previous incidents of this pattern, however, the meditation on this paradox demonstrates an important difference in the project at hand.

In the second and third meditations, the resolution of the initial error, the recognition that this had been a wrong turn, contributed to discoveries about the way forward for the meditative process. In the fourth meditation, however, this marks a shift in the meditative process itself insofar as the resolution of the paradox allows Descartes to posit features of his philosophy generally. As we have seen, the meditation on *first philosophy* has already been concluded and a new mission is at hand; the fourth meditation must be doing something else. Thus, the faux paradox introduced at the beginning of this meditation serves as the occasion to show how the principles of first philosophy will necessarily affect the way the meditation must now be conducted.

Instead of revealing the truth of the *cogito* or the intuitive nature of its certainty, therefore, the resolution of this seeming paradox sets the tone for the philosophical positions that Descartes wishes to develop later. In this case, there are three points that Descartes needs to clarify in order to put the discoveries of the previous meditations to good use: the ontological status of the human condition, the failure of teleological reasoning, and the limits of human understanding. In Descartes' philosophy these questions mark the transition from the axiomatic foundations of first philosophy to the foundational metaphysics of second (or practical) philosophy: the philosophy of the use of the faculties.

Error and non-being

Descartes characterises the initial problem thus:

I experience that there is in me a certain faculty of judgment, which, like everything else that is in me, I undoubtedly received from God. And since he does not wish to deceive me, he assuredly has not given me the sort of faculty with which I could ever make a mistake, when I use it properly. (AT7:53–4)

Already here we have the seeds of the solution, for it is the proper use of the God-given faculty that we must understand. Nonetheless, it remains true that I am given to errors and it is only by understanding how these errors arise – that is, through the improper use of my faculties – that I will be able to understand the *proper* use.

The initial insight that the meditator offers, therefore, is that this God-given faculty with which I err is not a faculty for producing error. That is, it is not the case, for example, that I have a thermometer that makes faulty reports about the temperature. Rather, it is more like having a thermometer that I do not know how to use. Indeed, just as it is a poor workman who blames his tools, it would not behove us to blame our faculties for the errors that arise. Once we know better how these faculties are to be used, we will understand the limits of their reliability.

Descartes is now faced with a new problem: how to explain that I do not have the innate mastery of my own faculties. While he will soon offer an explanation for why this happens to be a bad question, his initial answer focuses on the ontological distinction between infinite and finite being – between God and man. As infinite substance, God is pure being. Following the Platonic and Augustinian traditions, however, Descartes posits the necessity of a scalar opposite, pure non-being (nothingness), to stand over against God as pure being. We have already met a version of this move in the third meditation with the introduction of degrees of reality. Rather than speaking of the real, however, here Descartes characterises the distinction in purely ontological terms as the tension between what is (being) and what is not (non-being).

Plato uses this tension to account for the being of particular enti-ties that populate the world of experience. Where we previously spoke of these as more or less real, Plato notes that the world of particulars is marked by its participation in both being and non-being. A simple example will illustrate what he means by saying of something that it both is and is not. A schnauzer, for example, is big when compared with an ant and the same schnauzer is not-big when compared with an elephant. According to Plato, such an example is not trivial but marks out an important fact about all things in the world: each particular derives its being from its relation to something else. In Plato's language, whenever we say of a particular that it is something or other we are drawing a comparison to the form. Thus, when we say of something that it is a schnauzer what we mean is that it participates in important ways in the form of schnauzer – the really real schnauzer. Of course, there will be mixed-breed dogs that are *only part* schnauzer and there will be pure-breeds that are *more* schnauzer; but as we see in the case of dog shows even these schnauzers can be put on a scale of more or less schnauzer with only the ideal form being fully schnauzer.

In our case, the example of 'bigness' illustrates the tension that exists between being and non-being. Unlike such beings as schnauzers and elephants, the quality of bigness clearly operates on a scale which extends from being to non-being. That is, at one end of the scale of bigness is the infinitely big (that than which nothing bigger is possible) and at the other end is the infinitely small: nothingness. It is this notion that Descartes appeals to in the case of his own finite being (as a particular). I exist and therefore I am not nothing but I know that I am not infinite (am not God) and therefore I am not pure being. I exist in the middle ground between being and non-being and participate in both. Insofar as I am, I participate in being; insofar as I am not (everything) I participate in non-being.

The link between the Platonic ontological principle and the use Descartes makes of it is Augustine. For Augustine, the only pure being is God and therefore all of creation is in various ways a falling away from this pure being into nothingness. As we shall see, this is a crucial addition to the Platonic ontology because it adds an explicitly moral dimension. While it is true that for Augustine each creature is fallen, it is no less true that each creature ought to strive for a more perfect being. Thus, Augustine derives a moral philosophy out of the ontological fact of the fall away from pure being into nothingness. This position informs the fourth meditation in important ways and we will return to it later.

While Descartes does not explicitly follow Augustine in the theology of the fall, his diagnosis of the human condition is based on an understanding of the ontological relation between God (infinite being) and man (finite being). Moreover, it is out of the being of the human condition that error arises. As Descartes puts it:

insofar as I have been created by the supreme being, there is nothing in me by means of which I might be deceived or led into error; but insofar as I participate in nothingness or non-being . . . it is not surprising that I make mistakes. (AT7:54)

Part of the project, therefore, will be to determine what in me is divine – how I participate in pure being – and what in me falls short of this divinity. As this investigation will concern the (mental) faculties, the fourth meditation can be read as a sort of ontological psychology. That is, as I am thinking substance, it asks which of my faculties (of thinking) is most perfect – most God-like. Discovering this feature of my being will put me in a better position to order my less perfect faculties.

Critique of teleological reasoning

Of course, Descartes quickly realises that an important consequence of the difference between finite and infinite substance is a difference of perspective. By definition, my perspective as finite thinking substance will be limited. This basic fact calls into question the initial problem of explaining how it came to pass that my faculties are not fully reliable. For, while it is true that an infinite creator *could* have created me with perfectly reliable faculties, it would be presumptuous for me to assume that I *ought* to be so created. After all, understanding the mind of God is not something that is within the scope of a finite mind.

This opens the way for Descartes to offer two key insights into the human condition. First, when facing questions of the relation between finite and infinite substance, I ought to be cautious of teleological reasoning. Secondly, that which I see as an imperfection in my own being may in fact be a necessary feature of the total perspective. The first observation involves a critique of teleological reasoning generally and the second establishes a crucial fact of the human perspective on God's creation: that it is limited. While offered in passing and seeming to repeat well-worn theological doctrine, each of these points is important to our meditational project and Descartes' philosophical anthropology.

It seems a trite observation that a finite being will have a limited understanding of the divine. After all, in comparison with the infinite mind of God, my own understanding is not merely lesser but infinitely so. Thus, Descartes notes that God can 'bring about certain things the reasons for which I do not understand.' (AT7:55) Theologically, this is a version of 'God works in mysterious ways' but metaphysically this is a crucial critique of the science of ends, teleology, and indeed Aristotelian essentialism generally. Of the four 'causes' (or perhaps better '(be) causes') that govern Aristotelian explanatory science, the final cause (*telos*) is the one that is most clearly bound up with the notion of nature as destiny. And it is this notion that Descartes is keen to criticise.

According to Aristotle, as we have seen, our knowledge of a thing is based on answering 'why' questions, and our complete knowledge of something arises from our being able to answer four different types of these questions. Thus, a complete explanation will be constituted by four (be)causes. We might, for example, ask about the being of a statue: why is it as it is? The basic answers to this question will fall into line with four causes: material, formal, efficient, and final (*telos*). Thus, in answer to our question we might offer a material cause (because it is made of bronze) or an efficient cause (because it was made by Socrates). This is not the place for a full account of Aristotelian metaphysics. However, it is with the critique of teleological reasoning – that is, explanation in terms of final causes – that Descartes paves the way for the moral dimension of the fourth meditation.

It has been said that nature is destiny and this is certainly true of Aristotelian science. That is, based on an understanding of a thing's final cause – that to which something aims – one has an understanding of a thing's ultimate purpose. Thus, the final cause of a tool involves an understanding of what the tool is properly used for; the final cause of an organic entity (say an apple tree) tells us what a healthy apple tree ought to involve. In other words, unlike explanations involving the other causes, reasoning according to final causes – teleological reasoning – lends itself to normative claims. Knowing what a hammer was designed for allows us to identify misuses of the hammer; knowing what an apple tree is aiming at allows us to identify unhealthy or deformed apple trees. While this sort of reasoning has enormous practical benefits, it can become problematic if it is itself misused. To say that a hammer *ought* to be used to hammer nails is to deny its use as a breaker of windows; to say that an apple tree ought to produce apples is to devalue an apple tree that does not.

While Descartes is critical of teleological reasoning generally, within the context of the fourth meditation the force of this critique applies to the use of the faculties: in other words, to human activity. While it would not be appropriate for him to go into particular examples, it is easy to see how a misuse of teleology in the realm of human behaviour can be both restrictive and damaging. If we are willing to devalue an apple tree that does not produce apples, what of a human who does not measure up to the imagined final cause or purpose of being a human? If a human female 'ought' to produce children then society would be justified in arranging its laws and customs in light of this fact; if a human being 'ought' to have blue eyes and blonde hair then a society would be justified in arranging its laws accordingly. Of course, Descartes' key insight is that we are only *imagining* these final causes; we do not know them. Descartes is still operating at a level of abstraction that will not involve such specific examples but his critique of teleological reasoning lays the groundwork for a (science of) morals and politics that would necessarily preclude such claims.

The problem is, of course, that I am not a hammer. Unlike a hammer, which is a human creation, I am God's creation. We must keep in mind, however, that for Descartes God is not a personal being; God is a metaphysical being, infinite thinking substance. And therefore, unlike a hammer, I am not a personal creation. Moreover, as the mind of God is infinite, it is necessarily beyond the understanding of a finite mind such as my own. In other words, while we might assume that, as the creation of thinking substance, human being has a *telos* (purpose) it is necessarily something that I can only presume to know. The first moral precept of the fourth meditation, then, might be: do not presume to know God's plan.

In the context of the critique of my faculties of thought, this is crucial because it rules out teleological reasoning at the outset. If I did in fact know what the final purpose of God's creation was, then I would be able to understand the proper use of my faculties in accordance with this. However, as the final purpose of the creation of an infinite being is necessarily beyond my capacity to understand, I must discard teleological reasoning at the outset. The manner in which this critique plays out not only lays the theoretical groundwork for what follows, but, as we shall see, also provides a model for the moral reasoning that is at the centre of the fourth meditation.

Error and finitude

The final point Descartes makes in his diagnosis of the human condition is often, and quite appropriately, likened to Leibniz's theory of the best possible world. Descartes observes that one condition of finitude will be a limited perspective. Thus, it is unseemly for me to complain that I am imperfect if in fact my own imperfection is an essential feature of the 'big picture' that is God's creation. In other words, perhaps the functioning of my faculties only appears to be an imperfection from my limited perspective. Were this merely a formulation of what will become the best of all possible worlds principle in Leibniz, there would be little more to say on this topic. Fortunately, there are further consequences of this observation.

Introducing the 'big picture' at all poses an indirect challenge to the presumed solipsism of the second meditation. That is, rather than presenting an argument for the existence of something other than God and myself, Descartes poses a dilemma. Either I alone have been created by God and I am therefore unable to explain the fact that I have not been created as perfect, or I have been created with local imperfections that contribute to the greater global perfection. Of course, there is no reason to adopt this particular resolution to the paradox because the previous critique of teleological reasoning is sufficient to disarm the paradox without resolving it. However, this resolution is tempting insofar as it might very well offer the simplest solution. Thus, were we to follow Ockham, we would have reason to believe that I am not the whole of creation: my belief that I am the imperfect creation of a perfect creator suggests that there is more to creation than myself and God.

As elegant as this introduction of the possible existence of the external world is, however, this brief meditation on the possible role of my imperfection in creation primarily sets the tone for the rest of the fourth meditation. That is, rather than attempting to resolve the paradox we started with, we should set about understanding our own being as clearly as possible. There is no reason to believe that there is a paradox because there is no reason to believe that my own being is flawed in any meaningful way. Instead of thinking of myself as flawed I must simply keep in mind that I am finite. The problem is not so much that my finitude is an imperfection (although of course in some sense it is); rather it is that my finitude leads me to falsely understand myself as imperfect.

A particular condition of my finitude is that I will have a limited perspective on my own being in relation to both infinite being and any other being that happens to exist. It is the failure to recognise this limitation that leads me to ask such pseudo-questions as: how could it be that a perfect creator could create something that is imperfect? We have already seen how Descartes disposes of this sort of paradox without attempting to resolve it. However, this paradox is itself a model for all error. The false belief that we are meaningfully confronted with this paradox arises from a failure to understand our own limitations. Thus, in the course of the fourth meditation we will need to better understand the limitations that lead to this sort of error. In the end, of course, we discover that each error is the result of the failure to take these limitations seriously.

Thus, the red herring paradox that Descartes uses to spur on the meditation serves as a model for error generally. In the course of dealing with this paradox we discover important things that will serve us well in the remainder of the meditation. First, just as the paradox can be defused without being resolved, error can be remedied without recourse to truth. Secondly, just as a symptom of the paradox is blindness to the reality of the human condition of finitude, error is marked by a failure to take seriously the limits that this finitude imposes on us. Thirdly, just as the belief that there is a paradox necessarily involves a sort of hubris, so too does the belief that our faculties ought to be error free. And finally, this hubris in the face of God's creation imports an important moral dimension that will mark the exercise of my faculties. In short, Descartes has given us a précis of the fourth meditation in his treatment of the false paradox that seems to arise from his prior meditations.

The perfection of the will

At the close of the third meditation Descartes suggests that it is highly plausible that he had been made (in some way) in God's image. At the time, this suggestion plays out in terms of the trademark of God as craftsman. It is through the idea of absolute infinity (perfection) that we can come to understand God and that God exists. At that point in *Meditations* this likeness consists of nothing more than the common being as thinking (intellectual) substance. Of course, it cannot be denied that this likeness falls far short of identity because it is abundantly clear that my intellect is not infinite. When Descartes turns to the examination of the faculties in the fourth meditation, however, he is able to identify not only a likeness to God but a god-like faculty.

On its own, and despite its finitude, intellect is incapable of error. I discovered this during the second meditation where I was able to affirm that pure thought, intellect on its own, is fully certain: whatever else may be the case when I think something, it remains beyond the possibility of doubt that I do think that something. Thus, from the second meditation I am able to affirm that the 'I think' guarantees the reliability of all thought, that I cannot be in error so long as I merely report the content of my thoughts. In meditating on the faculties involved, therefore, we need only redescribe this fact in order to understand how error arises:

errors depend on the simultaneous occurrence of two causes: the faculty of knowing that is in me and the faculty of choosing, that is, the free choice of the will, in other words, simultaneously on the intellect and will. Through the intellect alone I merely perceive ideas about which I can render a judgement. Strictly speaking, no error is to be found in the intellect when properly viewed in this manner. (AT7:56)

I must therefore now examine the will, the faculty of choosing, if I am to understand how error arises. My initial intuition is that, as the intellect on its own is not culpable, the will must be responsible. Upon meditation, however, I discover that the case is more complicated. Where I can easily see that each of my other faculties is finite (and therefore imperfect) I discover that my will is in fact god-like. As a result, Descartes is prepared to expand upon his initial account of 'being created in the image of God'.

It is only the will or free choice that I experience to be so great in me that I cannot grasp the idea of any greater faculty. This is so much the case that the will is the chief basis for my understanding that I bear a certain image and likeness of God. (AT7:57)

While it is true that I share with God the ontological status of being intellectual substance, this cannot be the genuine source of my understanding of infinity for my intellect is not in fact representative of the infinite. Of all my features (faculties) as intellectual (thinking) substance, only my will exhibits the infinite to me directly.

That my will is perfect has less to do with the particularity of the human condition than with the nature of will itself. As Descartes points out, 'willing is merely a matter of being able to do or not do the same thing, that is, of being able to affirm or deny, to pursue or to shun. . .' (AT7:57) As a result, the will must be understood as simple: to have will at all is to have the capacity to choose and this capacity does not admit of degrees. For this reason we can also see that the common notion of 'free will' is entirely redundant. To have will is to have the freedom to choose; that circumstances and empirical limitations may restrict the efficacy of the will in no way impairs the will as a faculty. In other words, that I choose to believe or do something is not intrinsically influenced by the plausibility of the belief or the efficacy of the action. I may choose to walk through a brick wall (perhaps because I have chosen to believe that the wall is made of marmalade). I will probably fail in this endeavour (perhaps unsurprisingly in light of the implausibility of the belief), but I have chosen nonetheless.

Because of the redundancy of the notion of free will, therefore, Descartes is able to draw out an interesting feature of the determination of the will: we don't choose to walk through brick walls because we don't choose to believe that such things are made of marmalade. In the first meditation, of course, we met some people who might well make such choices but they are mad. Therefore, while the will is potentially unrestrained, the actually unrestrained will is a form of madness. But if, as we hope, we are not mad, then we must ask how it is that we do not make such unrestrained choices. For a full answer to this question we must await the sixth meditation, but at this point Descartes does offer a brief account of the determination (or inclination) of the will that might seem to violate the obsolete notion of free will but, in fact, is not in conflict with the notion of a perfect will.

Descartes continues his initial account of willing (cited above):

. . . or better still, the will consists solely in the fact that when something is proposed to us by our intellect either to affirm or deny, to pursue or to shun, we are moved in such a way that we sense that we are determined to it by no external force. (AT7:57)

Here the exercise of the will is opposed to an external force. In other words, will, properly understood, has only to do with those movements made in accord with internal force. In this way we preclude cases such as being swept away by a torrent – where the force is most clearly external. But this is not to say that we cannot be compelled by *internal* forces. That is, freedom is not incompatible with determination as long as that determination is internal.

Descartes' account of freedom includes a notion of determination thus:

In order to be free I need not be capable of being moved in each direction; on the contrary, the more I am inclined toward one direction – either because I clearly understand that there is in it an aspect of the good and the true, or because God has thus disposed the inner recesses of my thought – the more freely do I choose that direction. (AT7:57–8)

That is, when I find myself determined (inclined), for whatever reason, in one direction rather than another I am all the more likely to freely choose that direction. Hardly a paradox, this is a straightforward account of how the will works. We would be wrong to think that freedom is in conflict with such inclinations, for the inclinations are merely the background against which the will operates. I am never in a position to choose without such a background.

In the course of *Meditations* thus far we have seen two separate cases of the interaction of will and inclination. In the case of habit, we have seen how inclinations (for example naïvely to believe the reports of the senses) influence the will. But in the first meditation we have also seen how easily these inclinations can be overcome by the will. Of course this is only possible because the inclination here is in some sense external to us. That is, because sense is a hybrid faculty of both mind and body, the coercive power of the senses can be overcome by the proper exercise of the will. In contrast, in the second meditation we encounter an internally coercive situation in the case of the *cogito*. As a result of the operation of thought itself, I find myself coerced (determined/inclined) into believing, necessarily, that I exist. The belief in the certainty of the *cogito*, therefore, is the paradigm for the sort of determined choices that exemplify the freedom of the will properly understood. Once I see the truth of the *cogito* I am no longer free to believe that I do not exist; the discovery of the *cogito* overwhelmingly determines the choice I will make and yet, because this coercion is entirely internal to my being (thought), I make this choice in total freedom.

That my will is perfect/infinite/god-like is significant for a number of reasons. While this fact will play a crucial role in the development of the fourth meditation, perhaps the most significant result of this insight is retroactive: the perfection of the will validates the whole of *Meditations* thus far and the meditative process itself. That is, while the experience of the idea of perfection is the key to the culminating discovery of the third meditation, it is only by the exercise of my will that I can encounter the idea of perfection. Looking back, I realise that the whole of the first meditation is just such an exercise of my will: I choose to undertake the meditational journey 'once in my life'; in the course of the first meditation I continually choose to withhold judgement; I choose to treat as false that which is merely uncertain; and finally I choose to call upon the evil demon to bolster my will. I am now in a position to properly understand this last point as both a construct of my will and an example of the power of my own will.

Because of my bad intellectual habits, I may need to posit the evil demon as an external source of willpower. However, this 'external' source is entirely my own creation. That I choose to create this evil demon is an act of my own will. Even as I rely upon this external willpower to carry me through the withdrawal from habit, I exhibit precisely the strength of will that renders the evil demon obsolete. And this is the case because all of the power of the evil demon is derived exclusively from my choice to believe (strategically) in the possibility of this external power. The very solution I propose to overcome the weakness of my will (in the face of habit) is nothing other than an act of my own will in constructing and believing in the evil demon. Throughout the first meditation, therefore, I have done nothing other than exercise my will. Looking back it should be no surprise that through this method I discover the idea of perfection.

In the second meditation I begin to discipline my faculties by choosing always to preface my thoughts with 'I think'. That is, once again I deploy my will to limit my intellectual activity. When I come to the third meditation, then, it is no surprise that I have an idea of perfection for I have been exercising my own perfect faculty throughout. The fact that I have a perfect will, however, is not sufficient to account for my idea of perfection/infinity/God. Like the trademark that Descartes invokes, the exercise of will can only give me a taste of perfection. I am still burdened with all of my human finitude and my one perfect faculty will not be able to account for the objective reality of *absolute* perfection. That is, my will may be god-like and I can garner *some* understanding of God and perfection from the exercise of my will, but at best my formally real will would only be able to account for the objective reality of a perfect will – not of a perfect being.

Error and sin

Throughout the fourth meditation, Descartes draws parallels between error and sin. Indeed Descartes' account of the will provides an elegant explanation for the existence of evil in the world. One longstanding traditional account of this is that God created us with free will in order that we might choose to love and honour him. The downside, of course, is that once we have free will we might very well choose badly. Descartes' metaphysical account of will, however, goes further: without will we would have no way to ever discover God, let alone love and honour him. Will is the trace that God places in us so that we might discover his existence and nature. In other words, Descartes supplements the traditional account with an explanation of how the existence of will leads us inevitably to a greater understanding of the God we are meant to love and honour. Of course, this is not the main point of the fourth meditation.

While the basic structure involved in explaining why an all-powerful good God would allow evil to exist in the world is similar to the structure of the fourth meditation, the parallel is stricter. It is worth keeping in mind that I am a thinking being, that I am essentially thought. That is, the only actions that I can undertake are thoughts. With this in mind it is difficult to see how we could draw a meaningful distinction between error and sin. Theologically, of course, the Christian tradition makes no such distinction between a sin in thought and a sin in action; Descartes is taking this one step further, however. In the traditional model, the paradigm for sin is the action that transgresses. And while the church may stipulate that the sin committed only in thought is equally bad, what this must mean is something like 'thinking about stealing something'. In other words, because the action serves as the model, the only thoughts that are included under the category of sin are thoughts of sinful action. By taking thought as the model for action, however, Descartes has turned this system on its head.

In keeping with the general internality of the system, the transgression involved in error as sin is transgression against myself. That is, where sin traditionally involves a transgression against an externally established law, Descartes imposes the law upon himself. Error arises neither from the function of the intellect nor the function of will, for each is perfect in its own way. The intellect in itself only reports and the will in itself only chooses. Error, therefore, arises only out of the co-functioning of these two faculties; or, more to the point, error arises when will outstrips intellect.

Will can outstrip intellect in one of two ways: prejudicially or presumptively. The first case, typified by the sort of error I find myself in at the outset of *Meditations*, involves a sort of passivity. In effect, I allow judgements to be made without input from the intellect. This is prejudicial error because I judge before I have the facts and this is passive error because I do so without thinking. Thus, the prejudice that the reports of my senses are reliable is the sort of passive error that arises out of the naïve position. Either through habit or due to the coercion of opinions of sense, I succumb to the sorts of passive judgements that must be overcome in the first meditation. In the case of presumptive error, however, I ought to know better. I am not being lazy when I wilfully believe that if

I think I see a square tower there really is a square tower. After the first meditation, to continue to think this way requires an act of will: I must choose to make this assumption. But this assumption is presumptive insofar as it puts me in a position akin to God's through the unrestrained exercise of my god-like will.

This places the whole of *Meditations* in a moral light. That is, the project of avoiding error is a moral imperative that begins with the obligation 'once in my life to undertake such a project'. Failure to do so simply fosters the propagation of passive error, prejudice. But once this project is undertaken, it is incumbent upon me as a moral agent to avoid error; once I know the truths of first philosophy, weakness of will is no longer an adequate explanation for error. It will always be in my power to avoid error. Thus, in the course of *Meditations*, I first discover and then impose upon myself the limits within which judgements can be properly made. In the second meditation we have an example of the first (and safest) form of this self-imposed limit. By prefacing every judgement with 'I think' Descartes offers an initial model to work from.

In the second meditation the 'I think' delivers an extreme form of security that is appropriate given the extreme doubt of the first meditation. The 'I think' imposes a limit in a holistic or totalising way. Rather than projecting limits, the 'I think' draws the limits of the world in around me. In effect it achieves security by shrinking the universe to the realm of thought. In this way I eliminate the possibility of error by reducing the realm of discourse to interiority. In the fourth meditation Descartes is ready to give a more nuanced account.

I now better understand myself and the mechanism of error and thus I need not impose the extreme limit of 'I think'. Indeed, there are now certainties that do not need the protection of 'I think'. The *cogito*, of course, incorporates the 'I think' essentially and not merely protectively but after the third meditation I see that I do not add any certainty to the claim that God exists by buffering it with 'I think'. In this case, the certainty of the existence of infinite substance is guaranteed by the operation of pure intellect. As a result, I am able to affirm this without fear of transgression. But this is the key to understanding how the limit works in the fourth meditation. Instead of limiting myself to the consideration of that which I think, I now limit myself to judging only so far as I understand; rather than limiting my world by the imposition of 'I think', I align my ordinarily unlimited will with the limits of my finite intellect. This new self-imposed limit involves the will limiting itself and allowing my intellect to lead.

Inclination and indifference

Descartes characterises this gap between intellect and will in terms of the complementary notions of indifference and inclination. These are terms specific to this point in our meditational journey and so we must be careful not to associate inclination with the sort of lazy habit that we spent the first meditation overcoming. Instead, the source of inclination is intellect (understanding). As the proper way for me to exercise my faculties is for will to follow intellect, for judgement to follow understanding, intellectual inclination indicates a tendency to favour one choice over another. The paradigmatic case for such intellectually driven inclination is the overwhelming compulsion to affirm the certainty of the *cogito*. That is, once I understand the truth of 'I am, I exist' I cannot help but affirm this. As we have seen, Descartes is quick to point out that the overwhelming force of this inclination in no way interferes with the freedom of my choice; my will (power to choose) is not impaired by the necessity of this choice. Instead, the *cogito* serves as a model for the proper relation between intellect and will precisely because of this overwhelming compulsion.

Let us take a moment to consider what it would mean to wilfully choose against the affirmation of the *cogito*. On one level, this seems absurd: once I see the immediate and certain truth of my own existence it seems difficult (if not impossible) to think otherwise. Nonetheless, my will is infinite and as a result there is nothing that I cannot will in principle. In moral language, however, we might characterise such a use of the will as spiteful for we would be forced to choose in spite of and against the knowledge of the truth. Like a three year old who digs in his heels for no reason other than because he can, this wilful behaviour is to be frowned upon. And this is the key to understanding the link between the moral and the intellectual here: however one behaves, one ought to behave that way for a reason. Not only is there no reason for me not to affirm the truth and certainty of the *cogito*, but there is also overwhelming reason to affirm it.

In the extreme case of the *cogito*, finding compelling reasons in opposition seems unlikely and thus I would be forced to fall back on the sort of empty reason that a three year old might deploy: because I don't want to. But of course not all inclination is so overwhelmingly compelling; there is a scale of inclination on which the *cogito* is but one extreme. In highly, but not overwhelmingly, compelling cases I am always able to present a reason to choose against my own intellectual inclination. We have a name for this, however: bad faith. The case is simple: if I have an insight into the truth of something then my intellect inclines me to affirm it; if, however, I do not want to affirm this then I can tell myself a reason for not doing so. In traditional moral terms this is called a lie. Because I am telling the lie to myself, however, I can be said to be operating in bad faith: I know the truth because I, myself, discovered it and yet I lie to myself about this truth in order that I need not affirm it. This happens all the time: whenever there is something I know I ought to do but want to justify not doing it I create a reason for not doing it. When this 'something I ought to do' is 'something I ought to believe' then we have a textbook example of self-deception, bad faith.

Thus we can understand what Descartes means by inclination as a cause for the function of will. I am always free to choose against this sort of intellectual inclination but this exercise of the will would be inappropriate. Instead, the proper relation between my intellect and will is that I freely (joyfully) choose to follow the dictates of reason. What my intellect reveals to me admits of degrees, of course. There will be grey areas and lack of clarity but when, as in the case of the *cogito*, my intellect reveals a truth in absolute clarity then it would indeed be spiteful for me to reject this.

Clearness and distinctness revisited
In the third meditation Descartes attempts to posit a rule to govern the question of certainty: 'everything I clearly and distinctly perceive is true'. The problem with the notion of such a rule, we discovered, was that it was rendered redundant by the *experience* of clearness and distinctness. We now see that this redundancy can be understood in terms of inclination. Because of the clearness and distinctness of my (intellectual) perception, I am inclined to affirm something as true. In other words, in the third meditation Descartes attempted to formulate an *a priori* rule concerning clearness and distinctness when in fact, clearness and distinctness are descriptions of the experience of seeing the truth of something; it is the *a posteriori* inclination which drives me. With the compelling case of the *cogito* to guide me, I now recognise that the value of clearness and distinctness is as a guide in (and indeed a guard against) cases less determinate than the *cogito*. Thus, the rule of clearness and distinctness is an *a posteriori* rule of thumb.

This rule of thumb, this reminder that we ought to follow intellectual inclination, is necessary because there is a gap between my finite intellect and my infinite will. It is essential to the human condition that there be this gap and as a result there is the (human) possibility of indifference. Indifference is the complementary notion to inclination; it occurs when there is no inclination. That is, if my intellect provides no inclination to choose one way over another I am in a state of indifference with regard to these choices. Indeed, the possibility of indifference is characteristic of the human condition. A creature (perhaps an angel?) that always saw the truth would necessarily be inclined toward that choice and would never face the reality of indifference: 'Were I always to see clearly what is true and good, I would never deliberate about what is to be judged or chosen. In that event, although I would be entirely free, I could never be indifferent.' (AT7:58) The very possibility of indifference, therefore, is essential to the human condition as a result of the gap between my finite intellect and my infinite will.

As long as my will and intellect do not share a limit, situations will necessarily arise about which I have no reason to choose one option over another: I will be indifferent. Of course, this is precisely the moment that makes error possible. While it is possible for me to wilfully err by choosing in opposition to intellectual inclination, genuine (and not spiteful) error arises when, faced with a situation of indifference, I give rein to my will and choose with no reason. Here we see the guiding value of clearness and distinctness for if inclination and indifference exist as complements on a scale, clearness and distinctness can serve as indicators of where on the scale we stand.

At one end of the scale (the paradigmatic certainty of the *cogito*) I find overwhelming inclination and no indifference whatsoever; at the other end of the scale (the condition of ignorance) I find no inclination and total indifference. But in the vast grey middle ground I find my inclination tempered by my indifference; I am never totally indifferent but nor am I overwhelmingly inclined: there is room for doubt. Descartes characterises this middle ground in terms of clarity:

this indifference extends not merely to things about which the intellect knows absolutely nothing, but extends generally to everything of which the intellect does not have a clear enough knowledge at the very time when the will is deliberating on them. (AT7:59)

The danger here is that when I am mildly inclined I am likely to rush to judgement. Therefore, I must take care to observe the degree of inclination.

The problem is that in order to observe the degree of inclination I must have something with which to compare it. Ideally, this would simply require that I monitor the ratio of inclination to indifference. This is not possible, however, because indifference is not a positive quality but a privation. In other words, indifference manifests itself only as obscurity, as the cloud that renders the vast middle-ground between certainty and ignorance grey. Like the transition from day to night I cannot monitor the degree of dusk directly. Instead, at some point I discover that it is more difficult to make out objects and things begin to lose definition. Of course, this process of 'dusking' has been going on since noon; by degrees the finely etched pattern of a tree's bark has become less and less clear until at some point, much to my surprise, I see only a darkened silhouette. When did dusk happen? Were we to attempt to monitor dusk we would fail to find that single point where clearness and distinctness were lost; we would do better to monitor the clearness and distinctness.

Because inclination is a positive force, however, the temptation to continue to act well beyond the point of safety remains. Perhaps every child has experienced the challenge that dusk poses to a game. On long summer days my friends and I would play baseball long past the point when it was actually possible to play a meaningful game. The problem is that, as the definition of the objects fades by degrees, there is always the belief that we can play ten more minutes. Of course at some point it becomes evident that the ball is no longer visible; but on the long summer days of childhood this moment is inevitably discovered well after the fact.

The function of clearness and distinctness, therefore, is a positive marker on this scale. As I cannot observe the ratio between inclination and indifference directly, I must monitor the sign of my position on the scale. It is through attention to the degree of definition on the surface of the tree trunk that I mark my position on the scale between light and dark; it is through attention to clearness and distinctness that I regulate the relation between will and intellect. It is through attention to the clarity of the thrown baseball that I judge whether a meaningful game can yet be played; it is through attention to clearness and distinctness that I judge the degree of inclination and therefore the degree of certainty involved. For, while my will ought to follow my intellect, it is equally important that I am aware of just how far my intellect extends. An act born out of total indifference is much less common than one born out of insufficient reason.

Limiting the will

It would have been possible, of course, for God to have created us such that this tricky calculation would not be necessary. As we have seen, however, there is no good reason to question God on this. Moreover, whatever the reason for the human condition, I am stuck with it and I had better get on with dealing with it. Still, understanding the manner in which God could have created me casts light on the human condition that he did create.

The problem with the human condition is the gap between intellect and will. If I had been created with perfectly aligned faculties then there would be no problem. The nature of will, however, limits the possibility of this alignment to the extreme cases. That is, because will consists of only the power to choose, it is indivisible and it does not admit of degrees: it is a simple faculty that does only one thing and does it in an all-or-nothing manner. It makes no sense to say 'I sort of choose A' or 'I choose B a little bit'. Choice is total and simple; this is one of the reasons that will is necessarily infinite. In other words, once a creature has will, it necessarily has an infinite will for the power to choose is all or nothing.

As a result, if we are to imagine a manner in which God could 'repair' the human condition, it must be an all or nothing proposition: will and intellect cannot meet in the middle. Once I have will I have infinite will. Thus, in order for God to close the gap between will and intellect, either I would have to be created with infinite intellect to match my infinite will or I would have to be created with neither will nor intellect. In the latter case I would be an inanimate (and therefore soulless) creature such as a rock. In the former case I would be like an angel. These are the only options open to a God that wants to close the gap in the human condition *a priori*. In neither case would I be human.

This speculation, however, reveals that God has created me such that the gap can be closed. In the course of the fourth meditation, moreover, I have discovered that the human condition provides the resources for me to close the gap between finite intellect and infinite will myself. While will may be infinite in essence, it is not undetermined. That is, I have learned that the will can be restrained. Because I have an infinite will it is always within my power to restrain (or direct) my will. Furthermore, because of my meditation on the role of clearness and distinctness as markers for inclination toward truth I know *how* to direct my will.

Thus, as it is not in my power to know all things, it is always in my power to limit my will to that which I do know. While I do not have the capacity to perceive all things clearly and distinctly, I do have the capacity to limit my judgements to those cases in which I do perceive things clearly and distinctly. Indeed I have been practicing this informally throughout the first three meditations. In order to formalise this practice I will need only to posit a rule: 'I should never judge anything that I do not clearly and distinctly understand.' (AT7:61) In this way the original rule concerning clearness and distinctness is transformed into a rule for use.

Originally, Descartes had posited 'a general rule that everything I very clearly and distinctly perceive is true.' (AT7:35) Despite appearances, these rules are not equivalent. As is revealed in the language of its formulation, the initial rule violates the spirit of the subjective meditations by attempting to be 'general' and making claims about 'truth'. In other words, this first formulation attempts to legislate truth objectively and in advance. The transformation of this rule we find in the fourth meditation is a properly subjective and *a posteriori* rule: it is a rule for use. Unlike the rule from the third meditation, this rule can only be applied to cases before us; it cannot be applied before the cases arise. Similarly, this rule is a rule that I give myself as a way to regulate the faculties; it is not a way to regulate truth. As we have seen, truth can take care of itself; truth is revealed to the intellect and, in the form of inclination, compels the will. Clearness and distinctness have nothing active to do with truth: they reflect rather than determine it. Instead I can actively use them in order to regulate the will.

The final task of the fourth meditation is to remind the reader that this is in fact a meditative practice. Knowing the rule that ought to govern the will is not the same as applying that rule regularly. Thus, while it would be easier if God had imprinted this rule in my very nature, I can imprint this rule on myself through second nature: habit.

For although I experience a certain infirmity in myself, namely that I am unable to keep my attention constantly focused on one and the same item of knowledge [the rule], nevertheless, by attentive and often repeated meditation, I can bring it about that I call this rule to mind whenever the situation calls for it, and thus I would acquire a certain habit of not erring. (AT7:62)

Thus we discover that the meditative process is not merely a mode of discovery but of transformation. It is through the practice of meditation that I learn. More importantly, it is through the practice of meditation that I can (re)form myself into a person who is not given to error or sin.

The Fifth Meditation

When approaching the fifth meditation, the reader is confronted with a serious challenge because, perhaps more than any of the preceding meditations, this text looks like a standard formal treatise. The reader as meditator, therefore, must be on their guard against the temptation to reduce this meditation to a discourse on 'the essence of material things and the existence of God'. The danger, of course, is that as a reader who is accustomed to formal treatises and discourses in philosophy I will prematurely abandon the meditational practice that I have been so carefully cultivating up until this point. No doubt based on the assumption that I have internalised the appropriate meditative approach, the fifth meditation dispenses with all but a token meditative frame. Following a proper understanding of the fourth meditation, it is incumbent upon the reader to discipline their will so as to take up the meditative stance unprompted.

Entitled 'Concerning the Essence of Material Things, and Again Concerning God, That He Exists' it is natural to assume that these themes form the centrepiece of what is going on in the meditation. While this title is in fact a true reflection of the thematic content of the fifth meditation, it remains to be seen what role this meditation plays in the overall arc of *Meditations*. Moreover, approaching this meditation as one would approach a treatise proves to be baffling. On the one hand, the question of the essence of material things is dealt with in such haste and brevity that an enormous amount of elaboration, supplementation and indeed supposition is necessary to make sense of it. Hardly the model of detail and clarity, Descartes offers little more than a schematic account of material essences. On the other hand, however, the second declared theme of the meditation – the proof of the existence of God – is already a foregone conclusion after the third meditation. At best, this renders the fifth meditation superfluous; at worst, it is incoherent. Therefore, despite appearances, we should resist the urge to treat these themes as central to a supposed treatise.

Too tight a focus on these themes leads to a supposition of doctrinal commitment that is simply not borne out by the text. Among the doctrines of Cartesian philosophy that is often attributed to the fifth meditation is the theory of innate ideas. Perhaps because Locke's comprehensive disavowal of the doctrine of innate ideas is generally taken to be a response to Descartes rather than Cartesianism, Descartes has been saddled with the need to explain himself on this topic. And indeed, the fifth meditation is the closest he comes in *Meditations* to making a case for a theory of innate ideas. It is telling, however, that Descartes annunciates no such theory here and the word 'innate' is entirely absent from the meditation. Rather than allow ourselves to be guided by the presumption of doctrine, it is better to allow the text to guide our meditation and to show us how to integrate the fifth meditation into the overall project thus far.

The right use of the faculties

What, then, in addition to the content are we expected to meditate on? Following as it does on the heels of the fourth meditation, it is reasonable to suppose that the purpose of the fifth is not so much to prove anything as to demonstrate the proper use of the faculties: especially in proving things. The fourth meditation has only established the parameters of the relation between will and intellect in principle; the fifth meditation presents these principles in practice. In other words, the question of material essence, and especially the ontological proof, are occasions for the practical demonstration of the right use of the faculties. Thus, in addition to their results, we will pay particular attention to these demonstrations as themselves demonstrations of the proper use of the faculties.

Of particular interest here is the operation of the intellect as this is the first opportunity we have had to observe the intellect in action. We will recall that thus far the intellectual discoveries of *Meditations* have been the result of the prophylactic use of will (the deployment of 'I think') and the coercive power of particular ideas (the *cogito* and the idea of infinite substance). Neither is useful as a demonstration of the proper use of intellect because in neither case is the intellect genuinely used. The buffer 'I think' renders the intellect passive: accurately reporting the content of thought but doing nothing with it. Similarly, the overwhelming certainty of the *cogito* disqualifies it as a model for the use of my faculties because once I see it I cannot help but believe it. The intellect is reduced to a trigger for the affirmative operation of the will. The fourth meditation presents this fact in terms of intellectual inclination: in the extreme case of total conviction the inclination becomes necessarily compelling. Thus in the intellectual discovery of the *cogito* I do not have to do any work and the will and intellect are deployed in name only.

Borrowing a term from geometry, we might refer to this as a

degenerate case of the operation of the faculties. That is, while strictly speaking a point is a degenerate circle, we would do well to avoid using a point as a model for understanding the properties of circles. The case of the *cogito* is so extreme that it is simply not useful to understanding the proper use of the faculties. If it is inevitable that I affirm the truth of the *cogito* then this fails to provide a meaningful example of the harmonising of the faculties in a way that avoids error.

In the third meditation the idea of God functions in the same way. It is of course for this reason that the so-called proofs of the third meditation are superfluous. A clear and distinct perception of the idea of God/ infinite substance/absolute perfection is sufficient in the same way as the *cogito* is sufficient to compel belief. After clearing the view we have on this idea, the will and intellect have nothing to do. The 'proofs' that follow will be entirely unconvincing to someone who does not have (or does not have a clear view on) the idea of God, and entirely unnecessary to someone who does. At best these so-called proofs serve as elaborations of the idea of God and exercises for the meditator whose view of the idea of God is obscured in various ways.

It is only after the fourth meditation that I am in a position to attempt the use of my faculties in the vast grey area between these cases of absolute certainty and the nothingness of total doubt. Thus, while Descartes is no doubt interested in exploring the essence of material things and the existence of God, in both cases the real value is not in what is demonstrated but in the demonstration itself. As meditators it is up to us to learn how to use our faculties correctly so that we can discover for ourselves. It would be odd for Descartes to suddenly abandon his pedagogic principles and do the work for us by, for example, presenting doctrines to be adopted. Like a true scientist he may well be confident that we will validate his results for ourselves but without the proper understanding of our mental faculties no such validation is possible. For this reason, it is of the utmost importance that we understand the fifth meditation as a demonstration of the right use of the faculties.

Ideas of material things

Having determined, in principle, how to deploy my intellect reliably in an investigation, I return to my stock of ideas for a new object for meditation. Descartes begins by asking 'whether anything certain is to be had concerning material things.' (AT7:63) At this point it is crucial to recall that, while the title of the meditation points to 'material things', the only way in which Descartes is able to investigate these 'things' is through the ideas he has of them. While I do not need to deploy the 'I think' as rigorously as I did in the second meditation, it remains the case that the only materials I have to work with (even in the case of material things) are my ideas.

Descartes is explicit about this: 'before inquiring whether any such things exist outside me, I surely ought to consider the ideas of these things, insofar as they exist in my thought.' (AT7:63) Once again we are reminded not only that ideas exist but also that these and these alone are the proper objects of thought. Therefore, any investigation that begins from thought or mental activity must begin with the consideration of ideas. Moreover, as ideas exist (have being) they are subject to the rules of metaphysics. As we have already noted, ideas are in the first place thoughts representative of objects. As thoughts, of course, my ideas owe their being to my being as thinking substance; effectively, they are expressive attributes of me. These ideas, however, need not be simple. Rather, even as attributes, my ideas are articulated: they have properties. As such, my ideas provide a source for new knowledge if only I know how to analyse and examine them properly. As we shall see, the fifth meditation provides ample occasion to exercise the intellect in this project.

This brief phrase opening the enquiry also exemplifies an important and appropriate use of will in such examinations. If the fourth meditation focuses on the controlled use of will in relation to intellect at the back end of the process, so to speak, here we are reminded that throughout *Meditations* we have been employing the will at the front end. That is, in addition to the end-of-process use of will in affirming or denying results of intellectual activity, will is essential in properly framing the process of intellectual investigation at the outset. Descartes avoids overstepping the limits of proper intellectual enquiry by proactive application of will: before I investigate the things in themselves I ought first to investigate the ideas I have of these things. We have come a long way from the problems that opened the first meditation; I am no longer tempted to extend my investigation beyond the proper objects of thought: ideas. My impetuous will is now operating, as it should, in the service of intellect at both ends of the process: first by framing the investigation in a way that is appropriate to the function of intellect; secondly, by withholding judgement from those things under investigation which are not clearly and distinctly perceived by intellect.

Having directed his intellectual gaze upon the ideas of material things, we might expect to learn great things. The investigation itself, however, is so brief and sudden that if you blink you might miss the results:

> I do indeed distinctly imagine the quantity that philosophers commonly call 'continuous,' that is, the extension of this quantity, or rather of the thing quantified in length, breadth, and depth. I enumerate the various parts in it. I ascribe to these parts any sizes, shapes, positions, and local movements whatever; to these movements I ascribe any durations whatever. (AT7:63)

While there is much to chew on in this little paragraph, this is the extent of Descartes' treatment of the subject. For the purposes of summary rather than explanation it is useful to remember that Descartes understands the essence of matter to be reducible to extension and duration. Even in saying this much, however, Descartes comes very close to passing out of metaphysics and into the realm of physics. The fact that he elaborates on this theme elsewhere is worth noting but it is more interesting that he does not elaborate on it here.

Although, as we shall see, Descartes does not fully restrain himself in the sixth meditation, it is entirely proper that he stop short of physics in a text that professes to be on first philosophy. While we may have already passed from first philosophy proper to a foundational metaphysics, the outer limit of metaphysical enquiry is the question of essence and there is little more to say about the essence of material things. Instead, therefore, Descartes turns immediately to an examination of the experience of this discovery. In other words, rather than elaborate on the questions of extension and duration he reflects on the knowledge and certainty he has of these.

Innateness: the sense of certainty

The suddenness of this reflective move not only avoids the entanglements of physics but also sets the priorities for the fifth meditation. It serves as a reminder that the project of *Meditations* is the better understanding of understanding. The content discovered in this meditation will always be incidental to that which the discovery reveals about me and the use of my faculties.

Upon reflection, I note that I clearly and distinctly perceive extension and duration as essential in the ideas I have of material things. Therefore, I understand that the idea of a material thing inclines me to affirm that the essence of a material thing is extension and duration. It remains possible that no material thing exists at all. However, I cannot deny that I have ideas of material things and as a result of the examination of those ideas I can be certain that it would be essential to any existing material thing that it be extended and that it endure (that it exist in space and time).

The sense of certainty that arises from the examination of my ideas of material things, however, has a specific character that distinguishes it from the certainties encountered thus far:

> Their truth is so open and so much in accord with my nature that, when I first discover them, it seems I am not so much learning something new as recalling something I knew beforehand. In other words it seems as though I am noticing things for the first time that were in fact in me for a long while, although I had not previously directed my mental gaze upon them. (AT7:64)

Here Descartes distinguishes this sense of certainty qualitatively in two ways: in terms of the particular manner in which it arises, and in terms of the specific character of the experience.

Unlike the *cogito* or the existence of God, the essence of material things is revealed to Descartes as being in accord with his own nature. That is, while clearness and distinctness still function as markers for intellectual inclination, the inclination to affirm these qualities as essential to material things arises from my nature rather than from the idea itself. Within the context of *Meditations* this is significant because it characterises the certainty thus discovered as derivative (from my nature) rather than immediate. Put another way, of course, this means that the derivative quality of this sense of certainty sets it apart from the certainties I have thus far encountered.

The sense of certainty in the case of the *cogito* arises immediately and as a matter of course out of the function of my own thought; the sense of certainty in the case of the existence of God arises immediately and a matter of course out of my reflection upon the idea of God/infinite substance. In the present case, however, the sense of certainty arises out of my own nature. In other words, just as it is essential to material things (should they exist) that they exist in space and time, it is essential to my nature that it be in harmony with this categorisation of the world of material things: because of the nature of my being, it is natural for me to experience material things in space and time. Of course, I cannot know that there are material things that exist apart from my ideas of them; what I can know is that it would be essential to their being (should they exist) that they exist in space and time: otherwise my ideas could not correspond to these things. At this point I am limited to my experience of ideas and therefore whatever conclusions I might draw about a corresponding reality that exists apart from me will be entirely hypothetical. Nonetheless, by making the sense of certainty derivative of my being in this way, Descartes is able to qualitatively distinguish this sense of certainty from what might be called the pure certainties of the *cogito* and the existence of infinite substance.

Descartes also differentiates this derivative sense of certainty phenomenologically. That is, in addition to the difference of derivation, this sense of certainty is also experienced in a peculiar manner. Such a phenomenological account is only possible because for Descartes ideas are themselves objects of experience – or, in Descartes' terms, objects of perception. Indeed, given the parameters within which the meditational journey takes place, ideas are the only objects of perception. Thus, when Descartes turns his mind's eye on a particular idea this experience has a particular character. In this case, what stands out is the particular experience of certainty that accompanies the discovery of the essence of material things. While I may *know* that this certainty is in accord with my nature, I also *feel* this certainty differently than I do that of the *cogito* and the existence of God.

Keep in mind, what is distinctive about this experience of certainty is that:

> it seems I am not so much learning something new as recalling something I knew beforehand . . . as though I am noticing things for the first time that were in fact in me for a long while, although I had not previously directed my mental gaze upon them. (AT7:64)

This tribute to Plato's theory of recollection has not been lost on commentators and is often seen as a way into the supposed doctrine of innate ideas. We must take care, however, in how we interpret both Descartes and Plato on this point.

The emphasis in this passage is not on a doctrine of innateness but on the sense or feeling of innateness. That is, in the phenomenological examination of this sense of certainty, the notion of innateness is at best a way to describe the sense of intimacy involved; it is indicative of the feeling of remembering something rather than that of meeting it for the first time. In this sense, the fifth meditation has more in common with Plato's *Meno* than it does with the theory of recollection as it appears in the later dialogues (for example, in *Phaedrus*), where Plato links this theory more explicitly with the rest of his metaphysical idealism. Descartes already starts with ideas and therefore, unlike the later Plato, does not need to derive evidence of ideas from the experience of learning/remembering.

The fifth meditation is thus more in keeping with *Meno* where the theory of recollection is entirely incidental to the central investigation. In this dialogue, Socrates presents the theory of recollection as a way to explain the phenomenon of learning. As such, however, it is at best an explanatory hypothesis designed to further the dialogue with Meno by blocking the obstructionist objection that learning something for the first time is impossible in principle. In this regard, the strength of the theory of recollection lies in the way that it affirms the reality of learning while reframing the discussion in terms that are phenomenologically familiar: remembering what had been forgotten. Most importantly, for our purposes, it heightens the resonance between the phenomenon of learning and the phenomenon of remembering.

Playing out the allusion, then, in light of Descartes' interest in the phenomenon concomitant with the discovery of truths about essences (the feeling of certainty), we ought not to expect a full-fledged theory of innate ideas. Indeed, Descartes does not need such a theory for the phenomenon of this particular kind of feeling to be both real and useful. In other words, the actual status of the idea as innate (its history or origin) is entirely incidental to the experience involved in the discovery of certain truths about the idea. From the phenomenological perspective (the only one open to me at this point) the experience of an idea as particularly familiar and as being in accord with my nature is sufficient to differentiate these ideas from others. If this is all that is meant by 'innate' then we are on safe ground, whereas the imposition of a theory of innate ideas is both a distraction and a distortion of this limited sense of 'innate'.

The fifth meditation is much more agnostic about these ideas than the tradition makes out; it is worth noting, for example, that Descartes does not use the term 'innate' to describe these ideas here. Within the properly framed intellectual investigation of ideas, only the content of these ideas and the phenomenon of experiencing them as certain are at issue. Indeed, nothing more than this *can be* at issue. There is no perspective from which to determine the history or origin of an idea; therefore, the broader meaning of 'innate' as inborn necessarily eludes us. Fortunately, all that I need is the fact that it seems to me to be innate; but this seeming is nothing other than the experience of intimacy and familiarity outlined above. In short, the imposition of a theory of innate ideas at this point would violate the limits of enquiry that I have been at such pains to establish.

Nonetheless, Descartes has thus established the quality of the certainty that is characteristic of the experience of essences. This is no small thing, as such a certainty has been the goal since the first meditation. I now know that certainty, even if only in the experience of ideas, arises in accord with my nature and has a particular feeling of familiarity or intimacy. If clearness and distinctness are the markers for the intellectual inclination that ought to drive will in affirmation, this accord and familiarity guides the faculties in their operation.

Imagination and will in practice

In keeping with the agnostic position on innate ideas, Descartes limits himself to the declaration:

> What I believe must be considered above all here is the fact that I find within me countless ideas of certain things, that, even if perhaps they do not exist anywhere outside me, still cannot be said to be nothing. (AT7:64)

By abstracting from the idea of material things to the essence of material things (extension and duration) I have discovered a set of ideas that are marked by the sort of certainty outlined above. Having these ideas, I am now in a position to work with them. I have been deceived before, however, and I should take the time to reinforce this sense of certainty against possible doubt.

There is an obvious risk in pursuing a 'certainty' that is grounded in a sense of familiarity and seems to accord so fully with my nature. For one thing, what could be more familiar and more in accord with my nature than my own creation? In other words, the very ground for taking the ideas of essences seriously seems to point to the possibility that I am the author of these ideas, that these are my own fabrications. The second risk is that I really am remembering things that I have experienced before. In this case the danger is that I am mistaking acts of naïve sensation for acts of intellectual perception. That is, I might be succumbing to the familiar habit of accepting the reports of my senses without even recognising that I am doing so. It is therefore necessary to block these possibilities at the outset.

Given the nod toward Plato, it is unsurprising that the initial elaboration of the essence of material things is expressed in mathematical terms. In other words, the essence of a material thing, of existing in space and time, is that it is capable of mathematical description. Anything that has quantity as expressed in duration or extension is subject to the rules of mathematics and can be so described. More importantly, within the context of the fifth meditation, this fact allows Descartes to demonstrate that such essences are not mere fabrications of imagination.

As the primary source of fabricated ideas is the misuse of imagination of the sort I have encountered in the first and second meditations, it is essential that I come to understand how to use the imagination appropriately. Given the way the fifth meditation is shot through with visual language, it is unsurprising that the imagination plays such a central role. This visual language is already present in the initiation of the project Descartes sets for himself 'to see whether anything certain is to be had concerning material things . . . and to see which [features of these ideas] are distinct and which are confused.' (AT7:63) In thus turning my mental gaze upon my ideas of material things I quite appropriately call to mind an image: the imagination facilitates this examination by drawing an image of the particular idea under consideration. As we shall see, the function of the imagination has its limits but within the mental world of ideas it is an invaluable resource. That is, the calling to mind that the imagination facilitates is what allows me to focus my attention on one or another of my ideas. Thus it is that the statement of the essence of material things is prefaced by 'I do distinctly imagine. . .' (AT7:63)

The limit of the correct use of imagination is discovered when Descartes turns to triangles:

when I imagine a triangle, even if perhaps no such figure exists outside my thought anywhere in the world and never has, the triangle still has a certain determinate nature, essence, or form which is unchangeable and eternal, which I did not fabricate. (AT7:64)

Here we see the proper use of imagination in calling before the mind's eye a particular idea for examination by the intellect. However, when the imagination is thus deployed, the intellect discovers properties that had not been known prior to the exercise and therefore could not have been wilfully included in my imagined product. That is, imagination, properly used, is not a machine for creating new ideas, but the faculty for presenting an already existing idea to the mind for the purpose of intellectual examination. In this case, when I imagine a triangle I mentally construct it in the manner in which a geometer would; I do not create it in the way a fanciful artist would.

In order to construct the triangle, I must know certain properties of triangles in advance (for example, it must enclose a space by means of three straight lines). Once the triangle is constructed and presented to my intellect, however, I am able to demonstrate additional properties that were not known in advance (for example, that the three angles of the figure are equal to two right angles). And yet, if my demonstration is valid, each new discovery is accompanied by the same sense of certainty as the original certainty (i.e. that a triangle encloses a space by means of three straight lines). This certainty is, of course, marked by the sense of accord and familiarity: it is as if I had known all along that the sum of the three angles of a triangle would be equal to two right angles; once seen it is obvious.

For this reason, Descartes believes that the original construct of a triangle, even if called forth by the imagination, could not be a mere fabrication. For it to be such a fabrication I would have had to have known all those things in advance and deliberately included these properties in the original construct. It is also for this reason that it is imperative that we keep the sense or feeling of having known all along distinct from having actually known all along. The sense of familiarity always involves an 'as if' that remains steadfastly agnostic as regards the possibility of actually having known all along. Perhaps, as Plato suggests, this phenomenon marks an actual memory traumatically forgotten at birth; perhaps, as Freud might later suggest, this phenomenon marks an interaction between the conscious and the unconscious; perhaps, as the tradition of Cartesianism suggests, this phenomenon marks the existence of ideas implanted in my mind by God or nature. Nonetheless, in the fifth meditation, this phenomenon is a mark of intellectual certainty and nothing more.

This agnostic position with regard to these ideas reflects the moral commitment to the use of will from the fourth meditation. In addition, however, this example demonstrates the limit of the will in relation to these ideas of essences. Descartes begins his discussion of triangles with the observation that in one sense he is able to think of these ideas at will: it is the will that facilitates the proper use of imagination. That is, I will that I call a particular idea before the mind's eye. However, in another sense, once this idea is under examination there are things that happen even against my will: 'These [newly demonstrated properties] I now clearly acknowledge, whether I want to or not. . .'. (AT7:64) Therefore, the demonstration of geometrical truths by means of pure intellect exceeds the power of either the imagination (to construct) or the will (to deny – in good faith).

In this example, Descartes offers an exemplary instance of the harmony of the faculties in the operation of intellectual enquiry: guided by the principles of the fourth meditation, the will limits the enquiry to the field proper to the operation of intellect; the imagination facilitates the enquiry, where possible, by the construction of an idea as image for the mind's eye; the intellect examines this idea by means of the construct so provided and derives new truths for the will to affirm or deny; guided by intellectual inclination the will affirms these truths. In so doing, Descartes also presents geometric proof as a model for intellectual enquiry by presenting the rigors of mathematics in psychological terms.

The final worry – that the sense of familiarity that marks these ideas could be the mark of having been derived from the senses – is dealt with almost as an afterthought. We have travelled so far from our naïve position with regard to the opinions supposedly derived from sensation that the worry seems almost trivial. Compared to the possibility that my will and imagination have secretly conspired to deceive me, the possibility that I have fallen back into the habit of blindly following the senses is merely academic. Nonetheless, on the off-chance that the meditator has been backsliding, Descartes points out that there are numerous mathematical and geometrical demonstrations grounded in ideas available to the intellect that no-one would suspect to have been derived from the senses. Triangles, perhaps; but regular nineteen-sided figures?

As a result, these ideas (of essences) will not be subject to the sort of doubt that afflicts opinions derived from the senses. As we learned in the second meditation, the intellect cannot err when it operates exclusively within the frame of 'I think'. Now, however, we have learned that there are certain ideas (ideas of essences) that are marked by a particular sort of certainty and that within a prescribed field of thought, these ideas can be analysed and manipulated by the intellect to reveal new truths and certainties. In other words, in these passages we have witnessed a way for the intellect to be an active participant rather than merely a passive reporter of that which 'I think'. As such, the examination of 'innate' ideas offers an invaluable guide to the proper operation of the intellect.

The ontological proof

Descartes' next move is among the most controversial that he makes in the course of *Meditations*. Having established a method of intellectual demonstration that will preserve the certainty of perception from initiation to conclusion, Descartes embarks on an argument to prove the existence of God. For most commentators it is the ontological proof itself which is controversial. On its face, it does seem fishy and, as a result, many philosophers today accept some version of Kant's refutation of the proof. I happen to be less convinced by the refutation and less worried by the proof than most. However, as meditators, we should be worried not about whether the proof 'works' but about what the proof is doing here at all. If we have followed Descartes this far, then we have certainly put ourselves in the best position to understand the proof. Nonetheless, the proof, valid or not, sophistry or not, seems to be entirely superfluous. Not only has the existence of God been established in the third meditation but this has been established, without relying on argument, by immediate inspection of the idea of God. What, therefore, can Descartes be up to here?

The manner in which the ontological proof is floated is itself extraordinary. Thus, rather than attempt a schematic reconstruction of the proof, it is useful to see what is actually said in the fifth meditation. The first hint that this is something other than a poorly transcribed schematic proof is that the whole project is framed by a question:

But if, from the mere fact that I can bring forth from my thought the idea of something, it follows that all I clearly and distinctly perceive to belong to that thing really does belong to it, then cannot this too be a basis for an argument proving the existence of God? (AT7:65)

Positioning the ontological proof as following on from such a speculative question leaves the status of the proof decidedly undecided. As we shall see, the proof itself fails to conclusively resolve this issue and the suspension of the opening question lingers in the subjunctive mood that closes the paragraph.

The proof itself, as it appears in *Meditations*, is fairly straightforward:

Clearly the idea of God, that is, the idea of a supremely perfect being, is one I discover to be no less within me than the idea of any figure or number. And that it belongs to God's nature that he always exists is something I understand no less clearly and distinctly than is the case when I demonstrate in regard to some figure or number that something also belongs to the nature of that figure or number. Thus, even if not everything that I have meditated upon these last few days were true, still the existence of God ought to have for me at least the same degree of certainty that truths of mathematics had until now. (AT7:65–6)

Put this way, the thing that is most striking is the modesty of the claim. On the one hand, in keeping with the meditative process, it limits itself to the subjective claim, *for me*. On the other hand, despite what we already know about the certainty of the existence of God from the third meditation, this proof only allows the same degree of certainty as we have previously attributed to mathematics.

This final point is worrying insofar as Descartes has gone to great lengths to differentiate the certainty of mathematics from the 'pure' certainties of the *cogito* and the existence of God. Moreover, we recall from the first meditation that the question of mathematical truth has been suspended due to the possible existence of an omnipotent (and possibly deceiving) God. If we divorce the fifth meditation from the third meditation things seem to go horribly awry. That is, without the prior certainty that God exists (and is no deceiver) then the certainty of mathematical truths remains forever contingent. The best the fifth meditation can do on this point is establish that the sense of certainty I have about these mathematical truths is familiar and in accord with my nature. In other words, without the prior guarantee that my nature is not deeply flawed and that I can in fact trust this sense of 'innateness' that I feel about mathematics, all I have thus far established is the sort of internally coherent system that I identified in the first meditation.

With this in mind, the role of the ontological proof is even more perplexing. It would seem that without recourse to the prior certainty that God exists, the proof actually establishes a lesser certainty than we wanted. Like the truths of mathematics, the existence of God would be guaranteed only as internally cohering with my mental universe. But with the prior certainty, the proof is not only superfluous but superseded.

That the ontological proof, as delivered in the fifth meditation, fails to secure the sort of certainty one might expect suggests that, in fact, there is something amiss. Given the necessity of the prior certainty of the existence of God in order to make the meditation function as advertised, it is not surprising that Descartes' elaboration of the ontological proof reverts to the sort of coercive certainty that we see in the third meditation. In other words, the notion that the ontological proof follows on from the mathematical demonstrations of the fifth meditation is a false start that leads us back to what we already knew. After all, *Meditations* is littered with illustrative false starts and Descartes himself seems far from convinced by this approach to the question of God. Thus, it would not be too much to say that Descartes anticipates Kant's refutation of the ontological proof insofar as it turns out that speculative reason is incapable of securing the level of certainty that the mere understanding of the idea of God imparts immediately and intuitively.

Thought and existence

Descartes' elaboration of the ontological proof is couched in a series of possible objections to the proof itself. In each case, however, the resolution of these doubts serves to realign the proof rather than bolster it. That is, by the end of Descartes' ostensibly defensive elaborations, we are brought to the point where we realise that what grounds the ontological proof is not the activity of pure speculative reason, but the clear understanding of the idea of God in question. This subjective ground returns me to the third meditation and demonstrates the limits of my intellectual faculties. In this way, the by-pass through the ontological proof validates the intuitive certainty of the third meditation by establishing the limits of reason. In the process, however, the order of the fifth meditation is reversed. In the end, it is not mathematical certainty that validates the existence of God. Rather, the proper understanding of how the certainty of the existence of God underwrites the ontological proof feeds back to ground the certainty of mathematics.

Descartes first observes that the proper view on the ontological proof is obscured by intellectual habit. 'Since in all other matters I have become accustomed to distinguishing existence from essence, I easily convince myself that it can even be separated from God's essence and, hence, that God can be thought of as not existing.' (AT7:66) Certainly, this is the case with the triangle that we have been studying: I am free to imagine a triangle and then to demonstrate necessary truths about this triangle without committing myself in any way to the existence of triangles in the world. In other words, I suspend judgement about existence in order to study the essence. Moreover, this is the very habit of mind that I have been employing since the first meditation. The purpose of the method of doubt was to bracket off questions of existence in order to understand what remained true at each stage of doubt. This method became formalised in the second meditation through the use of 'I think'. Unfortunately these self-enforced habits now block the efficacy of the ontological proof.

That they are self-enforced is useful to keep in mind, for if they are willed by me then they are not absolute: habits can be broken. Nonetheless, the habit was instituted for a purpose and it has been useful. There must be good reason to allow the ontological argument to violate this proscription. Unsurprisingly, the reason for this exception to the rule is grounded in the nature of the idea of God. Descartes' solution will not appeal to those who are looking for a ground in speculative reason, but is entirely fitting given the subjectivism of *Meditations*:

> But nevertheless, it is obvious to anyone who pays close attention that existence can no more be separated from God's essence than its having three angles equal to two right angles can be separated from the essence of a triangle. . . (AT7:66)

Thus, at the first hurdle, Descartes abandons the hope for a speculative proof.

Instead, Descartes appeals to 'our attention' and to 'the nature of the idea of God'. In this way, Descartes brings the ontological proof back into line with the third meditation. If we properly understand the idea of God then we will not be able to think God's essence without existence. For a meditator who has already passed through the third meditation, this is appealing; as a way to bolster the validity of the ontological proof, this is devastating. By appealing to the attention of the meditator, Descartes ostensibly grounds a weak leg of the proof but in fact obviates the need for a proof at all. If close attention to, and proper understanding of, the idea of God is sufficient to establish the necessary existence of God in the third meditation, then it is unsurprising that it will be able to establish that God's essence is inseparable from God's existence. Nonetheless, this does give Descartes the opportunity to demonstrate an important feature of intellectual reasoning that will inform the whole of the fifth meditation.

The next objection that Descartes treats seems trivial and, as we can see where this is going, it is tempting to skip ahead. However, as meditators we know that this is about process and not product, and Descartes still has quite a bit to show us in the process. It is clear to Descartes that from the fact that he cannot think of a valley without a mountain this does not establish that any such mountain and valley actually exist. All that is guaranteed is that if there is a valley that does exist in the world, it must be accompanied by a mountain. The objection is thin indeed as it is clear that the parallel case (God) involves existence as one of its conjoined features. However, the mountain and valley example fails because 'my thought imposes no necessity on things.' (AT7:66) In other words, from the fact that I *think* the mountain and the valley together I cannot infer that the mountain and valley exist. This is not a power of thought.

We have made this little detour through mountains and valleys, however, because Descartes would like to emphasise that *my thought imposes no necessity on things*. That is, Descartes is not foolish enough to believe that the power of thinking something can make it so. To imagine that this is the sort of magic involved in the ontological proof would indeed be a mistake. Nonetheless, it is because of this incapacity of my thought that the proof – insofar as we can still call it a proof – works at all.

But from the fact that I cannot think of God except as existing, it follows that existence is inseparable from God and that for this reason he really exists. Not that my thought brings this about or imposes any necessity on anything; but rather the necessity of the thing itself, namely, of the existence of God, forces me to think this. (AT7:67)

As we anticipated, the ontological proof derives its force and validity from the idea of God itself: in the face of the idea of God (clearly understood) I am powerless to think of God without the idea of existence. And thus we have returned to the third meditation and rendered the ontological proof superfluous.

This is an extraordinary reversal insofar as it denies the power of speculative reason to establish this certainty by proof. Any proof to be had is driven not by my active intellect but by the unfolding of the idea of God. That this notion of proof is entirely alien to modern liberalism is captured in the declaration: 'For I am not free to think of God without existence. . .'. (AT7:67) For what it is worth, this one phrase insulates Descartes' version of the ontological proof from a refutation (such as Kant's) that enshrines the Enlightenment values of intellectual freedom. In order for speculative reason to operate, I must be free to entertain ideas at will; but for Descartes there is one idea in the face of which I am not free.

That this runs counter to Enlightenment principles, however, is not to revert to dogmatism. Rather, we have what might be called a conflict of freedoms. That is, the Enlightenment project of which we are the direct heirs believes in objective (i.e. non-subjective) freedom; *Meditations*, however, operates on the assumption of subjective freedom. As a meditator, I am asked to examine my own storehouse of ideas; I am asked to examine the idea of infinite substance/God/infinity that I find there; I am asked to spend time with this idea. Descartes believes that when I do this, I will, in fact, come to the same conclusion that he does, but he does not impose this conclusion upon me. Nor is this process dogmatically stipulated. As we shall see, the whole of the meditative process is geared toward the use of my faculties to make possible 'clear sight'. At root, Descartes' ontological proof amounts to this: once you see the idea of God clearly, you will also see the necessity of God's existence.

The idea of God

Descartes readily admits that I am not compelled to see, clearly and distinctly, the idea of God. Indeed, as we shall see, this is among the most difficult things to do. Given the mess that is the human condition, it would be much easier to rely on revelation to get the job done. I might never consider the idea of God; or I might entertain only a confused idea of God; or, entertaining a clear and distinct idea of God, I may fail to consider all the necessary attributes of this idea. In the end, all that Descartes insists upon is that once I consider the idea of God clearly and distinctly and note all the necessary attributes of this idea (including existence) I am then powerless to deny the existence of God.

To illustrate this point, a parallel with geometry is in order. It is not necessary that I ever consider right triangles; it is possible that I have considered right triangles but have vast misconceptions about them (for example, that a right triangle always has three sides of the same length); it is possible that my idea of a right triangle does not involve such misconceptions and yet is not complete (I have not considered all the properties of right triangles). In the end, however, if I am working with a clear understanding of what a right triangle is then once I have considered the manner in which the hypotenuse relates to the other two sides of the right triangle I will be powerless to deny the validity of the Pythagorean Theorem.

Drawing out the parallel with Plato's *Meno*, Descartes implies that, as humans, we are in the same position in regard to the idea of God as Meno's slave boy is to the ideas of geometry: we are ignorant rather than stupid:

as far as God is concerned, if I were not overwhelmed by prejudices and if the images of sensible things were not besieging my thought from all directions, I would certainly acknowledge nothing sooner or more easily than him. (AT7:69)

At this point the promise of the subtitle is fulfilled. The whole of *Meditations* up to this point has been an exercise in clearing away prejudices and the distractions of the sensory world. Just as Socrates guides the slave boy toward a grasp of the Pythagorean Theorem, Descartes has been guiding us toward a clear view of the idea of God.

It is worth noting, however, that Descartes must be very careful in how he presents this for he is advocating a number of potential heresies. If we ask what sorts of prejudices are confusing our idea of God and how the sensory world might be interfering with our understanding of this idea, the answers are likely to upset certain long-standing religious opinions. It is easy to shrug off the sort of childish prejudice about God that he lives on a cloud and has a long beard. It is less easy to shrug off the incarnation of Christ as a mere prejudice. And yet this is precisely what Descartes is asking us to do. A clear and distinct perception of what is essential to God (as infinite substance) precludes such things as bodily appearance, spatio-temporal location, in short, any aspect of the personal God central to Christian doctrine. Nor does the Lutheran reformation help here for the word become scripture is no less prejudicial than God become man. Descartes' God, the God established in the third meditation and by the ontological proof, is a purely metaphysical God. Moreover, it would seem that prejudices of religion, at least in part, obscure the discovery of this God.

God and mathematics

We should be careful of the parallel with mathematics, of course, because it is the certainty of God's existence that underwrites the validity of mathematics itself (and the related knowledge of essences). As noted above, the status of validity in mathematics is limited to one of internal coherence. The idea of God, by means of the necessity of his existence, transcends this internal coherence and thus provides an external around which to orient the truths internal to the system. It is easily said that God guarantees the certainty of my reasoning with regard to mathematics and essences; it is less easy to understand what this might mean once God is no longer in a position to act by fiat.

The first thing to note is that Descartes is explicit about the reversal of dependence:

> although I needed to pay close attention in order to perceive [the idea of God], nevertheless I now am just as certain about this as I am about everything else that seems most certain. Moreover, I observe also that certitude about other things is so dependent on this, that without it nothing can ever be perfectly known. (AT7:69)

Thus, it is not the certainty of mathematics that contributes to the certainty that God exists but vice versa.

When it comes to establishing knowledge, Descartes notes that God is at once the source and the remedy for my confusion. God, however, does not act to guarantee my knowledge but acts to guarantee my nature. That is, God as creator is responsible for the better part of my nature: 'that, while I perceive something very clearly and distinctly, I cannot help believing it to be true.' (AT7:69) The problem, of course, is that human nature falls short of the divine in significant ways. Thus, 'my nature is also such that I cannot focus my mental gaze always on the same thing, so as to perceive it clearly.' (AT7:69) Put another way, humans are easily distracted. Therefore, in creating me, God has provided a means to attain knowledge via attention and clear perception; this, however requires great effort on my part and it is easy to lose track of the knowledge previously demonstrated. This experience is, unfortunately, all too common to students of geometry for whom the truth of the geometric proof was perfectly clear *the night before* the exam!

Proper knowledge of God solves this dilemma of distraction by guaranteeing that once demonstrated the results can be trusted. That is, with the knowledge that God is my creator and that he has given me a nature capable of knowledge, I will not need to re-prove a theorem every time I want to use it. This is particularly significant for a science built up from principles over time as it would be inordinately cumbersome to reinvent the wheel every day.

> Once I perceived that there is a God, and also understood at the same time that everything else depends on him and that he is not a deceiver, I then concluded that everything that I clearly and distinctly perceive is necessarily true. (AT7:70)

Similarly, the idea of God (infinity) stands as a stable point of reference that gives meaning to the internally coherent truths of mathematics.

God need not intervene in each arithmetic calculation to guarantee the result because I can develop a theory of mathematics entirely based on my intellectual reasoning. What I cannot guarantee is that this mathematical system in any way reflects the nature of the universe. The metaphysical God Descartes has proposed is the infinite limit of calculation, series, figure and representation. It is not the case that God designed the universe according to mathematical rules. It is the case that the universe can be described according to mathematical rules because of the nature of God as infinity.

This complete description of the idea of God marks the culmination of first philosophy insofar as without this idea no knowledge, and therefore no physics, would be possible. Thus, it is no accident that the fifth meditation leads us back to the third meditation. It is only after the fourth meditation that I am able to realise the full and proper potential of the first philosophy developed in the second and third meditations. But the fifth meditation also marks the limits of reason by showing that the ontological proof cannot in fact be grounded in speculative reason alone: thought imposes no necessity on things. If I am to escape the solipsism of the second meditation, I will need a touchstone external to my own thought. For God to provide this touchstone, he must guarantee his own existence without the aid of mere speculative reason.

The Sixth Meditation

The sixth meditation is a somewhat anomalous conclusion to *Meditations on First Philosophy* in that it has little to do with first philosophy and has abandoned the meditational approach we have been cultivating. Compared with the other meditations, the sixth meditation is a sprawling text in which it is easy to lose one's way. Descartes as the guide to our meditation is conspicuously absent. Instead we are, for the first time, presented with a text that is genuinely more discourse than meditation. As in the fifth meditation, it is appropriate that Descartes is no longer guiding my meditation as, if I have been keeping up, I ought by now to be able to do this on my own. Moreover, if the shift to a more formal discourse is not entirely appropriate as a conclusion to *Meditations*, it is a fitting transition beyond the questions of metaphysics to those of physics. Indeed, Descartes indulges in some physics along the way here. In keeping with its content, it is unsurprising that the sixth meditation is a hybrid of metaphysics and physics, of meditation and discourse; as we shall see, the main points of this meditation centre around the hybrid faculties of imagination and sensation.

In the fifth meditation we learned that the appropriate faculty for first philosophy is the intellect. At the same time we learned the limits of this faculty. On the one hand, it is only appropriate for the examination of essences; on the other hand it is not capable, on its own, of generating proofs of external existence – even that of God. As a result, if I wish to examine whether material things exist, I will need to expand the field of enquiry to include the senses and imagination. This means that I will be moving beyond first philosophy and the examination of mere essences. This also means that I will have to overcome the intellectual mistrust of these faculties. Without recourse to these faculties, I am unable to launch an enquiry beyond that which I concluded in the fifth meditation. For this reason, the sixth meditation can be read as a cautious rehabilitation of the faculties I have had the least faith in thus far.

In the second meditation, Descartes first proposes that the senses and imagination are faculties that seem to have something to do with both the mental and the material. At the time, that was good reason to reject them in favour of the pure mental faculty of intellect. With the fifth meditation, however, we have reached the limit of what the pure intellect can accomplish. Expanding the investigation to include sensing and imagining, of course, involves some risk. It is important, therefore, to handle these with care. As a result the approach to these dangerously hybrid faculties will be oblique.

Imagination

Descartes first turns to imagination because 'from the faculty of imagination, which I notice I use while dealing with material things, it seems to follow that they exist.' (AT7:71) That is, the operation of the imagination *suggests* the existence of material things; material things seem to be implicated in the use of imagination. It is important to note that Descartes does not endorse the reports the imagination makes about material things; this would be to succumb to pure fancy. As we have seen, however, we often learn more by reflecting upon the operations of the mind than we do from these operations themselves. Thus, in keeping with the spirit of *Meditations*, Descartes' desire to better understand himself, his first approach is to better understand imagination (what it is and how it works) because this seems to offer the most likely results: 'For to anyone paying very close attention to what imagination is, it appears to be simply a certain application of the knowing faculty to a body intimately present to it, and which therefore exists.' (AT7:71–2)

In order to take up this reflective perspective on imagination it will be necessary to disentangle it from the intellect. That is, in many of the basic examples we have thus far encountered, imagination and intellect seem to work hand in hand. Take the example of a triangle: 'when I imagine a triangle, I not only understand that it is a figure bounded by three lines, but at the same time I also envisage with the mind's eye those lines as if they were present. . .'. (AT7:72) In this case, I both understand by means of the intellect and I envisage by means of imagination. Indeed, the habit of employing imagination in the aid of intellect is so strong that it can be difficult to consider a triangle *without* calling up a mental image of some triangle or other. Nonetheless, they need not operate in unison and in the process of disentangling them we see how quickly the intellect outstrips the imagination.

Descartes jumps straight to a chiliagon (a thousand-sided figure) to make his point. As meditators, however, we ought to be able to establish the limits of imagination by a simple mental exercise. Try to imagine a triangle. Not hard at all. But now, let us continue the series: imagine a square; a pentagon; a hexagon; a heptagon is harder; stop signs make it easy to imagine an octagon; but most people drop out of the running at nonagon. Even if someone were to insist that they had a clear and distinct image of a ten- or twelve-sided figure, this exercise makes it very clear that at some point the imagination will give out. And yet, someone who is adept at mathematics will be able to demonstrate properties of ten-, twelve-, even thousand-sided figures because they are each still available to pure intellect.

Descartes uses the example of a chiliagon and myriagon (ten-thousand-sided figure). I, no doubt, can call to mind an image of each of these but if I am honest I will admit that I am unable to tell the difference between the two images or even see that they are representative of the figures so described. Moreover, while it is helpful to call up a pentagon in the mind's eye to facilitate the operation of the intellect, it is not at all helpful to call up such a vague and confused image in the case of a chiliagon. In this case, intellect is on its own and would do better to ignore the image proposed. In this way Descartes establishes that the intellect can function independently of the imagination and that it is up to the will to disentangle them so that I can better understand what is going on in the operation of imagination.

Once disentangled, the first thing that Descartes notes is that the operation of the imagination involves a sort of effort that is absent from the operation of the intellect. To be clear, Descartes does not say that the operation of the intellect is effortless. Rather, there is a distinctive effort involved in the application of imagination that serves as a first way to differentiate these two faculties. We probably encountered this sort of effort when we got to heptagon in our mental exercise, and perhaps we even noted a drop off in effort when we moved on to the more familiar octagon. For Descartes, the effort manifests itself in the way we can turn the mind's eye successively around an imagined figure. When imagining a pentagon, for example, I can imagine the whole figure or, by mental effort, I can inspect each of the sides on its own whilst keeping the whole image of a pentagon in mind. Thus, in addition to being separable in principle, intellect and imagination can be differentiated phenomenologically.

Once I consider the imagination on its own, however, I discover that this power, insofar as it is distinct from my intellect, is not essential to my being. This is not entirely surprising given the fact that imagination was sequestered in the second meditation. Still, in the second meditation I did concede that I am a thing that doubts, understands, wills, and also imagines and senses. After the fifth meditation, however, I realise that, while I am a thing that imagines, imagination is not part of my essence. This is no small discovery as it distinguishes the acts *appropriate* for me as a thinking thing from those essential acts that *make* me a thinking thing. Upon reflection I recognise that imagination is not essential to my being – even as a being that thinks: 'For were I to be lacking this power, I would nevertheless undoubtedly remain the same entity I am now.' (AT7:73)

In disentangling imagination from intellect I was able to establish that my intellect can operate without the aid of imagination. This allows me to recognise that nothing changes about my ability to think without imagination and therefore imagination cannot be essential to my being. Thus, even though I do happen to imagine, and imagination happens to facilitate intellectual activity in certain cases, and imagination is a proper mode of thought, it is not essential to me, for I can exist without it. Given the fact that imagination will shortly turn out to be a blind alley in attempting to prove the existence of material things, it is worth noting the manner in which Descartes makes this conceptual move of distinguishing imagination from my essence. Unlike intellect, or even will, imagination is an extra feature. That it can be excised in reality is shown by the fact that I have excised it in thought. And that it can be excised at all shows that it is not essential. This pattern of reasoning will resurface later in the meditation when Descartes turns to the real distinction between mind and body.

For our purposes here, however, this exploration of imagination is quickly petering out. From the fact that imagination is not essential to my being, Descartes concludes that it is likely that 'the power of imagining depends upon something distinct from me.' (AT7:73) From this we go straight into the realm of hypothetical speculation:

And I readily understand that, were a body to exist to which a mind is so joined that it may apply itself in order as it were, to look at it any time it wishes, it could happen that it is by means of this very body that I imagine corporeal things. (AT7:73)

That is a lot of 'ifs' and Descartes knows it. We might have learned something about imagination, and we certainly have learned something about how to establish real distinctions, but we are not likely to learn anything conclusive about material things in this way.

On the chance that we establish this hypothesis by some other means later in the meditation, Descartes does propose a way in which to understand the relation between intellect and imagination:

As a result, this mode of thinking may differ from pure intellection only in the sense that the mind, when it understands, in a sense turns toward itself and looks at one of the ideas that are in it; whereas when it imagines, it turns toward the body and intuits in the body something that conforms to an idea . . . (AT7:73)

Keep in mind, this is pure speculation as he has been unable to establish through the examination of imagination that any such body exists. Nonetheless, this is a striking image of the operation of the mind at the barrier between the mental and the physical. And as the sixth meditation is attempting to negotiate this barrier, this image does a good job of illustrating the difficulties involved. At this point, however, Descartes is forced to abandon the route through the imagination; at best, all it has achieved is the 'probable conjecture' that body exists.

Sensing

From imagination, Descartes moves on to an examination of the faculty of sensing. While imagination is apt for the positing of corporeal and geometric features, the other hybrid faculty, sensing, has the advantage over imagination with regard to such features as colours, sounds and pain. That is, even when I do imagine these things, 'I perceive these things better by means of the senses, from which . . . they seem to have arrived at the imagination.' (AT7:74) Of course, Descartes has not forgotten that he has been hostile to the senses for the whole of meditations and so we will proceed cautiously. First Descartes will rehearse why it is that he once believed the senses so uncritically. Then he will review the manner in which he found fault with this naïve position before returning with a critical reappraisal of the senses in order to see what may be salvaged.

Descartes breaks down the inventory of what the senses report in a pre-meditational naïve state. Most obviously, my senses reported that I had a body which I called mine and that this body was one among several such bodies existing in the world. These other bodies seemed to interact with my body in various ways. In particular, my body was affected by these other bodies in ways that I judged to be beneficial or harmful to my body. I recognised these effects by the sensations I call pleasure and pain. These sensations are the first among those that might be called 'inner sensations' insofar as they seem to inhere in my body in a way that 'outer sensations' do not. I recognise other inner sensations such as appetites (e.g. hunger and thirst) and bodily tendencies (e.g. mirth, sadness and anger). In addition, there are those sensations that seem 'outer' insofar as they do not seem to me to be inside my own body but to impinge upon it from without. Among these outer sensations, Descartes identifies those that report the essential features of matter (extension, shape and motion) as well as those that report tactile and visual qualities. This, in summary, is the naïve account of the reports of the senses.

With this in mind Descartes turns his attention to the fact that, for his pre-meditational naïve self, these reports compelled belief in an extra mental world. As he puts it, 'it was surely not without reason' (AT7:75) that these sensations should lead him to suppose that they proceeded from bodies in the world. That is, without judging the validity of drawing such a conclusion, Descartes wishes to enumerate the reasons that seemed so compelling once upon a time.

While it is clear that these reasons are not conclusive, they are, on the face, compelling, and it is easy to see how one could be led into the habit of believing in the existence of material bodies on their basis. The first point is probably the most compelling but we should remember that Descartes is indulging in naïve experiential reasoning here as it is clear to the serious meditator that what he actually writes is incoherent:

> For I knew by experience that these ideas came upon me utterly without my consent, to the extent that, wish as I may, I could not sense any object unless it was present to a sense organ. Nor could I fail to sense it when it was present. (AT7:75)

To the naïve realist this claim is absolutely clear: in the absence of a hot stove (or something else that is hot) I cannot feel heat; in the presence of a hot stove I cannot help but feel heat. That this so obviously begs the question (by including the existing object in the description) is ample evidence for the failure of the reasoning; and yet, it is clear how someone in the naïve pre-meditational state could find this compelling.

In addition to the fact that these sensations seem entirely oblivious to my will, however, they are also marked by a certain vivacity that marks them off from similar ideas 'deliberately and knowingly formed through meditation' (AT7:75) or found in memory. As a result, I am, in my naïve state, inclined to believe that they did not come from me. Moreover, on reflection, I come to believe that the ideas of sensation antedate reason and that it is the senses that provide the raw data for reason. While no one of these reasons is conclusive, their sheer weight might be sufficient to compel belief in the existence of external bodies.

Moreover, I have reasons to distinguish this body I call 'mine' from other bodies and to grant it a sense of priority because of this special relationship. After all, I find I cannot be separated from this body in the same way I can from, say, the chair I am sitting in. More importantly, however, appetites and feelings of pleasure and pain seem to be in the service of this body: it seems that I have been 'taught by nature' to recognise the sensation of hunger as a sign that I ought to eat. From these observations, however, I am further compelled to believe in the existence of other bodies because if I follow 'taught by nature' as a guide with my own body, why should I deny it when I am also taught by nature to believe in material things? This observation, however, brings us to the brink of the first meditation.

What follows is a rehearsal of the method of doubt. This version, while briefer than the first meditation, is enhanced in response to the richer description of the world of sense Descartes has just put forth. For our purposes, the key move in response to the general claim that I am taught by nature to believe the reports of the senses, is that I now recall that one of the reasons I doubted the testimony of the senses in the first place was that I had been taught by nature to do so. That is, when all is said and done, the method of doubt begins from the experience of having been taught by nature that the senses are not entirely reliable. If for no other reason, the conflict inherent in 'taught by nature' ought to lead me to doubt the naïve position.

Once elaborated, even the most intimate of sensations seems to be misleading. Thus, Descartes supplements the basic examples of circumstantial error with the extreme example of phantom limb phenomenon. If the sensation of pain can arise in the absence of a limb and yet compel belief in the existence of that limb then what hope do we have with the less intimate sensations? In short,

As to the arguments that used to convince me of the truth of sensible things, I found no difficulty in responding to them. For since I seemed driven by nature toward many things about which reason tried to dissuade me, I did not think that what I was taught by nature deserved much credence. And even though the perceptions of the senses did not depend on my will, I did not think that we must therefore conclude that they came from things distinct from me. . . (AT7:77)

Thus Descartes brings us up to the end of the first meditation and I remember why I abandoned the senses in the first place.

Crucially, there have been four more meditations since that moment of disorienting doubt. And thus Descartes is now prepared to mount a critically informed rehabilitation of the senses:

But now, having begun to have a better knowledge of myself and the author of my origin, I am of the opinion that I must not rashly admit every thing that I seem to derive from the senses; but neither, for that matter, should I call everything into doubt. (AT7:77–8)

The worry that drove me into the total doubt of the first meditation was that I could not be certain that I did not have (or had not been created with) a faulty nature. Indeed, some of the examples listed in this meditation certainly do call for these sorts of worries. Now, however, because I have a better idea of my own nature, I am in a position to begin a sober re-assessment of the role and reliability of 'taught by nature'.

Separability of mind and body

Thus far we have been pursuing the question of material bodies. The title of the sixth meditation, however, also announces that we will find the real distinction between mind and body. In the second meditation we explored the nature of mind on its own, but at that point Descartes explicitly deferred the question of the distinction between mind and body, having offered only a first tentative approach. However, as we have just seen, much has changed since then. As a result, the first thing Descartes is willing to posit in preparation for his re-assessment of 'taught by nature' is that mind and body are really, not merely theoretically, separable.

In the second meditation, I established that I am thinking substance and that matter is extended substance. There, however, the focus was really on the question of being and, more importantly, my being. That is, while the question of matter arose in the second meditation it did so largely as an aside in the course of a meditation about my being as a thinking thing. The discussion of the wax, we will recall, served as an exemplar of my thought of substance rather than an account of material substance *per se*. Moreover, while terms of the family 'essence' occur in the second meditation, the focus is generally on what it means to be a thinking thing rather than an analysis of the question of essence. After the fifth meditation I understand how to think about essences explicitly and about material essence in particular. Thus, in the sixth meditation, I am prepared to synthesise these various strands in order to establish the real distinction between mind and body as promised in the title of *Meditations*. Because this is a mere synthesis, the 'proof' here is exceedingly, and to some excruciatingly, brief.

As we have seen in the treatment of imagination and intellect, 'my ability clearly and distinctly to understand one thing without another suffices to make me certain that the one thing is different from the other, since they can be separated from each other, at least by God.' (AT7:78) The analysis of imagination and intellect that opens the sixth meditation shows how this works. Although I generally do think of the operation of my imagination and intellect as intertwined, I am capable of intellectual thought without the aid of imagination. Not only are there occasions where the imagination fails to arrive on the scene, but it is possible to think of my intellectual activity without imagination in any circumstance. That is, by an act of will, I can suppress the urge to imagine a triangle when thinking of the Pythagorean Theorem – and nothing changes in either the operation of my intellect or indeed my being as a thinking thing.

This example is crucial to understanding the real distinction between mind and body because the cases run in strict parallel. Like the imagination and intellect, I understand my mind and body to be constantly intertwined; as we have seen in the second meditation, it is possible to understand my being (as a thinking thing) without the body; the process of meditation itself assures me that I have sufficient willpower to 'withdraw from the body' at least for a time; and while my will might fail, God's will would not. Therefore, I can be certain that my mind is distinct from my body and can, in principle, be separated from it.

To be separable in principle, however, is a reflection of the essential being in question. That is, from the above observations I now know something more about my essence:

> from the fact that I know that I exist and that at the same time I judge that obviously nothing else belongs to my nature or essence except that I am a thinking thing, I rightly conclude that my essence consists entirely in my being a thinking thing. (AT7:78)

Just as we were able to separate the faculty of imagination off from the essence of intellect, we have now separated the body off from the essence of mind.

Like the imagination, my body is intimate to me. Nonetheless, this is not sufficient reason for thinking that the body is essential to me. This is reinforced by my understanding of matter:

> although perhaps . . . I have a body that is very closely conjoined to me, nevertheless, because on the one hand I have a clear and distinct idea of myself, insofar as I am merely a thinking thing and not an extended thing, and on the other hand I have a clear and distinct idea of a body, insofar as it is merely an extended thing and not a thinking thing, it is certain that I am really distinct from my body and can exist without it. (AT7:78)

And thus the second promise of the title of *Meditations* is fulfilled: all that is necessary to establish the possibility of the immortality of the soul is that the soul is not required to perish with the body.

Of course, as we shall see, disentangling mind from body is not as easy as disentangling imagination from intellect. But that I lack the power to disembody myself by an act of will is not at issue. My will, while infinite in itself, is not infinitely efficacious: there are many things that I can choose to do but that I cannot accomplish; indeed, in the elaboration of the fifth meditation I acknowledged that thinking it does not make it so. Nonetheless, were I to have a sufficiently efficacious will, then the *actual* separation of mind and body could be accomplished. Fortunately, I know of one being with a will that is both infinite and infinitely powerful: God.

Faculties and modes

At first glance, it is difficult to see how reinforcing the divide between mind and body could possibly help in establishing the existence of material bodies. It would seem I have merely made bodies more distant from what I am in a position to know. This purification of my being, however, is absolutely necessary for the argument that follows. Ironically, as long as there is the slightest suspicion that I am essentially material, either in whole or in part, I will be unable to establish the existence of matter. This is because the approach used to establish the existence of the material world is modelled on the approach used in the third meditation to show the necessary existence of God.

In the third meditation, Descartes initiates the investigation into the existence of an other – who turns out to be God – by examining his ideas: if he finds that he has an idea that he could not be the cause of, then there must be some other being that is the cause of that idea. In the sixth meditation, the investigation turns to faculties rather than ideas. That Descartes begins with the hybrid faculties might seem to indicate that he is hoping they will somehow straddle the divide between mind and body in a revelatory way. Indeed, this would be in keeping with Descartes' first abortive attempt to use the imagination to bridge this gap. There is a reason, however, that the first attempt is aborted: it does not lead anywhere. Descartes is not repeating the same failed strategy but, somewhat confusingly, using the faculties of sense and imagination to illustrate an important general point about faculties. For it is via the nature of the faculties in general that we will be proceeding.

While I have no problem understanding myself without the faculties of imagination and sensation, as they are not essential to me, when I turn to an examination of the status of these two faculties I note a difference: 'I cannot understand them clearly and distinctly without me, that is, without a substance endowed with understanding in which they inhere, for they include an act of understanding in their formal concept.' (AT7:78) In other words, I cannot conceive of imagination, for example, without some reference to mind because the imagination does actually produce images in the mind. What would it mean to have an understanding of imagination in the abstract? Without mind?

From this observation Descartes draws an important conclusion about the ontological status of these faculties: 'Thus I perceive them to be distinguished from me as modes from a thing'. (AT7:78) On its own this gets us no closer to bridging the divide between mind and body but it does tell us something about the ontology of faculties. What follows is perhaps the most abstruse move in the whole of *Meditations* – particularly for us as modern readers to whom substance metaphysics is almost wholly alien.

To say that a faculty is a mode of a thing is already saying a great deal. A mode, we recall, is an expressive modification of substance. We have already seen a link between the faculties and modes of thinking in the second meditation. There we learned that thought is a mode (expression, modification) of thinking substance. Thus far in *Meditations* we have been talking of the faculties of thought (intellect, will, imagination, and so on) as *ways* of thinking; we have not actually enquired into the ontological status of these faculties. However, already in the second meditation we ought to have recognised that the distinction between what thinking substance is and what it does is at best a question of perspective and at worst entirely spurious. To say 'I think' is already to say 'I am' because it is the act of thinking that is essential to my being. Why should things be any different when it comes to the various specialised faculties if I am ready to admit that each of these is also in fact thinking?

In identifying mental faculties with modes of thinking substance, Descartes opens the way for an analysis of modes and faculties generally. For our purposes, the most important feature of the mode-substance relation is that modes are not capable of independent existence. Hence, if faculties are modes then the existence of a faculty indicates the existence of a substance in which it inheres. Just as it is nonsensical to think of imagination entirely divorced from thinking substance, it is nonsensical to think of any faculty/mode entirely divorced from some substance or other. Descartes' next move is to identify certain faculties (modes) 'such as those of moving from one place to another, of taking on various shapes, and so on. . .' (AT7:78), which we recognise from the wax example. Calling them faculties rather than modes may at first be misleading but is actually entirely appropriate in the current context.

One of the things that this discussion brings out is that the difference we think we see between faculties and modes is illusory. Rather than being grounded in a proper metaphysical understanding of the relation to substance, this apparent difference arises out of the nature of the substance involved. It would seem equally absurd to say of a fish that it has wings or of a bird that it has fins, but on closer inspection of the relation of the (pectoral) fin/wing to the body of the fish/bird it is not hard to see that, both functionally and anatomically, these are remarkably similar. We are initially misled in this case because we do not normally think of fish as flying and birds as swimming. In the same way, we speak of faculties of thought and modes of matter without realising that, ontologically speaking, these bear the same relation to substance.

This is crucial because the model Descartes is using to understand the faculty/mode relation to substance is that of imagination (and sensing) to mind. Therefore,

it is clear that these faculties [of moving, taking on shape, etc.], if in fact they exist, must be in a corporeal or extended substance, not in a substance endowed with understanding. For some extension is contained in the clear and distinct concept of them, though certainly not any understanding. (AT7:79)

As mind has no part in extension, and a clear understanding of shape and movement necessitates extension, the appropriate substance would have to be one whose essential feature was extension: thus, matter. As this is merely a hypothetical argument, of course, this does not establish the existence of matter. If, however, we have good reason to believe that the faculties (modes) of matter exist then we will know that matter exists.

The existence of the material world

Descartes next turns to the faculty of sensation which he now qualifies as passive: 'there clearly is in me a passive faculty of sensing, that is, a faculty for receiving and knowing the ideas of sensible things . . .' (AT7:79) There is a little slippage in the argument here as it is not immediately clear that he is justified in characterising the faculty of sensing as passive. Upon reflection, however, it is clear that Descartes has the resources to justify this move even if he fails to deploy them explicitly. One way that he could establish this is by proving the distinction between imagination and sensation in the manner in which he established the distinction between imagination and intellect.

He has not made this argument, but it is clear that he could have as it is not difficult to see that what distinguishes imagination from sensation (and therefore establishes them as really different faculties) is the role of active will involved. Indeed, imagination and sensation are remarkably similar except that in the functioning of imagination I seem to be active, and in the functioning of sensation I seem to be passive. Descartes provides a hint of this back-story later in the passage when he reminds us that what initially made the reports of the senses so compelling is that the ideas of sense arise even against my will.

One way to understand the passivity of the faculty of sensation, therefore, is to note that at the same time that Descartes announces this supposedly new quality, he also specifies that this is 'in me'. That is, we have been treating sensation as a hybrid faculty. Now Descartes is once again focussing on the faculty of sensation insofar as it exists in me, in the mind, as opposed to in the (hypothetical) body. Once the possibility that I am merely confusing imagination for sensation has been blocked, the passivity of the faculty of sensation *in me* provides a clue for the existence of a corresponding active faculty *not in me*. Indeed, it is crucial that the active faculty of imagination is excluded from this analysis in order to secure the necessity of an activity arising from a faculty that is not in me.

Thus, of the passive faculty of sensation, Descartes notes that: 'I could not use it unless there also existed, either in me or in something else, a certain active faculty [mode] for producing or bringing about these ideas.' (AT7:79) This active faculty (mode) will have to inhere in a substance. It cannot inhere in me (as a thinking thing) because it does not involve understanding in any way and it happens even against my will. 'Therefore the only alternative is that [this active faculty] is in some substance different from me, containing either formally or eminently all the reality that exists objectively in the ideas produced by that faculty. . .'. (AT7:79)

The obvious candidate for this substance other than me is, of course, God. After all, this is the only other substance I know to exist. Moreover, as an omnipotent being, God would have no problem whatsoever in supporting this active faculty. For Berkeley, in fact, this is the proper conclusion to draw: God actively intervenes to create the idea of the world in our minds at every moment. Berkeley, however, has dropped most of the substance metaphysics that renders this an unsuitable conclusion for Descartes. If God were to support the active faculties that produce the ideas of sense in my mind then, for Descartes, this would be for God to produce these ideas eminently rather than objectively – and this would make God a deceiver.

Not being an extended substance, God does not have properties such as size and shape. There is no doubt that an omnipotent God is capable of producing in me the ideas of size and shape via sensation. But my senses lead me to believe that the ideas of size and shape so produced are formally present in the substance that actively produced them. In other words, if God did this he would be deceiving me. Fortunately, in the third meditation we established that God is not a deceiver. Therefore, neither of the two substances I know to exist could be supporting the active faculty (mode) necessary to the fact that I have sensations. As a result, there must be a substance, heretofore unknown to me, that is supporting this active faculty (mode). Moreover, this substance must contain, formally, those properties of extension, shape, motion and so on: in other words, this substance would be matter.

To our post-empiricist ears this sounds strange: certainly there is nothing active in the nature of the stone that makes me sense it as hard. If we pause a moment, however, this is not as strange as it sounds. What Descartes is suggesting is that material substance can be modified such that it produces sensations. Put this way, we are more likely to accept Descartes' point. After all, it is nothing other than a modification of the structure of limestone that differentiates hard marble from soft chalk. That we think of this as active, therefore, need not result in some form of animism.

The active faculty that Descartes is trying to identify is not the sort of activity that has matter doing things like walking around or skipping rope; it is the sort of activity that causes sensations – nothing more. Nor should we be troubled by the imposition of causality here, for this causality is similarly limited to the interaction that gives rise to ideas in the mind. All that Descartes has established is that there is something other than me that exists and that it exists as a corporeal being. The only activity that we can as yet ascribe to it is the sort of interaction with my passive faculty of sensation that will give rise to the ideas of sense.

We should not get too excited, however, because Descartes makes the modesty of this discovery immediately clear: 'Nevertheless, perhaps not all bodies exist exactly as I grasp them by sense, since this sensory grasp is in many cases very obscure and confused.' (AT7:80) In the fifth meditation we established that, if material things exist, they would have to exist in space and time and they would be describable by mathematics.

Now, we have proven that material things do exist but we must still be careful to limit ourselves in accord with the fifth meditation: 'But at least they do contain everything I clearly and distinctly understand – that is, everything, considered in a general sense, that is encompassed in the object of pure mathematics.' (AT7:80)

Taught by nature

It should be stressed that this brings us only to the point where we affirm the formal features of material reality. The senses have provided the basis for the deduction that material things exist but this deduction does not validate the specific information the senses provide. That is, the deduction of the sixth meditation actually only serves to transform the hypothetical claims about the essence of matter from the fifth meditation into certainties. I am still in the dark as to the validity of the content of any particular ideas delivered by the senses. Put another way, if we have been working our way backwards through the stages of doubt in the first meditation, we are still more or less behind the dream argument.

Even in dreams, we recall, the laws of mathematics and the basic features of experience hold true; what I cannot be certain of are such details of particular experience as 'I am now seeing a chair' or 'this chair is red'. Thus at this point in the sixth meditation, Descartes notes:

As far as the remaining matters are concerned, which are either merely particular (for example, the sun is of such and such a size or shape, and so on) or less clearly understood (for example, light, sound, pain, and the like), . . . these matters are very doubtful and uncertain. . . (AT7:80)

In order to establish the veracity of the senses, or at least the limits of this veracity, some other approach will be necessary. Moreover, now that the pure speculative power of the intellect has been exhausted (in the fifth meditation), and the metaphysical deduction via the faculties has run its course (earlier in the sixth meditation), we should be prepared to lower our expectations in this regard. The best options for certainty are already at an end.

The best resource remaining is the fact that I am God's creation and that God is not a deceiver. The very fact that I make errors, of course, shows that this approach will have limits. For this reason, Descartes dedicates the remainder of *Meditations* to understanding these limits so as to facilitate the highest possible probability of certainty. Thus Descartes returns to 'taught by nature' as a starting point as this does seem to deliver some degree of certainty in day-to-day experience. Moreover, upon reflection it is clear that nature is no less a creation of God than I am. In other words, if I take 'nature' in its most general sense 'I understand nothing other than God himself or the ordered network of created things which was instituted by God.' (AT7:80) Given this, while I may not be in a position to understand the overall plan of this network, I would not be wrong to assume that some patterns or other should be available to my understanding.

More particularly, 'By my own particular nature I understand nothing other than the combination of all the things bestowed upon me by God.' (AT7:80) With this notion of human nature in place I turn to those things that (my own) nature teaches me most intimately. Thus we turn to those inner sensations that we noted earlier. At this point, however, I am ready to explore the possibility that these most intimate sensations are indicative of more than mere sensation:

> There is nothing that this [human] nature teaches me more explicitly than that I have a body that is ill disposed when I feel pain, that needs food and drink when I suffer hunger or thirst, and the like. (AT7:80)

That is, by these inner sensations, nature teaches me about the condition of my body and thus brings my body into relation with the rest of the world.

These intimate sensations also teach me something about the relation between my being (as a thinking thing, a mind) and the body I call mine. The phenomenology of these experiences teaches me that I am not conjoined to my body in a haphazard or circumstantial way. I am not merely present in my body the way a sailor in a ship is; rather I am 'most tightly joined and, so to speak, commingled with it, so much so that I and the body constitute one single thing.' (AT7:81) If I were merely present in my body, then I would discover damage to my body the way that a sailor would discover damage to his ship: by inspection. In contrast, the sensation of pain, for example, is immediate, intense and indeed personal in a way that damage to a ship could never be to even the most dedicated sailor. It is worth noting that, in relation to his own body, this positions Descartes in opposition to the ordinary use of 'have'. That is, even though my body is not essential to me, it is part of me. I do not have a body in the same way that I have a coat or baseball bat: it is *more* than my property; yet it is not of my essence.

In addition to these objects of inner sensation, however, I am also taught by nature that there are other bodies in the world. Moreover, nature teaches me by various signs that some are to be pursued and others avoided. These signs, of course, are the variety of ideas of sensation: colours, odours, degrees of heat, tastes, and the like. For example, one might learn through (hard) experience – be taught by nature – not to eat the meat that is green; and given the intimate sensations associated with the eating of green meat we have good reason to trust this lesson. Nonetheless, Descartes is keen to remind us not to step beyond this merely phenomenal conclusion.

It is clear that nature teaches us a regular correspondence between features in bodies and features in sensation. However, it also clear that it does not, because it need not, teach us anything about likeness. That is, for the purposes of protecting the body from harm, all that is required is a link between a particular sensation and a painful effect; this is entirely sufficient to keep me from eating meat that appears to me to be green. Nature need teach us nothing about whether the meat really is green.

There are of course occasions when the lessons of nature seem to mislead me. Indeed, it was the observation of this fact that led me into the method of doubt in the first place. As Descartes patiently reminds us, however, more often than not the fault lies not with nature, but with us. As we learned in the fourth meditation, intellectual error arises through rash and reckless judgement: I jump to conclusions. If I eat an apple one day and get violently ill that same day, I may decide that the apple caused my illness. I may decide that nature has taught me by sure signs never to eat apples; I would likely be wrong in this judgement and were I to give the case careful consideration I might revise my conclusion. I might, for example, decide that only this particular apple was poisonous; or I might decide that the apple was not the real cause of my illness but was merely coincidentally present at that time. These, of course, are questions for physics and not metaphysics. Nonetheless, I should be careful that I do not make the *metaphysically* rash judgement of rejecting the value of 'taught by nature' because of such cases.

I could, however, make another sort of error in using 'taught by nature'. I could attempt to derive information about the nature of the thing in itself. Strictly speaking, my knowledge of the thing as it is, rather than as it appears, is limited to what I can learn by *the light of nature* – intellectual reasoning. But, as we have seen, this is limited to the knowledge of essences expressed in pure mathematics. Thus, from 'taught by nature' I am not able to draw any conclusions about the thing in itself;

all I can know are the phenomena and their various associations. Of course, I am given to rash judgements in this area as well.

Descartes illustrates the proper limits of 'taught by nature' in this regard with the example of heat and fire:

> although I feel heat as I draw closer to the fire, and I also feel pain upon drawing too close to it, there is not a single argument that persuades me that there is something in the fire similar to that heat . . . [on] the contrary, I am convinced only that there is something in the fire that, regardless of what it finally turns out to be, causes in us those sensations of heat or pain. (AT7:83)

Thus, while I have found a role for the sensations, I have also marked the limit of what they have the right to report. Beyond the reporting of phenomena, all the senses can tell me is that there is a something-I-know-not-what that causes these phenomena. If intellectual inspection is unable to elaborate on this, then my investigation must come to an end at this point.

Leaving meditations behind

Toward the end of the sixth meditation, Descartes ceases to merely dabble in physics and crosses the line entirely. The remaining passages are given over to the question of how error can arise due to the nature of mind-body interaction. That is, rather than the purely mental error of judging beyond the limit of intellect, or the error of misjudging the lessons of nature, Descartes now turns to those cases where the body is in some sense responsible for faulty sensation. We have already encountered the example of the phantom limb and Descartes now sets about offering a physical account of this sort of bodily error. All that need concern us in these discussions is: that this is a necessary feature of mind and body being so tightly conjoined; and that this is properly a discussion for physics.

In these cases, as well, however, the metaphysical lesson is the same. Whether the cause of the error is mental or physical, it always remains in our power to withhold judgement and to base even our contingent judgements on the best possible evidence. In these final sections we can observe Descartes the scientist putting these principles into practice to explain the phantom limb phenomenon and dropsy. And while we may have reason to approve or disapprove of the results of his scientific investigation, it is clear that Descartes the scientist is proceeding on the basis of his previously established metaphysical commitments. In the end, if there is one practical lesson that *Meditations* teaches us, it is that for all things we do, believe, judge or hypothesise we must have reasons and these ought to be subject to scrutiny.

For this reason, one of the final points Descartes makes in *Meditations* is that there simply is no good reason to adhere to the dream argument: 'the hyperbolic doubts of the last few days ought to be rejected as ludicrous. This goes especially for the chief reason for doubting, which dealt with my failure to distinguish being asleep from being awake.' (AT7:89) Descartes' account of the obvious differences between these two states need not trouble us because, as meditators, we no longer need the hyperbolic doubt of the dream argument. Once *Meditations* has been traversed I know enough about myself, my faculties and God that I am able to avoid error through care, attention and modesty. The abandonment of the dream argument does not grant free license to my intellectual judgement because, in part due to the power of the dream argument, I now know my own limits and can act accordingly. In other words, there once was good reason for the dream argument but those reasons have expired.

Thus, if I have learned these lessons, I am able to hear the words that opened the first meditation in a new way because I have fulfilled my obligation to undertake *Meditations* once in my life.

3. Study Aids

Glossary

adventitious ideas
Ideas that are neither fabricated by imagination nor derived exclusively from my nature (innate); often taken to be sensory ideas, in *Meditations* these are treated more generally as those ideas that come to me from beyond me (have an external origin). *See* innate ideas.

Cartesian Circle
The problem, often attributed to Descartes' metaphysics, of needing to establish the existence of God in order to secure the reliability of the criteria of clearness and distinctness while requiring the reliability of criteria of clearness and distinctness in order to prove the existence of God.

clearness
The quality of a perception being present and open to the attentive mind. *See* distinctness.

cogito
Literally 'I think'; although the term does not appear in a meaningful way in *Meditations*, it has come to stand for the existence of the self discovered in the second meditation.

distinctness
The quality of a perception being so precise and separated from all others that it involves nothing which is not clear. *See* clearness.

epistemology
The philosophy of knowledge; often taken to be a main theme of *Meditations*.

God
Infinite Substance. *See* infinity, substance.

infinity
That than which nothing greater can be; in *Meditations* this is taken to be an absolute and should not be confused with either the very large or an additive notion of infinity. *See* God.

formal reality
That the being of which is not representational; loosely, what we would call really existing. *See* objective reality.

foundationalism
The epistemological position sometimes attributed to *Meditations* that attempts to ground knowledge claims on axiomatic or indisputable foundations and thereby derive the reliability of knowledge from the certainty of these foundations.

imagination
A hybrid faculty of mind capable of producing images or representational ideas; properly used in the aid of intellect or reason.

innate idea
An idea derived exclusively from my nature; often assumed by the tradition to be 'written on the soul' by God or pre-existing experience in some way; in these latter senses only the idea of infinity/perfection/ God is technically an innate idea; in *Meditations* the term applies to all ideas that are neither fabricated by the imagination nor adventitious; examples of innate ideas include the *cogito*, 'thing', 'truth' and 'thought'. *See* adventitious ideas.

mind-body dualism
The metaphysical position that divides reality into two irreducible substances (thought and matter); often used to describe Descartes' metaphysics despite his inclusion of a third substance (God). *See* God, substance.

objective reality
That the being of which is merely representational. *See* formal reality.

ontology
The philosophy of being including questions of essence and existence.

res cogitans
Literally 'thinking thing'; the basic term for thinking substance. *See* substance.

scepticism
Any of a variety of philosophical attitudes that call certainty into question and thereby, either as a goal or a means, withhold assent to truth claims.

substance
That which is capable of independent existence; also the bearer of attributes (or properties); in *Meditations* we find two finite (matter, mind) and one infinite (God) substance. *See* God.

will
The faculty of choosing; in Meditations this faculty is taken to be infinite (or perfect) in the sense that choice is absolute.

Types of Question You Will Encounter

Essay and Exam questions on *Meditations* tend to fall into certain categories.

1. The most basic type of question asks for an explanation of a particular argument or position in the text (e.g. the method of doubt, the distinction between mind and body, etc.). In answering these questions it is important that you are clear what the argument is trying to establish or what purpose the position serves. This provides the frame in which your explanation makes sense. Otherwise you will simply be rehearsing the text. More often these sorts of expositional questions are supplemented by evaluation or comparison.

2. An evaluative question asks that, in addition to explaining a part of the text, you judge whether or not this argument is successful or this

position tenable. In these cases it is crucial that you do more than give an arbitrary opinion. A good evaluative answer includes an outline of the criteria being applied to reach this final judgement. These might be internal or external to the text. Internal criteria are those that the text imposes on itself (e.g. Descartes uses the method of doubt to find an opinion that cannot be doubted); external criteria are those that you apply to the text (e.g. Descartes' project has undesirable consequences). In the case of external criteria it is crucial that you explain what is at stake and why we should care but it is also important to note that these values are not necessarily those of the text.

3. A comparative question will ask you to bring *Meditations* into dialogue with some other philosopher (or commentator) usually in order to evaluate which one has the more compelling answer to a particular question. Here it is crucial that you make certain that the grounds of comparison are at least compatible. For example, both Kant and Descartes are troubled by the problem of the external world and so it is reasonable to ask about the relative success of their solutions to this problem. This sort of comparison, however, almost always reveals a difference that may overshadow the commonalities. For example, Kant's concern with the external world is more epistemological and Descartes' more ontological. This is important to note because a good answer allows the differences to frame the comparative approaches.

4. There are also questions that ask you to relate problems or arguments from *Meditations* to contemporary debates in a related field. For example, you might be asked how Descartes' understanding of mind and body informs contemporary debates in cognitive science; or you might be asked what light Descartes' commitment to subjectivity casts on a current debate in phenomenology. On the whole, these sorts of questions ask you to use *Meditations* as a resource for a particular problem and as a result certain liberties can be taken with the original text; positions, arguments and debates will be applied to new contexts and so the original context is of less import.

Tips for Writing about *Meditations*
1. There are always difficulties when using a philosophical text in translation but these are redoubled in the case of *Meditations* as English translations come in three varieties. Because *Meditations* was published

in both Latin and French during Descartes' lifetime, English translators have used either the Latin or the French or a combination of the two as their source text. Worse still, many English editions do not make it clear which 'original' is being translated. This text uses a translation from the Latin but there are reliable translations of the French as well. It is crucial that you know which form of translation you are using because there are differences.

2. References from *Meditations on First Philosophy* are usually noted by the pagination of the modern standard edition of Descartes' works edited by Charles Adam and Paul Tannery and are therefore designated by 'AT' followed by the volume and page number. The volume for the Latin edition is 7 and that of the French is 9a.

3. Remember that many of the terms that Descartes uses have a technical meaning that differs even with the technical meaning these might have in contemporary discourse. Apart from certain terms from scholastic philosophy, however, Descartes rarely deploys a term without explaining it as he does so. Therefore it is important that you pay attention to the use of seemingly non-technical terms like 'God' as much as you do to obviously technical terms like 'formal reality'.

4. Because of the meditational nature of this text, it is important that you are aware of the rhetorical valence of passages you are quoting. Many of the things Descartes says in *Meditations* are provisional and some simply do not reflect the beliefs of Descartes. In the course of the text many of the positions that Descartes takes are in the process of revision and some are abandoned entirely. Therefore, it is important to note the context in which a position is put forth and ask yourself what purpose this might be serving here. Otherwise, you might discover you attribute a position to Descartes that he disavows a few paragraphs later.

5. When writing about such a rhetorically rich text there is the temptation to attempt to echo the style of the author. This is not the purpose of an essay on a philosophical text. Your essay should not be an attempt to recreate the effect of the original: *Meditations* does that very well. Rather, given the effect of that text, you should attempt to explicate, elaborate or apply the main points of the text as appropriate.

Further Reading

Translations of *Meditations*

Descartes, R. *Discourse on Method and Meditations on First Philosophy*, trans. Donald A. Cress (Indianapolis, IN/Cambridge: Hackett, 1998)

Descartes, R. *Meditations, Objections, and Replies*, ed. and trans. Roger Ariew and Donald Cress (Indianapolis, IN/Cambridge: Hackett, 2006)

Descartes, R. *Meditations and Other Metaphysical Writings*, trans. D. Clarke (London: Penguin, 2000)

Descartes, R. *Meditationes de prima philosophia, Meditations on First Philosophy: A Bilingual Edition*, ed. and trans. George Heffernan (Notre Dame: Notre Dame University Press, 1990)

Descartes, R. *Meditations on First Philosophy, with selections from the Objections and Replies*, ed. and trans. John Cottingham (Cambridge: Cambridge University Press, 1996)

Translations of Descartes' Works

The Philosophical Writings of Descartes (in 3 volumes)
— Vols. 1 and 2 trans. John Cottingham, Robert Stoothoff, and Dugald Murdoch (Cambridge: Cambridge University Press, 1984)
— Vol. 3 *The Correspondence* trans. John Cottingham, Robert Stoothoff, Dugald Murdoch, and Anthony Kenny (Cambridge: Cambridge University Press, 1991)

Descartes, R. *Philosophical Essays and Correspondence*, ed. Roger Ariew (Indianapolis, IN/Cambridge: Hackett, 2000)

Descartes: Philosophical Writings trans. Norman Kemp Smith (New York: Modern Library, 1958)

Elisabeth, Princess of Bohemia, and Descartes, R. *The Correspondence Between Princess Elisabeth of Bohemia and René Descartes*, ed. and trans. Lisa Shapiro (Chicago: University of Chicago Press, 2007)

Historical Perspectives and Voices

Ariew, R., Cottingham, J., and Sorell, T. (eds) *Descartes' Meditations: Background Source Materials* (Cambridge: Cambridge University Press, 1998)

Ariew, R., and Grene, M. (eds) *Descartes and His Contemporaries: Meditations, Objections, and Replies* (Chicago: University of Chicago Press, 1995)

Atherton, M. (ed.) *Women Philosophers of the Early Modern Period* (Indianapolis, IN/ Cambridge: Hackett, 1994)

Malebranche, N. *Dialogues on Metaphysics and on Religion*, trans. Nicholas Jolley and David Scott (Cambridge: Cambridge University Press, 2008)

Poullain de la Barre, F. *Three Cartesian Feminist Treatises*, trans. Vivien Bosley (Chicago: University of Chicago Press, 2002)

Spinoza, B. *Principles of Cartesian Philosophy*, trans. Samuel Shirley (Indianapolis, IN/Cambridge: Hackett, 1998)

The Spiritual Exercises of Saint Ignatius trans. George E. Ganss, S.J. (Chicago: Loyola Press, 1992)

Commentaries and Monographs

Alanen, L. *Descartes's Concept of Mind* (Cambridge, MA: Harvard University Press, 2003)

Beck, L. J. *The Metaphysics of Descartes: A Study of the Meditations* (Oxford: Clarendon Press, 1965)

Bordo, S. (ed.) *Feminist Interpretations of René Descartes* (University Park, PA: Pennsylvania State University Press, 1999)

Chappell V. (ed.) *Descartes's Meditations: Critical Essays* (Lanham, MD: Rowman and Littlefield, 1997)

Cottingham, J. (ed.) *Descartes* (Oxford: Oxford University Press, 1998)

Cottingham, J. *Descartes* (Oxford: Blackwell, 1986)

Cottingham, J. (ed.) *The Cambridge Companion to Descartes* (Cambridge: Cambridge University Press, 1992)

Curley, E. *Descartes Against the Sceptics* (Cambridge, MA: Harvard University Press, 1978)

Evans, J. C. *The Metaphysics of Transcendental Subjectivity: Descartes, Kant and W. Sellars* (Amsterdam: Verlag B.R. Grüner, 1984)

Flage, D. E. and Bonnen C.A. *Descartes and Method: A Search for a Method in "Meditations"* (London and New York: Routledge, 1999)

Garber, D. *Descartes Embodied* (Cambridge: Cambridge University Press)

Gaukroger, S. (ed) *The Blackwell Guide to Descartes' "Meditations"* (Oxford: Blackwell, 2006)

Hatfield, G. *Routledge Philosophy Guidebook to Descartes and the Meditations* (London and New York: Routledge, 2003)

Matthews, G. B. *Thought's Ego in Augustine and Descartes* (Ithaca, NY: Cornell University Press, 1992)

Menn, S. *Descartes and Augustine* (Cambridge: Cambridge University Press, 2002)

Rorty, A. (ed.) *Essays on Descartes' Meditations* (Berkeley: University of California Press, 1986)

Rozemond, M. *Descartes's Dualism* (Cambridge, MA: Harvard University Press, 1998)

Sesonske, A. and Fleming, N. (eds.) *Meta-Meditations: Studies in Descartes* (Belmont, CA: Wadsworth Publishing, 1965)

Wilson, M. D. *Descartes* (London and New York: Routledge, 1978)

Woolhouse, R. S. *Descartes, Spinoza, Leibniz: The Concept of Substance in Seventeenth Century Metaphysics* (London and New York: Routledge, 1993)

Original Responses and New Directions

Bordo, S. *The Flight to Objectivity: Essays on Cartesianism and Culture* (Albany: SUNY Press, 1987)

Brodsky Lacour, C. *Lines of Thought: Discourse, Architectonics, and the Origin of Modern Philosophy* (Durham, NC: Duke University Press, 1996)

Derrida, J. "Cogito and the History of Madness" in Derrida, *Writing and Difference*, trans. Alan Bass (London: Routledge, 1978)

Foucault, M. "My body, this paper, this fire" in Foucault, *History of Madness*, trans. Jonathan Murphy (London: Routledge, 2006)

Husserl, E. *Cartesian Meditations: An Introduction to Phenomenology* (Dordrecht/Boston/London: Kluwer Academic Publishers, 1997)

Irigaray, L. *Speculum of the Other Woman* (Ithaca, NY: Cornell University Press, 1985)

Irigaray, L. "Wonder: A Reading of Descartes, *The Passions of the Soul*" in *An Ethics of Sexual Difference* (London: The Athlone Press, 1993)

Marion, J-L. *Cartesian Questions: Method and Metaphysics* (Chicago: University of Chicago Press, 1999a)

Marion, J-L. *On Descartes' Metaphysical Prism: The Constitution and the Limits of Onto-theo-logy in Cartesian Thought*, trans. Jeffrey L. Kosky (Chicago: University of Chicago Press, 1999b)

Marion, J-L. *On the Ego and on God: Further Cartesian Questions*, trans. Christina M. Gschwandtner (New York: Fordham University Press, 2007)

Maritain, J. *The Dream of Descartes*, trans. Mabelle L. Andison (London: Philosophical Library, 1946)

Rorty, R. *Philosophy and the Mirror of Nature* (Princeton, NJ: Princeton University Press, 1980)

Valéry, P. "Presenting Descartes", trans. Harry Lorin Binsse in *The Living Thoughts of Descartes* (London: Cassell and Company, 1948)

Zizek, S. The Ticklish Subject: The Absent Centre of Political Ontology (London and New York: Verso, 1999)

Index

Adderson, P., 69; *see also* Goti, V.
ad hoc revisionism, 17–19
adventitious ideas, 103, 105, 107; *see also* idea
affect, 101–2
anima see soul
Anselm, 5, 97
appetite, 181–2
Archimedean point, 51, 83, 93
Arianism, 115
Aristotle, 9–11, 40, 60–1, 64, 66–7, 108, 140
    essentialism, 139
    metaphysics of, 9, 84, 87, 108, 112, 140
    Metaphysics, 9
    science, 19, 25, 40, 63, 139–40
    substance, 130
Augustine, 5, 129, 138
    Augustinian philosophy and tradition, 6, 137

being qua being (being of being), 9, 12; *see also* ontology
Berkeley, G., 29, 189
brains in vats, 46–7
'by the light of nature', 106, 193; *see also* 'natural light of reason'

Cartesian Circle, 88–9, 122–5
Cartesianism and Cartesian Philosophy, 1, 86, 156, 164, 174
    metaphysics of, 70, 128
    post-Cartesian philosophy of mind, 86, 95
Cartesian subjectivity, 62; *see also* subjectivity
cause (*aita*), 9–10, 139–40
    efficient cause, 10, 140
    final cause, 10, 139
    formal cause, 10
    material cause, 10, 140
    telos, 10, 139–41; *see also* teleology
Certainty
    experience of, 93–4, 106, 124, 162
    sense of, 74, 160–2, 164, 166, 169
    see also innateness
Christian philosophy and tradition, 6, 148; *see also* scholastic philosophy and tradition
clearness and distinctness, 88–94, 104, 117, 123–5, 131, 151–5, 161, 164
    experience of, 92, 151
    clear and distinct perception, 88–9, 91, 94, 117, 131, 158, 174; *see also* perception

clearness and distinctness (*cont.*)
    rule of, 91–2, 94, 106, 117, 123–4,
        151, 155
cogito, 14–15, 27, 34, 47, 49–50,
        54–8, 61–2, 68–9, 72, 83, 90,
        92–3, 104, 106, 124, 131,
        134–6, 146, 149–52, 157–8,
        161–2, 169
cognitive revolution, 7
conservation of being, 110–11

daimon, 46; *see also* evil demon
deceiving God, 28, 39, 41–2, 44, 74,
        89, 91, 106, 133, 169
    deceiving God hypothesis, 42–4,
        47, 65, 89, 91, 132
    existence of, 42
doubt, 21–3, 27–31, 35–6, 40, 42, 44,
        49, 51–3, 68, 76, 87, 98, 102,
        106, 120, 132, 143, 149, 164,
        167–8
    frame of radical doubt, 66, 69, 74,
        76, 79; *see also* frame
    hyperbolic, 49, 195
    of the existence of God, 41; *see also*
        God
    radical, 48, 59, 62, 64–9, 71, 74–7,
        79, 106
    total, 49, 158, 183
dream argument, 28, 34–40, 42, 47,
        89, 92, 106–7, 191, 195
dream experience, 36–7, 39–40,
        114
duration, 160, 164–5

ego, 11
Elisabeth of Bohemia, 3
empiricism, 2, 77, 121
    empiricist tradition, 72

Enlightenment
    project, 2, 173
    values, 172
epistemology, 2, 11, 46, 88, 143
    epistemological bias, 2
    epistemological foundationalism,
        55
error, 30, 92, 102–3, 135–8, 141–4,
        147–9, 152, 155, 158, 193–5
    bodily, 194
    circumstantial, 91, 106, 183
    intellectual, 193
    passive, 148–9
    presumptive, 148
    sensory, 28–9; *see also* senses
    see also sin
esse, 87, 108; *see also* essence
essence, 87, 108, 154, 160, 163, 165,
        170, 174, 177, 179, 184–5, 192
    experience of, 164
    ideas of, 164, 166–7
    knowledge of, 174, 193
    of thought, 87
    see also esse, ousia
evil, problem of, 147–8
evil demon (evil deceiver, evil genius),
        44–7, 49, 55, 58, 146–7; *see also*
        daimon
expression, 72–3, 95–6, 112, 131–2,
        134–5, 187
    thought as modal expression, 112,
        131–2, 187; *see also* mode
extension, 39, 75, 80, 95, 109, 160,
        164–5, 181, 188, 190
external world, 76, 88, 113, 142

fabrication, 103, 164–6; *see also*
        imagination
faculties, 26–7, 29, 31, 41–4, 91, 107,

114, 117, 133–7, 139, 140–1,
    143–4, 146–8, 150, 154–5,
    157–8, 160, 164–5, 170, 173,
    177, 179, 186–7, 189, 191, 195
active, 189–90; *see also* imagination
as modes, 186–9; *see also* mode
harmony of, 135, 158, 167
hybrid, 74, 146, 177, 181, 186,
    189; *see also* imagination,
    sensation
of choosing, 144; *see also* will
of imagination, 70–2, 80, 83,
    103, 177, 185, 189; *see also*
    imagination
of perception, 76, 117; *see also*
    perception
of reason, 93; *see also* intellect
of sensation or sensing, 41, 80,
    103, 177, 180, 186, 188–9; *see*
    also sensation
ontology of, 187–8; *see also*
    ontology
passive, 188–90; *see also* sensation
proper or right use of, 83, 134–5,
    137, 141, 157–8
reliability of, 32, 37, 44, 117, 139
sense faculties, 31, 33, 37; *see also*
    senses
fall, theology of the, 138
Feuerbach, L., 121
first philosophy, 2, 8–12, 20, 50, 85,
    129, 134–6, 149, 160, 176, 177;
    see also metaphysics, ontology
frame, 33, 35–7, 59
framed coherence, 34
freedom, 144–6, 150, 173
    intellectual, 172
    objective, 173
    subjective, 173

Freud, S., 166
Foundationalism *see* epistemology

Galileo, 114–15
God, 5–6, 11, 20, 27, 40–4, 53–4,
    84–5, 88–90, 93, 96, 101, 107,
    114–18, 120, 123, 125–35,
    137–9, 141–4, 147–9, 154–5,
    166, 169–70, 172, 174–7, 186,
    189–91, 195
    as creator, 40–1, 43, 117, 125–6,
        128, 133, 135, 175
    Deist 'Watchmaker God', 118
    existence of, 20, 41, 43, 84–5, 87,
        89, 94, 96–8, 114, 117, 121,
        123–5, 131–2, 156, 158, 161–2,
        168–71, 173, 186
    God's essence, 170–1
    God's existence, 85, 87–8, 97, 116,
        171, 173–4
    idea of, 41, 85, 101, 114–26, 128,
        130–4, 147, 158, 161, 168,
        170–6
    mind of, 139, 141
    personal, 115, 141, 174
good God hypothesis, 42

Hegel, G. W. F., 118
human condition, 136, 138–9, 141,
    143–4, 152, 154, 173
Hume, D., 1–2, 121–2

'I', 13–14, 56, 61, 67–9, 71, 73–4
idea, 99–102, 104–5, 107, 109,
    112–15, 119–20, 122–4, 131,
    160–7, 172–3, 186, 189
    of perfection, 121, 146–7
Ignatius of Loyola, 5–7
    Spiritual Exercises, 5–8

imagination, 70–4, 79–81, 83, 94,
    99–100, 103, 114–15, 135,
    164–7, 177–81, 184–9
inclination, 145–6, 150–5, 157, 161,
    164, 167
indifference, 150, 152–3
infinity, 118–19, 121, 123, 144, 176
    absolute, 121–2, 143
    additive notion of, 121
    idea of, 118–24, 147, 173, 175
    idea of absolute, 122, 143
innate idea, 103–5, 163–4, 167; *see
    also* innateness
    theory or doctrine of, 156–7,
    162–4
innateness, 160, 162
    sense of, 162, 169
    see also innate idea
intellect, 19, 25, 135, 143–4,
    148–55, 157–9, 165–7, 172,
    177–80, 184–5, 187–8, 191,
    194
    finite, 149, 151–2, 154
    infinite, 154; *see also* God
    pure, 115, 149, 167, 177–8
'I think', 73, 75–7, 82–3, 87, 89, 91,
    127, 132, 143, 147, 149, 157,
    159, 171
    frame of, 77, 81, 94, 99–100,
    102–3, 167

judgement, 82–3, 93–4, 101–5, 109,
    134, 146, 148–50, 155, 159,
    170, 193–5

Kant, I., 1–2, 104, 168, 170, 172,
    200
    refutation of the ontological proof,
    168, 170, 172

law of conservation of energy, 111
law of preservation (of being), 126–7
Leibniz, G. W., 1–2, 72, 141
    best of all possible worlds, 141
Lichtenberg, G. C., 69–70, 72–3
Locke, J., 1–2, 156

madness, 31–6, 145
    madness hypothesis, 32, 34–5,
    42–3
material essence, 156–7, 184; *see also*
    matter
material falsity, 122
material things, 158–61, 177, 180,
    182, 190–1
    essence of, 156, 158, 160–2,
    164–5
    existence of, 177, 179
    idea of, 158, 160–1, 164–5
    see also matter
mathematics, 24–5, 39–40, 88, 91–2,
    117, 165, 167, 169–70, 174–6,
    178, 190–1, 193
    truths of, 24, 89, 92, 169, 175
matter, 10, 12, 83, 109, 160, 181,
    184, 186, 188, 190–1
    essence of, 160, 191
    see also material things
meditational practice, 8, 49, 62, 156
meditational text, 5, 7–8, 27–8, 35,
    45, 51, 64
metaphysics, 8, 10, 12, 20, 72, 100,
    107, 129, 136, 159–60, 176,
    193
    Descartes', 11, 45, 72
    expressivist, 72; *see also* expression
    foundational, 136, 160
    metaphysical knowledge, 6
    practical, 134

subjectivist, 127
substance, 72, 84, 86, 88, 94–5,
    107–8, 187, 189
method of doubt, 17–18, 20–3,
    25–32, 34–7, 39, 41–2, 44–5,
    47, 49–52, 54–9, 66, 76, 83,
    113–14, 170, 182–3, 193
    stages and staging of doubt, 27–8,
        30–2, 41, 44, 170
    test of doubt, 23–4, 59, 65
    see also doubt
mind, 2, 6–7, 48, 54, 60, 64, 72,
    81–3, 86–7, 96, 101, 180, 184,
    187–90, 192
    finite mind, 139, 141
    mens, 60, 63, 65, 67
    mind and body, 80, 146, 180,
        184–7, 194; see also mind-body
        dualism, mind-body interaction
    philosophy of mind, 2, 84, 86, 95
mind-body dualism, 60, 63
mind-body interaction, 194
mode, 72, 87, 95–6, 111, 131, 135,
    187–91
    of thinking, of thought, 95, 107,
        179–80
    substance-mode relation, 98, 187
modern liberalism, 172
morality and morals, 20, 23, 34, 135,
    138, 140–1, 143, 149–51, 166
    moral agent, 31, 149
    moral imperative, 149
    moral reasoning, 141

'natural light of reason', 93, 106; see
    also 'by the light of nature'
Newtonian physics, 127
Nietzsche, F., 72
nothingness see pure non-being

Occasionalism, 118
ontological proof, 157, 168–74, 176
ontology, 2, 11, 87–8, 107, 134, 138,
    187; see also first philosophy
ousia, 87, 108; see also essence

painter's analogy, 37, 99, 103
perception, 48, 76, 80–3, 91, 94, 99,
    117, 120, 151, 162, 164, 168,
    175
    as act of the mind, 81–2, 91
physics (science, natural philosophy),
    10, 12, 129, 160, 176, 193–4
    second philosophy, 12, 129
Plato, 2, 5, 7, 40, 107–9, 129, 137–8,
    162–4, 166, 173
    forms, 108, 138
    Meno, 162–3, 173
    Phaedrus, 163
    Metaphysics of, 108
    Theory of Recollection, 162–3
post-Kantian philosophy, 72, 84
post-Lockean philosophy, 84
Pythagorean Theorem, 25, 173, 184

rational animal, 60, 64, 66–7
rationalism, 2
reality, 39, 75, 91, 107–11, 120, 131,
    133, 137, 162, 180
    formal, 109–14, 119, 128, 131
    mark or feature of, 36–7
    material, 191
    nominal, 123
    objective, 109–15, 119, 122–3,
        131, 147
    sensory, 37, 39
    thought independent, 76
representation, 107, 110–11, 115,
    176

representation (*cont.*)
  representational objects, 112
  representational content, 112–14,
    131
res cogitans, 67, 69, 70–2, 129–30; *see
    also* thinking thing
Robinson Crusoe, 96–8, 112–13, 116

scepticism, 20–1, 55, 90
schnauzer, 108, 137–8
Scholastic philosophy and tradition,
    9–10, 13, 97, 100
scientia, 18, 20
sensation, 25, 32–3, 48, 65–6, 75,
    80–3, 99, 103, 105, 164, 167,
    177, 182–3, 186, 188–90, 192–4
  inner sensation, 181, 192
  outer sensation, 181
  see also senses
senses, 19, 24–6, 28–32, 36–8, 42, 44,
    47, 53–4, 70, 76, 78–9, 82–5,
    87–8, 91, 100, 102–3, 105, 135,
    146, 167, 177, 181–3, 190–1,
    194
  ordinary sense experience, 36
  reliability of, 29–32, 37, 148, 183
  reports of, 29–30, 33, 82, 94,
    100–2, 104–5, 146, 148, 164,
    181, 183, 189
  sense experience, 37–8, 40
  sense organs, 65, 73
  sensory illusion, 28, 30; *see also*
    error
  testimony of, 29–33, 183
  see also sensation
sin, 135, 147–8, 155; *see also* error
Socrates, 46, 163, 174
solipsism, 90, 98, 122, 132, 142, 176
  epistemological, 87–8

ontological, 87–8, 90, 94–8
solipsistic bind, 92, 116
solipsistic meditator, 166
solipsistic position, 87, 94, 98,
    105–6
solipsistic subject, 93, 116; *see also*
    subject
soul, 7, 12, 20, 48, 63–8, 83, 185
  anima, 60, 63–7, 71, 73, 77, 80
  animus, 65, 67
  distinction of the soul from the
    body, 12
  immortality of, 12, 185
  soul and body, 65–6, 68
  soul-body dualism, 63–4, 68
space and time, 161–2, 165, 190
Spinoza, B., 1, 72, 128–30
  metaphysical monism, 129
  metaphysics of, 129–30, 130
spirit, 6–7
Stoics, 5, 81
subject, 61, 64, 69–72, 74–5, 127
  subject-agnosticism, 72
  thinking subject, 74, 77, 130
subjectivity, 2, 61–2, 73–7, 93, 97–8
  perspective of, 64, 75, 97–8
  philosophy of, 48, 61, 69, 75
  pure, 61
substance, 12, 25, 72–3, 87, 95–6,
    104, 108–9, 111, 114–15, 118,
    126, 128–30, 132–3, 135, 184,
    186–90
  extended, 184, 190; *see also* matter
  finite, 128–9
  idea of infinite substance, 118, 157,
    173
  infinite, 117–20, 125, 128–9, 132,
    135, 137, 139, 141, 149, 157–8,
    161–2, 173–4; *see also* God

intellectual, 118, 143–4
limited, 128
material, 95–6, 113, 118, 184, 190;
    see also matter
relative, 118, 128–30
thinking, 72, 87–8, 94, 96, 104,
    112–14, 118, 126–32, 134–5,
    139, 141, 143–4, 159, 184, 187;
    see also res cogitans

'taught by nature', 106–7, 182–4,
    191, 193–4
teleology, 139–40
teleological reasoning, 136, 139–42
thinking thing, 59, 66–73, 76, 86, 96,
    104, 114, 179, 184–5, 189, 192;
    see also res cogitans
trademark, 131–2, 143, 147

trademark argument, 118, 122,
    130
transcendental deduction, 104–5
transgression, 148–9; *see also* sin

volition, 101–2; *see also* will

wax example/experiment, 76–7, 80,
    82, 187
will, 31, 44–5, 47, 101–2, 105, 109,
    134, 143–59, 164, 166–7, 179,
    182, 184–7, 189
    determination of, 145; *see also*
    inclination
    free, 144–5, 147
    freedom of, 146
    see also volition
Wittgenstein, L., 82